Embedded Systems Fundamentals with ARM Cortex-M based Microcontrollers

D1293056

Embedded Systems Fundamentals with ARM Cortex-M based Microcontrollers

A Practical Approach

Alexander G. Dean

ARM Education Media

ARM Education Media

ARM Education Media is an imprint of ARM Ltd., 110 Fullbourn Road, Cambridge, CB1 9NJ, UK

ISBN: 978-1-91-153103-6

British Library Cataloguing-in-Publication Data
A Catalogue record for this book is available from the British Library

Library of Congress Cataloging-in-Publication Data
A Catalog record for this book is available from the Library of Congress

For information on all ARM Education Media publications, visit our website at armedumedia.com

To report errors or send feedback please email edumedia@arm.com

Contents

Foreword

Alex Dean and I worked together at United Technologies in the early 1990s helping companies such as Otis, Pratt & Whitney, Carrier, and Sikorsky improve their embedded computing practices. Since then we have both chosen embedded systems as a career path, and have both done dozens of design reviews on real industry projects. Sometimes we have been able to team up on an especially important product review, which is always a blast. Whenever we chat, he tells me about his latest cool project, usually involving gadgets for his sailboat. Alex has seen the real world of embedded system design as few other professors have, and has gotten his hands dirty building real stuff. This book reflects that experience.

We are in an era in which most technologists seek to specialize, but being a good embedded system designer requires breadth across both Computer Science and Computer Engineering. Beyond that, many of the tradeoffs for embedded systems are quite different from those for desktop and enterprise systems. This book does an admirable job of covering the embedded computing design space, balancing the opposing forces of hardware versus software, depth versus breadth, and performance versus constraints. Embedded computing is usually about being highly constrained on cost, speed, memory, power, and pretty much everything else. Yet it is also about building systems that can be life-critical, or potentially put a company out of business due to the cost of a product recall if the software has a defect. Most of those who have not worked in the area do not realize how pervasive this technology is, nor how difficult it is to do well.

To give an example of how much we depend on embedded computers without necessarily realizing it, consider a server farm used for Big Data. Everyone knows there are lots of multicore big CPUs there. But there are also embedded computers and mission-critical embedded software in at least the following places in that same machine room complex: network interfaces, disk controllers, storage box controllers, board-level power supplies, rack-level power management, power distribution switchgear, backup battery controllers, backup-diesel engine controllers, temperature monitors, air handlers, cooling compressors, cooling expansion valves, humidity controls, lighting controls, network switches, a badge swiping system, a security video system, an alarm system, a fire suppression system, vending machines to keep the operators happy, status monitors for many of those systems, and ... well, you get the idea. Without embedded computing, the high-tech world as we know it simply would not exist. And that example is just the starting point. Embedded systems are everywhere, and I am continually astonished at the places I find not only microcontrollers, but whole teams of engineers designing and maintaining embedded systems. The difference between an embedded system that works somewhat and one that really works can easily be the difference between a product that succeeds or a product that makes the headlines (or worse) because it failed. If you doubt whether embedded system design can be a big deal if you get it wrong, consider the billions of dollars that have been spent on lawsuits because of badly written software or poor choices about what a system did.

The sweet spot for this text is for students who have seen many of the pieces before, but need a structured way to put all the pieces together. So that means they already know how to program, how a CPU works in general, and how programs execute. But probably they have seen all this in a desktop computing environment in their introduction to computing hardware and to software systems courses. This book takes those pieces and puts them together into a coherent whole. It also helps students un-learn some of the habits that are appropriate only for big-system computing. In embedded systems, memory is not "free", nor can you simply throw more cores at a problem if you have a $1 CPU that has to run on a coin battery cell for five years. Getting these systems right requires a blend of both science and engineering, with a healthy respect for the realities of the marketplace and the messiness of interfacing to the real world.

This book gives a big picture on diverse topics, including:

- Computer organization and assembly language. If you do not understand how interrupts work, you should not be building embedded systems. (There is more, but that is a good starting point.)
- Digital design and how software interacts with bare metal hardware. Modern embedded systems are all about working with peripheral circuits to maximize system capability at minimum total cost.
- Analog I/O. The real world is not digital. (You knew that, right?)
- How to program in C. Regardless of what you think about the language, most embedded code is in C or a suspiciously C-like subset of C++, and it is the rare project that is not built on top of an existing code base.
- Tool chains and support software. Developers have to understand how compilers, real-time operating systems, and other building blocks work to use them effectively. (Hint: Most embedded micros in real products do not run Linux. Or any other OS you are likely to know.)
- Time. The computer's job is to keep up with the real world, not the other way around, and doing so creates all sorts of problems that must be understood.
- Respect and understanding for what is really going on in both the hardware and the software. The best embedded system designers understand how to exploit the strengths of both hardware and software.

The book uses the ARM Cortex-M0+ processor, which has a nice selection of peripherals while still giving the feel of a resource-constrained embedded system. Beyond that, the examples have a strong dose of Alex's experience working in industry, and deal with many of the practical issues that arise in real products.

This book takes an integrated approach to putting the pieces together, rather than simply presenting the various pieces in isolation. Each chapter has well-illustrated working examples based on a real MCU evaluation board. These activities start early, with Chapter 2 showing how to read switches and light LEDs using GPIO and C code. Concurrency and responsiveness also appear early, and weave through the various examples throughout the rest of the book, working up from busy polling to preemptive task scheduling. In addition, the examples work through a progression of getting things work in a simplistic way and then improving performance by using peripherals instead of a brute force software approach. An analog waveform generator provides a running example, going from software-only timing through using DMA data transfers to the DAC.

Finally, this book emphasizes having students understand what is really going on under the hood of the compiled C code. While most embedded systems are written in C instead of assembly language these days, students need to appreciate what the compiler is doing to make their code too big, too slow, or too vulnerable to race conditions. They also need to be able to debug optimized compiled code and write the occasional low-level optimized loop that links to a C program for that 1% of the code where speed is everything. Or even better, understand what is happening well enough to trick the compiler into generating an efficient code for them.

If, after reading this book, you are still thinking of using another book, do yourself a favor. Check the index of that other book. If the word "watchdog" does not appear, put the book down and back away from it slowly. It is not really an embedded computing book if it does not talk about watchdog timers, and you would be surprised how common that is. (Yes, Alex does cover watchdog timers in this book.) I look forward to the chance to use this book in my teaching.

For those of you who are students, pay attention to what is in this book. You have probably already looked at several of the ever-popular cut-and-paste-the-code books. They can be expedient, but you will not really learn what is going on from them, or from the books that just rehash the data sheet. Alex's book is different. It will help you put all the pieces together, so that you *understand* what you are doing, which is the great thing about having the opportunity to study and learn at a university, isn't it?

Professor Phil Koopman, Carnegie Mellon University

Pittsburgh, PA, January 2017

Preface

Introduction

It is an exciting time to develop embedded systems! Modern microcontrollers (MCUs) offer remarkable performance at a very low cost. The Internet provides an abundance of source code and documentation. The combination of inexpensive hardware platforms (e.g., Arduino, Raspberry Pi, and Beaglebone) with the right software (to abstract away details and guide users) has helped lower the barriers to embedded system development, allowing experimentation without requiring encyclopedic knowledge.

Unfortunately, these supports become shackles when trying to scale up to a larger, more complex system with tighter constraints. Industrial designers of embedded systems draw from a large toolbox of technical methods in order to meet requirements such as speed, responsiveness, cost, weight, reliability, or energy use.

Many of the hardware tools are built into the MCU: a central processing unit (CPU) to execute software, an efficient interrupt system enabling quick responses to events, fast memory to hold the program and data, and specialized hardware peripheral circuits to reduce the need for a high-speed CPU. Hardware peripherals can often signal and control each other, eliminating the need to involve software on the CPU. MCUs offer a range of low-power modes so the designer can trade off performance and power consumption as needed.

Other tools are provided by the software, which is typically written in C or C++ and compiled to run in the processor's native machine language. This avoids the run-time delays and memory overhead of interpretation or scripting. Multitasking software is scheduled on the CPU using interrupts and a scheduler, which may be cooperative (e.g., state machines) or preemptive (e.g., a real-time kernel).

To summarize, successful embedded system designs use peripherals and well-structured software on the CPU with light-weight context switching to provide responsive concurrency. This textbook aims to explain how to develop microcontroller-based embedded systems using these industry-standard methods and practice these with the most widely used processor architecture in embedded computing today: the ARM Architecture.

Challenges of Embedded Systems Education

There are several interesting challenges to learning (or teaching!) embedded systems in a college or university. First, the field builds on concepts from several areas: computer engineering (CPE), electrical engineering (EE), and computer science (CS). Some students will be able to study joint degrees, or even double or triple major, but most will not. Second, these concepts and their solutions must target embedded system design spaces, which are quite different from the mainstream general-purpose or high-performance computing design spaces covered by most courses. Third, there are so many areas to cover that it is easy to concentrate on the familiar, which crowds out the unfamiliar. Presenting the areas with just enough detail (but not too much) can be difficult.

Challenge 1: Spanning Electrical and Computer Engineering and Computer Science

Successful embedded system designers need a variety of skills from CPE, EE, and CS, but not too much, and the right version given the context. These skills are typically split across ECE (electrical and computer engineering) and CS departments. To make things worse, CPE and CS courses are constantly pulled toward higher performance computers and higher levels of abstraction (to manage the increased application complexity enabled by the increased performance). This widens the gap with the embedded system design space.

The following areas in CPE and EE are the most critical for students in the field of embedded systems:

- Computer organization and assembly language programming are fundamental to an understanding of the CPU, memory, peripherals, and interrupt system.
- Digital design is necessary to understand not only how the CPU works, but more importantly to understand how peripheral circuits work. These digital circuits (e.g., GPIO, timers, DMA) provide cheap concurrency because they operate independently of the CPU. A good design will offload computationally expensive software tasks to allow a relatively slow MCU to provide precise timing and predictable performance at a low cost and with little power consumption.
- Basic analog circuit design and analysis skills are needed for adding external circuits such as LEDs, switches, and sensors. Knowing how to use an oscilloscope or logic analyzer to examine and understand the timing of events within a system is essential for effective debugging.

The following areas in CS are the most critical for students in the field:

- C language programming is necessary because it is the dominant language for programming embedded systems.
- Compilers and assembly language programming provide an understanding of how a CPU really does the work specified by the source code. Knowing how the program is compiled and structured helps with avoiding errors (e.g., preemption), debugging, designing efficient systems, and improving performance.
- Operating systems' task scheduler concepts enable students to understand how to share a single CPU among the multiple concurrent activities of the embedded system. These topics include multitasking, preemption, and prioritization. Students need to understand how to design multitasking systems using intertask communication and synchronization to avoid common bugs such as data race hazards.

Challenge 2: Targeting the ES Design Space

For each area mentioned, the practical solutions depend on the design space. The design spaces for most embedded systems are quite different from those of general purpose and high-performance computing, because of different drivers and constraints. For example:

- Computer Organization: Embedded processors typically do not need the raw speed sought in general-purpose or high-performance computing systems. As a result, they don't require high clock speeds and the deep processor pipelines and multilayer memory systems to support them.
- Operating Systems: OS courses generally target a resource-rich Linux system that features a preemptive scheduler, ample compute and memory resources, a virtual memory system with hardware support, and user and supervisor modes. This type of system does not offer the precise timing control needed for many embedded systems and is often too complex, power-hungry, and expensive. Students must be able to apply the concepts of task scheduling, synchronization, and communication to a system built on interrupts, peripherals, and a simple scheduler (whether a preemptive real-time kernel or a cooperative scheduler).
- Programming: Embedded systems use compiled languages instead of scripted or interpreted languages for reasons of predictability, efficiency, and compactness. Because of this history there is a large installed base of C/C++ development infrastructure. However, many programming curricula target Java (or even a scripted language). This abstracts away low-level and implementation issues that can make or break an embedded system.

Challenge 3: Providing Sufficient (but Not Excessive) Coverage

With all of these areas to cover, it is easy to emphasize the familiar, crowding out the unfamiliar. Furthermore, the hands-on nature of embedded systems courses often slows down the progress as the student or instructor tries to get a code example working to demonstrate an important concept.

This book tries to present the areas with just enough detail (but not too much) and with practical solutions for the design space. This book does not try to present an exhaustive, complete education of all possible ways to do something. Instead, it presents the most practical options given the constraints.

Notes to the Instructor

Why Use This Book?

In this textbook, I have sought to present the most important topics for embedded systems using a coherent, compelling, hands-on format.

First, the textbook uses a hands-on approach to get students excited and motivated. Each chapter has illustrated, working examples based on a real MCU evaluation board. These activities start early, with Chapter 2 showing how to read switches and light LEDs using GPIO and C code.

Second, the textbook introduces concepts of concurrency and responsiveness early. Chapter 3 uses a running example of scanning LEDs according to switch positions to introduce concepts important for creating modular, responsive, and efficient systems. By stepping through and evaluating these improvements, the student is given a solid foundation on which to investigate real-time kernels (in a later course). Concurrency and responsiveness are introduced using the following sequence:

1. Starting with a simple program with software to poll switches, flash LEDs, and delay using busy-waiting
2. Restructuring the software into tasks
3. Scheduling the tasks cooperatively
4. Improving the responsiveness of cooperatively scheduled tasks by using state machines to break up long operations
5. Using interrupts and event-driven software to replace polling of switches
6. Replacing busy-waiting delay loops by using a timer peripheral
7. Prioritizing tasks
8. Scheduling tasks preemptively

Third, the textbook covers how to improve performance by using peripheral hardware in place of software. An analog waveform generator is used as a running example. It is introduced as an application of the digital-to-analog converter, with timing fully dependent on software execution speed. It reappears in the timer chapter, with a timer-driven periodic ISR updating the DAC to improve timing stability. The final appearance is in the DMA chapter, in which the DMA controller under timer control automatically copies data from a memory buffer to the DAC.

Fourth, the textbook covers C code as implemented in assembly language by the compiler. The main goals are to help students understand why their code is slow or large, how to make it faster or smaller, to understand preemption risks for shared data, and to help debug programs by working at both the source and object code levels. This textbook does not expect students to program in assembly language, although they may do so in a later course, given this foundation.

Course Material Linkage

This textbook is designed to be used for a one- or two-semester course introducing students to embedded systems. It complements the Efficient Embedded Systems Design and Programming Education Kit from the ARM University Program. If you are an instructor, you can receive a donation of this Education Kit by emailing university@arm.com. The Education Kit includes lecture materials and licenses to ARM's Keil MDK-ARM professional software. Students need prerequisite knowledge in C programming, digital design, and basic circuit theory.

Target Platform

This textbook targets the ARM Cortex-M0+ processor, which executes the instructions of the program. The processor is a component within the microcontroller, which adds circuits to clock the processor, memory to hold the program and data, and peripheral devices that simplify programs and improve their performance. This processor is available in microcontrollers from a wide range of manufacturers.

The target platform is the FRDM-KL25Z development board from NXP Semiconductor, with a list price of under $20. It uses the NXP KL25Z128VLK4 microcontroller from the Kinetis L ultra-low-power family. This device features a Cortex-M0+ processor capable of running at up to 48 MHz, and contains 128 kB of flash ROM, 16 kB of RAM, and a wide range of peripherals. The development board adds a USB debug interface (OpenSDA), power supplies, and input and output devices. A three-axis accelerometer is used to detect acceleration. Because it also senses the force of gravity, it can be used to determine the inclination (tilt) of the board. A touch-pad slider can measure the position of a fingertip using a capacitive sensor. A three-in-one output device is included: three high-brightness LEDs (red, green, and blue). These LEDs can be lit with varying levels of brightness to produce a full range of colors.

The material in this textbook can be used with other Cortex-M0+ platforms. Four of the first five chapters are essentially independent of the MCU's peripherals and apply to all Cortex-M0+ processors. The remaining chapters and the Appendix are closely integrated with the peripherals by necessity. NXP's other Kinetis MCUs use many of the same peripherals as the KL25Z, making it easier to use those MCUs and their associated FRDM evaluation boards. Targeting an MCU family from a different vendor will require porting the peripheral examples.

Software Development Environment

Software examples in this textbook are written in C and compiled to run without an operating system. ARM's Keil MDK-ARM integrated development environment is used throughout the textbook. The free version of MDK-ARM supports all of the code examples in this textbook and associated course materials. Note for instructors: If the object code size limitation of the free version (currently 32 KB) is a constraint, please request a license donation from ARM for the full professional version of MDK-ARM.

Organization

The textbook is organized as follows:

Chapter 1 introduces students to the concepts of MCU-based embedded systems, and how they differ from general-purpose computers. It then introduces the ARM Cortex-M0+ CPU, the Kinetis KL25Z MCU, and the FRDM-KL25Z MCU development board.

Chapter 2 presents the general purpose I/O peripheral to provide an early, hands-on experience with reading switches and lighting LEDs using C code. It also introduces the CMSIS hardware abstraction layer, which simplifies software access to peripherals.

Chapter 3 introduces multitasking on the CPU, with the goals of improving responsiveness and software modularity while reducing CPU overhead. The interplay of interrupts, peripherals, and schedulers (both cooperative and preemptive) is examined.

Chapter 4 presents the ARM Cortex-M0+ processor core, including organization, registers, memory, and instruction set. It then discusses interrupts and exceptions, including CPU response and hardware configuration. Designing software for a system with interrupts is discussed, including program design (and partitioning work), interrupt configuration, writing handlers in C, and sharing data safely given preemption.

Chapter 5 first gives an overview of toolchain, which translates a program from C source code to executable object code. It then shows side by side the source code and the object code the toolchain has generated to implement it. Topics covered include functions, arguments, return values, activation records, exception handlers, control flow constructs for loops and selection, memory allocation and use, and accessing data in memory.

Chapter 6 presents analog interfacing, starting with theory and ending with practical implementations. Quantization and sampling are presented as a foundation for both digital-to-analog conversion and analog-to-digital conversion. The DAC, ADC, and analog comparator peripherals are presented and used.

Chapter 7 presents timer peripherals and their use for generating a periodic interrupt or a pulse-width modulated signal, or for measuring elapsed time or a signal's frequency. Watchdog timers, used to detect and reset an out-of-control program, are also discussed. The SysTick, PIT, TPM, and COP timers are examined.

Chapter 8 discusses serial communication, starting with the fundamentals of data serialization, framing, error detection, media access control, and addressing. Software queues are introduced to show how to buffer data between communication ISRs and other parts of the program. Three protocols and their supporting peripherals are investigated next: SPI, asynchronous serial (UART), and I²C. UART communication is demonstrated using the FRDM-KL25Z's debug MCU as a serial port bridge over USB to the PC. I²C communication is demonstrated using the FRDM-KL25Z's built-in 3-axis accelerometer with I²C interface.

Chapter 9 introduces the direct memory access peripheral and its ability to transfer data autonomously, offloading work from the CPU and offering dramatically improved performance. Examples include using DMA for bulk data copying, and for DAC-based analog waveform generation with precise timing.

An Appendix covers how to measure the power and energy use on the FRDM-KL25Z board, including disconnecting the debug MCU to reduce power. Methods to measure energy consumption using an ultracapacitor are highlighted.

Acknowledgments

I would like to thank the following people for their help:

- Khaled Benkrid, Melissa Good, and the reviewers at ARM for supporting this project.
- Bill Trosky, Phil Koopman, Alan Finn, and Chris McClurg for opening so many doors to me in the embedded systems world.
- The development teams who welcomed me in as an outsider to review the embedded software for their products. They helped me understand their design goals, technical and non-technical constraints, and day-to-day challenges.
- The students who helped me sharpen my message and identify the fundamental issues at stake. Their enthusiasm and creativity are always a powerful, positive force.
- My wife and daughters for support, encouragement, and the quiet time needed to complete this work.

Author Biography

Dr. Alexander G. Dean has been a faculty member of the Department of Electrical and Computer Engineering at North Carolina State University (NCSU) since 2000. He received his BS (1991) from the University of Wisconsin, Madison, and his MS (1994) and PhD (2000) from Carnegie Mellon University.

Dr. Dean has developed four courses on embedded systems at NCSU, ranging from fundamentals to architecture and design to optimization. He has created course packages targeting five different MCU families for the university programs of three companies, including the Education Kit on Efficient Embedded Systems Design and Programming for ARM Education.

Dr. Dean's research involves using compiler, operating system, and real-time system techniques to extract more performance from commodity microcontrollers in embedded systems while reducing clock speed, energy, and memory requirements. His research also includes applying these methods for low-cost control of switch-mode power converters.

Dr. Dean has worked at United Technologies Research Center developing embedded systems and their communication network architectures. He holds three patents in the area. He has performed over 60 in-depth, on-site embedded software reviews for industry both domestically and internationally since 2001.

1

Introduction

Chapter Contents

Overview

In this chapter we introduce the basic motivations and key concepts for embedding a computer into another system. We examine the design of the hardware and software for the embedded systems and also the constraints that designers face. Finally, we examine the target hardware platform we will use in this textbook.

Concepts

Why Control a System?

Improving how a system is controlled can provide better performance, extra features, reduced purchase or operating costs, and more dependability. An embedded computer system is a computer that has been embedded into a larger system in order to improve it in some way, typically by controlling it.

Figure 1.1 shows an electric hot plate that is used to cook food. The control knob on the front allows the user to turn on or off the hot plate and to set its temperature. Let's examine the existing control system, determine its weaknesses, and consider how we can improve it.

Figure 1.2 shows the internal components of a hot plate: a black control knob, a heating element (covered by a silver metal circle), a red indicator lamp, and a temperature control system. The indicator lamp is connected in such a way that it lights when the heating element is powered.

The temperature control system, shown in Figure 1.3, is very simple and is based on a single component: a temperature-sensitive (thermostatic) switch. One of the switch contacts is made from two different types of metal so that it bends as it grows hotter. When the switch gets hot enough, the contact bends so far that the switch disconnects the heating element from the power. The heating element and then the switch start to cool down. Eventually the switch will cool down enough to bend back and make contact. The control knob adjusts the distance between the switch contacts, setting the temperatures at which the switch will open or close. How well does this control system work? Let's find out.

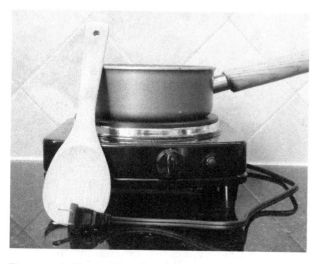

Figure 1.1 Electric hot plate for cooking food. Photo by author.

Figure 1.2 Internal components of hot plate. Photo by author.

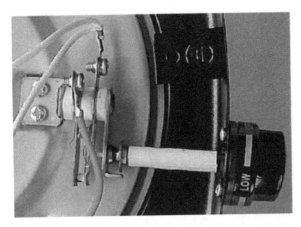

Figure 1.3 A detailed view of the thermostatic switch used to control the heating element. Photo by author.

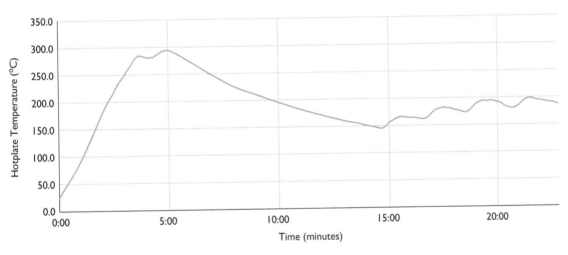

Figure 1.4 Hot plate temperatures measured over time.

How Good Is the Hot Plate's Temperature Control?

The temperature of a hot plate cooking surface can be measured using a thermocouple, a type of electric thermometer. Figure 1.4 shows the temperature over time. At time $t = 0:00$, the control knob is set to Low to turn on the heating element. The temperature rises to nearly 300°C over the next 5 minutes. The heating element turns off briefly at $t = 4:00$ and then for a longer time at $t = 5:00$. The hot plate then takes the next 10 minutes to cool down to about 150°C at about $t = 14:40$. After this start-up period, the temperature starts rising in steps as the switch cycles on and off with a roughly 2-minute period, eventually reaching a range centered near 190°C. Notice the temperature never actually stabilizes, but rises or falls within a range of about 20°C based on whether the switch is open or closed.

Although the control system is simple and low cost, it does not control the temperature of the hot plate very well. Consider the following points:

- The actual temperature swings wildly in the first 15 minutes. Variations in temperature will make it harder to cook food consistently. The temperature finally starts to stabilize after 15 or 20 minutes, which is a long time to wait before starting to cook.
- The actual temperature of the hot plate cooking surface is not measured. Instead, the switch measures a combination of the temperatures of the metal shield and the internal air.
- There is a delay between when the metal shield and the internal air temperatures change and when the switch temperature changes, as the heat must be conducted to the switch contact.
- The control system is not calibrated. The control knob is marked with settings OFF, LOW, MED, and HIGH instead of actual numerical temperatures.

Why Use Electronics and an Embedded Computer?

Using electronics can improve the temperature control of this hot plate in many ways:

- We can reduce the delay between a temperature change and the control system's response by using a smaller sensor that changes temperature quickly.
- We can mount the smaller temperature sensor on the bottom of the hot plate itself to further reduce the delay. This would save time and power by eliminating the large temperature overshoot at 5 minutes.
- We can switch the heating element on and off more frequently, reducing the temperature ripples shown starting at 15 minutes in the graph.
- If we do this switching fast enough, we can control the fraction of time the heating element is on, giving us a wide range of heat outputs rather than the simple on/off of the current system.
- An electronic approach allows us to measure the temperature precisely instead of relying on the simple above/below information that the thermostatic switch provides.
- Coupling the precise temperature measurement with the proportional heating control, we can use a better control scheme. For example, we can turn on the heater a little bit if the temperature is only slightly below the desired set point, but turn it on more fully if the temperature is far below the set point. This will improve response and reduce the temperature overshoot.
- Adding multiple temperature sensors would allow us to monitor temperatures at multiple locations on the hot plate, not just one. This will further help control the temperature.

We could design a dedicated electronic control circuit to apply these methods, but it is almost always more practical to use an embedded computer because it provides greater flexibility with low cost and a quick development time. The exceptions are devices with extreme requirements (e.g. processing speed, power consumption, or unit cost).

Embedded computers use specialized *integrated circuits (ICs)* called microcontrollers that have features to simplify the monitoring and control of a system. A *microcontroller unit (MCU)* has a *central processing unit (CPU)* that runs a program made of *instructions*.

> integrated circuit (IC)
> Electronic circuit with components built into single piece of silicon, enabling extreme miniaturization, mass production, and cost reduction

> microcontroller unit (MCU)
> Integrated controller hardware circuit containing CPU, peripherals, support circuits, and usually memory

> central processing unit (CPU)
> Hardware circuit which executes a program's instructions

> instruction
> Command which a processor can perform (execute). Consists of an operation and optional parameters called operands.

An MCU makes it easier to add sophisticated control methods at a low cost per product. We customize the computer to our application by writing software for the application and designing simple hardware to interface with the system. The recurring hardware costs are low because embedded computers typically use MCUs, which are inexpensive because they are produced in such high volumes. MCUs also reduce system costs because they include circuits to interface with the system, greatly simplifying the hardware development effort and circuit complexity. The main cost for embedded systems is generally the development of the control software, not the hardware itself.

Once there is an MCU in the system, it becomes much easier to add other useful features to improve and differentiate the product:

- Automatically turn off the hot plate for safety after a fixed time with no temperature knob changes.
- Provide calibrated temperature control with actual temperatures on the knob rather than LOW, MED, or HOT.
- Flash the lamp to indicate when the hot plate temperature is at or near the set point.
- Display the current temperature and the desired (set-point) temperature on a panel display.

How to Embed a Computer?

Let's examine how to improve the hot plate by adding an embedded computer. Figure 1.5 shows a block diagram of our improved, computer-controlled hot plate. We will use an MCU as the controller to read the desired and actual temperatures and decide on how to control the output. The MCU reads inputs to determine the state of the system being monitored and controlled. For the hot plate, the inputs include the temperature control knob position (desired temperature) and the hot plate temperature. That temperature is measured with a sensor that provides a signal whose voltage varies proportionally with temperature. The MCU may need to convert this signal into a form it can use.

We will use a simple on/off signal to control the heating element. Because the output signals from the microcontroller are low voltage and low current they are not capable of powering the heating element. We need to use a driver circuit to step up the signal from the microcontroller to an adequate level.

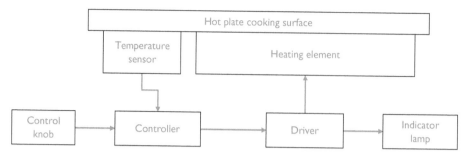

Figure 1.5 Block diagram of a computer-controlled hot plate.

The heating element and the indicator lamp operate at a line voltage, such as 110 V or 220 V. However, the microcontroller operates at a much lower level: 3.3 V. We need to use a power supply to convert the input voltage down to 3.3 V. This power supply is not shown in the diagram.

The main job of the software in the controller will be to compute the error between the desired temperature (the set point), as indicated by the control knob, and the actual temperature, as measured by the temperature sensor. The controller will then adjust the amount of power delivered to the heating element in order to reduce that error.

Examples of Embedded Systems

Let's examine two more examples of embedded systems to get an idea of the variety of devices and their different design goals and constraints.

Figure 1.6 shows a quadcopter, which is a small, remote-controlled toy aircraft. The user flies the quadcopter using a wireless remote control that sends commands to change altitude; rotate; travel forward, back, or sideways; or even flip over 180° and fly upside down. The quadcopter has four motors that drive four rotors to provide lift. By adjusting the speed of the motors individually, the quadcopter can be made to move in different ways. However, it is too difficult for the user to control each motor's speed directly. Instead, the quadcopter's embedded computer translates the user's remote control commands into motor speed commands. This translation depends on the current orientation and motion of the quadcopter, which can change very quickly. The quadcopter has a set of accelerometer sensors to detect acceleration in three directions (up/down, left/right, forward/back) and a set of gyroscopic sensors to detect rotation in three directions (roll, pitch, yaw).

Figure 1.7 shows a refrigerator with a freezer, an ice maker, and a water chiller. Figure 1.8 shows its control panel and display and part of the chilled water and ice dispenser. The refrigerator needs to maintain temperatures within specified ranges in two compartments, allow the user to change those temperatures, light the compartments when its door is opened, make ice, and dispense chilled water, ice cubes, or crushed ice. Other features include sounding a chime if the door is left open for too long and indicating when the water filter needs to be replaced.

Looking at the Hardware Inside

Let's take a look inside the quadcopter. The *printed circuit board (PCB)*, shown in Figure 1.9 and Figure 1.10 is about 4.5 cm long. The two large black squares in Figure 1.10 are the MCU (above) and the acceleration and rotation sensors (below). The corners of the PCB hold four *light-emitting diodes (LEDs)* and wires to the four motors. A radio interface chip is hidden

Figure 1.6 A remote-controlled quadcopter toy. Photo by author.

Figure 1.7 A refrigerator with a freezer, an ice maker, and a dispenser for water and ice (not shown). Photo by author.

Figure 1.8 A user control panel above the chilled water and ice dispenser. Photo by author.

underneath the white glue and silver cylinder to the right of the MCU and sensors. Most of the small black rectangles with three legs are transistors that drive the four motors. The battery cable plugs into the large orange connector on the left.

printed circuit board (PCB)
Board which holds electronic components and uses conductive traces for connections

light-emitting diode (LED)
Electronic component which emits light. Used for indicators, backlighting, and general illumination

Figure 1.9 The front of a quadcopter controller board. Photo by author.

Figure 1.10   The back of a quadcopter controller board. The large black squares are the MCU (top) and
the accelerometer/gyroscopic sensor (bottom). The black wire is the radio antenna. Photo
by author.

Now let's examine the refrigerator's PCB. Figure 1.11 and Figure 1.12 show the front and back
of the main PCB, which is about 25 cm long. The MCU is located on the back of the PCB and
is just one of many electronic components. These other components convert power, amplify
and condition signals from input devices, and drive output devices. Here are the major input
and output devices:

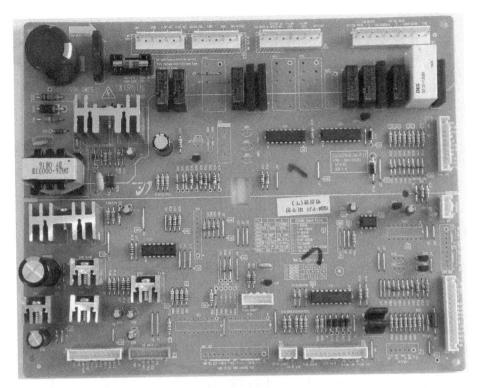

Figure 1.11 The front of a refrigerator controller board. Photo by author.

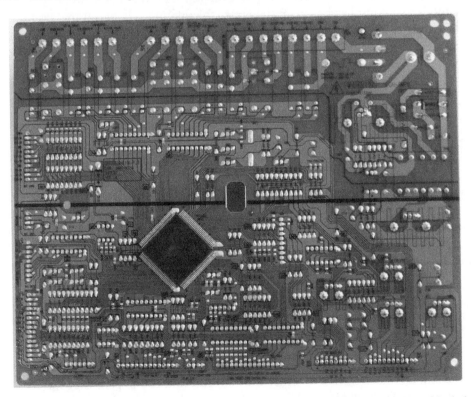

Figure 1.12 The back of a refrigerator controller board. The microcontroller is the large black diamond.
Photo by author.

- Inputs
  - Switches: user control panel, compressor overload protection, freezer door, refrigerator door, ice bucket full, water/ice dispenser lever, cube motor position, ice maker test, ice route motor position.
  - Temperature sensors: external air, freezer, freezer defroster, refrigerator, refrigerator defroster.
- Outputs
  - Lights: freezer, refrigerator, dispenser.
  - Indicators: user control panel.
  - Heaters: freezer defroster, refrigerator defroster, water pipe, door cap, dispenser, water tank.
  - Motors: compressor, ice route, auger, cube, ice grinder, freezer fan, condenser fan, refrigerator fan.
  - Water valves: water solenoid, icemaker solenoid, water stepper motor.

You probably didn't expect a refrigerator to be so complex.

Typical Embedded System Software Operations

To do their work, embedded systems typically perform one or more types of operations:

Closed-loop control involves controlling an output variable based on one or more input measurements. For example, the refrigerator controller maintains the temperature by turning on the compressor if the refrigerator compartment is too warm and turning it off if it is too cold. Similarly, the quadcopter controller keeps the craft flat and stable by adjusting the power to its rotor motors based on measurements of acceleration and rotation. There are more sophisticated control methods that consider the size of the error (the difference between the desired value and the actual measured value), how quickly it is changing, and how long it has persisted.

Sequencing involves controlling an output through a sequence of steps. For example, the ice-maker follows several steps to make ice:

- Fill the ice tray with water.
- Chill the ice tray until the water is frozen.
- Heat the ice tray to allow the ice to separate from the tray.
- Eject the ice from the tray.

Signal conditioning and processing may be used to average together multiple sensor readings or filter out noise from motors or other devices. For example, the quadcopter's four motors vibrate as they run, introducing noise into the acceleration and rotation readings. Taking multiple readings and averaging them can reduce the impact of this noise, improving accuracy.

Communications and networking allow the device to interact with subsystems or other systems. The quadcopter receives packets of control data sent by radio from the controller. The MCU needs to decode each packet of data to determine which commands and parameters have been sent.

Embedded System Attributes

Now let's examine some attributes of embedded systems and the impact they have on the software and hardware. These attributes lead to different design approaches and decisions than for personal computer application programs.

Interfacing with Inputs and Outputs

Embedded computers typically need to sense the environment and then control devices in response. To do this, specialized circuits are needed to get the information to and from the CPU, which executes instructions. We have seen examples of input and output devices for the refrigerator and the quadcopter. MCUs consist of a CPU surrounded by specialized *peripheral* hardware circuits that perform much of this interfacing. Any remaining interface circuits are added externally on the PCB.

Many of the external devices use *analog* signals in which the voltage (or current) can take on a continuous range of values to convey information. For example, a temperature sensor might indicate its reading by setting its output signal's voltage to 0.05 V/°C. A reading of 0.5 V would indicate a temperature of 10°C. This analog signal must be converted to a *digital* value for the program to process it; this is done using an *analog-to-digital converter (ADC)*. To generate sounds accurately, the MCU must generate analog voltage signals to drive headphones or speakers. The digital values representing the sound signal can be converted to an analog voltage using a *digital-to-analog converter*.

peripheral
Hardware circuit which helps CPU by interfacing or providing special functionality

analog
Capable of taking on an infinite number of values

digital
Capable of taking on a limited number of values

analog-to-digital converter (ADC)
Circuit which converts an analog value (e.g. voltage) to its corresponding digital value

digital-to-analog converter (DAC)
Circuit which converts a digital value to its corresponding analog value (e.g. voltage)

Often signals must be processed before they are converted to the digital domain for the CPU. For example, weak signals need to be amplified, high-voltage signals need to be scaled down to safe levels, and noise must be filtered out. Similarly, the MCU may not be capable of driving power-hungry output devices (e.g. motors and solenoids), so amplification is needed. Consider again the refrigerator controller's main PCB, as shown in Figures 1.11 and 1.12. The MCU is not powerful enough to drive the heaters, motors, and valves directly, and so it uses various devices (e.g. the black blocks and the white block along the top of the PCB) to do the job. This also protects the circuit by isolating low-voltage components like the MCU (which operates at 3.3 V) from the mains voltage (e.g. 120 V or 220 V).

Concurrency

Embedded controllers must typically manage multiple activities concurrently, often with precise control of the timing:

- For example, the quadcopter MCU must accept user commands by radio while also monitoring rotation (about three axes) and acceleration (in three axes), controlling the speeds of four motors to maintain stable flight, flashing indicator lights, and monitoring battery voltage.
- The refrigerator must control the temperature in the refrigerator compartment, the temperature in the freezer compartment, manage the ice-making process, display information on the front panel, accept user commands, and perform diagnostics.

Adding more features to a system increases the software's complexity. A graphical liquid crystal display (LCD) may require several software components to (1) manage the user interface's windows, menus, and screens, (2) translate text, graphics, and images into pixel values, and (3) update the display's memory with these pixel values. Other examples of such features are WiFi and Bluetooth communication and removable storage devices such as Secure Digital flash cards and USB drives. The maker of a complex peripheral IC may provide a software module (driver) to make interfacing easier. Embedded system developers frequently use third-party software components for such tasks to simplify the development process.

Microcontroller units provide concurrency by sharing the CPU among different parts of the software (including interrupt handlers, tasks, threads, and processes), and also by performing some processing in hardware peripherals that run independently of the CPU.

The scheduler determines what piece of software to run next on the processor and switches execution contexts as needed to make it happen correctly. There is a wide range of schedulers available. The most basic schedulers are simple to use and impose little overhead on the processor. They work best for simple systems and only provide limited help to the developer. More advanced schedulers provide better responsiveness (described next) and more features to help in program development. Real-time operating systems (e.g. RTX from Keil) typically use such schedulers. However, they require more of the processor's time and memory, ruling out the use of some low-performance MCUs. In addition, the presence of additional features introduces some performance variability. A full-fledged operating system (e.g. Linux) provides a wide range of features and services to help the embedded system developer. Such an operating system (OS) requires even more processor time and memory, so a much more powerful MCU is required.

Responsiveness

One challenge for embedded system developers is providing enough responsiveness while sharing the CPU's time across many activities. The field of real-time systems studies this aspect of design and performance.

If an embedded controller does not respond to commands and changes in the environment quickly enough, the system may damage itself, people, or other equipment. Often, embedded systems have requirements that specify deadlines for a response to a given input command. Consider the quadcopter: if there is a one-second delay between your changing the flight controls and the quadcopter acting on that command, the aircraft will be much harder to control.

There are two aspects to making a system responsive: raw processing speed and task scheduling.

First, the processor must be **fast enough** to complete the critical processing before its deadline. There are different ways to approach this. One is to make the code efficient so it can do the necessary work with very few instructions. Making the code efficient is called **optimization** and is a common task in embedded system development. Another approach is to use a fast processor so that those instructions are executed very quickly. And of course, both can be used.

There are trade-offs involved here: it takes developers more time to optimize code, increasing the development costs but not the recurring per-unit costs. Using a faster processor (usually) does not increase the development costs, but it does increase the recurring per-unit costs. A faster processor is more expensive, and it may also require more careful circuit design methods. Once the processor speed exceeds 50 MHz, the flash memory will not be able to keep up, forcing CPU designers to modify the memory system to hide this delay.

Second, the processor needs to **stay focused** on the **critical processing** rather than being distracted by other processing, which will introduce delays. If possible, the critical processing should be performed by hardware peripherals to prevent any software interference. Otherwise, some kind of software scheduling approach is needed. Simple scheduling approaches provide moderate responsiveness, but to get the best responsiveness, a system needs to use interrupts and a preemptive scheduler (e.g. a real-time kernel or a real-time OS). Stepping up to an OS (e.g. Linux) reduces the system's responsiveness because now there are many activities that could delay the critical processing. Scheduling methods are discussed in Chapter 3.

Some embedded systems have such high processing demands that they use multicore processors, which are able to execute instructions from multiple programs (or parts of the same program) simultaneously. Other such systems may use multiple single-core processors to get higher performance.

Finally, some embedded systems use multiple processors to simplify design, rather than to get raw processing speed. Separating the processing reduces timing interference among the software components. Many commercial off-the-shelf modules (e.g. a WiFi interface) contain an integrated MCU to do the work.

Reliability and Fault Handling

Embedded systems are expected to work correctly and reliably. Unlike personal computers, the user does not expect to have to reboot an embedded computer. If something fails, the system should minimize the impact of that failure rather than cause further problems.

Providing reliability and appropriate fault handling are very much dependent on the specific application. Which components are most likely to fail? There may be methods to detect actual or impending failures and shut down the system before there is more trouble. For example, sensors can be added (e.g. a thermal sensor to detect an overheating motor, a current sensor to detect short-circuited output), the circuit can be designed in a way to make failures easy to detect in software, or the software may be able to analyze historical data to determine failures. Embedded systems software typically contains large amounts of fault-handling code to deal with these exceptional cases.

The quadcopter does not need a long-term, highly reliable operation because it is a toy and the expected lifetime is short (perhaps 6 months). The mechanical components of the quadcopter will likely fail before software faults occur. However, note the white glue in Figure 1.10 which keeps larger, loose objects from vibrating and weakening their connections to the PCB.

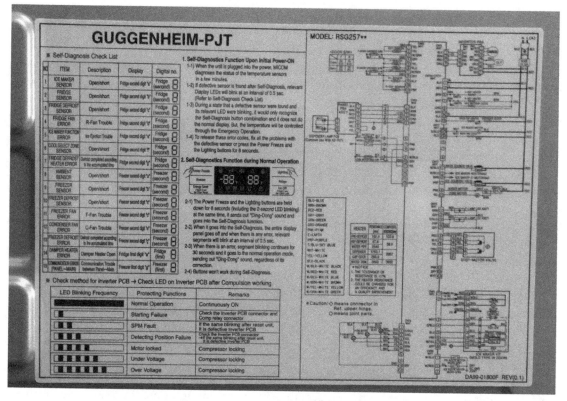

Figure 1.13   The label on the back of a refrigerator provides diagnostic and connection information for service personnel. Photo by author.

Diagnostics

For some systems, it is very important to be able to find and repair faulty components quickly and easily. One good example is the refrigerator: the manufacturer wants to minimize costs and time for its service personnel. The embedded computer system can help by providing diagnostic support to test the system and identify which components have failed.

The left half of the label shown in Figure 1.13 is dedicated to explaining the refrigerator's self-diagnosis capabilities. This allows the manufacturer's service personnel to spend less time identifying the problem, reducing service call costs. The PCB in Figure 1.11 is designed to simplify diagnosis and repair; most connections are labeled and a legend labeled "SENSOR Check-Point" explains where to measure the eight different temperature sensors.

Constraints

Constraints placed on the resulting embedded system design limit the designer's options when trying to meet the system's functional requirements. The embedded system must not be too expensive, large, heavy, power-hungry, and so forth.

Parts **costs** are important for many embedded systems. The quadcopter and its controller sell for about \$30, so the cost for parts (electronic, mechanical, etc.) needs to be under about \$8. There is great pressure to use the least expensive parts that are adequate for the job. In this case, the MCU used is an STM32F031K6, which contains a Cortex-M0 CPU running up to 48 MHz, with 4 KB of SRAM and 32 KB of flash ROM. Most embedded systems are programmed in the C or C++ languages, in large part because these languages can be compiled into code with precise control of the hardware, and yet use small amounts of memory. Similarly, most embedded systems do not use a complex OS such as Linux to share the computer's resources among the parts of the program. The main reasons are that the Linux OS requires large amounts of memory and a fast processor for good performance. There are alternative methods that can use a much less expensive embedded computer and still meet the performance requirements.

Some embedded systems have constraints on **power**. Power constraints limit the system's rate of energy use. For example, the amount of power that a photovoltaic (PV) cell can generate depends on the ambient light. If the circuit tries to use more power than the PV cell can provide, the cell's voltage drops and the system stops working.

Energy constraints limit the total amount of energy that can be used. For example, a battery holds a limited amount of energy. That energy can be used quickly or slowly, but there is only a limited amount available. Flying the quadcopter faster will discharge its battery faster, reducing the maximum flight time possible. So one goal for its developers was to use energy-efficient motors, lights, radios, and MCUs.

Some applications are **weight**-sensitive. Heavier objects take more energy to lift, move, and stop. For the quadcopter, lightness is important because a heavier quadcopter uses energy faster. In order to lift a heavier quadcopter, more lift is needed, so the motors will need to spin faster, drawing more power, and discharging the battery sooner. The quadcopter uses very small components in order to reduce the weight.

The quadcopter also has **size** constraints. Notice how small the components on the PCB are and how closely packed together they are. Compare this with the much larger and more sparsely packed PCB for the refrigerator. The refrigerator's MCU is about 35 mm × 35 mm and takes about 1,225 mm² of the PCB area. This is far larger than the quadcopter's MCU, which at 10 mm × 10 mm takes only 100 mm².

Embedded systems are often expected to operate reliably over a wide range of **temperatures**. Electronic components for consumer applications are expected to operate with ambient temperatures of 0°C to 70°C. Components for the more demanding industrial and automotive applications are expected to handle ranges from –40°C to 85°C.

Target Platform

Overview

Now let's take a look at the hardware platform that we will be using. We will start with the CPU and work our way out.

This textbook targets the ARM Cortex-M0+ processor shown on the left side of Figure 1.14. The processor executes the instructions of the program.

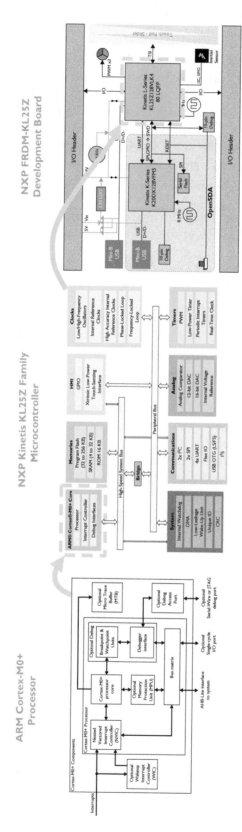

Figure 1.14   An overview of a processor, microcontroller, and development board. Courtesy of ARM Ltd. and NXP Semiconductors N.V.

Figure 1.15   FRDM-KL25Z development board from NXP Semiconductors N.V. Photo by author.

The processor is a component within the microcontroller, shown in the center of Figure 1.14. The MCU adds circuits to clock the processor, a memory to hold the program and data, and peripheral devices that simplify programs and improve their performance. The NXP KL25Z128VLK4 MCU is used here.

The microcontroller is mounted on a FRDM-KL25Z development board, shown on the right side of Figure 1.14 and Figure 1.15. This PCB adds a debug interface, power supplies, and various input and output devices.

Processor

The Cortex-M0+ processor, shown in Figure 1.16, executes the instructions that make up the program. At the center of the Cortex-M0+ processor is the processor core, which communicates with the memory to get the instructions it executes and hold the data it processes. The memory is located outside the processor in the microcontroller and is connected via the AHB-Lite interface. The bus matrix shares the memory bus among multiple possible readers and writers. An optional memory protection unit enables the system to restrict a task to using only a limited region of the memory, limiting the effects of bugs.

Interrupts come to the processor core through the Nested Vectored Interrupt Controller (NVIC), which prioritizes and filters them as needed.

The optional Wakeup Interrupt Controller cuts power consumption by letting the NVIC and the rest of the processor go to a low-power sleep mode and waking them up if an interrupt is requested. Several modules provide debug support, including downloading code to the MCU's

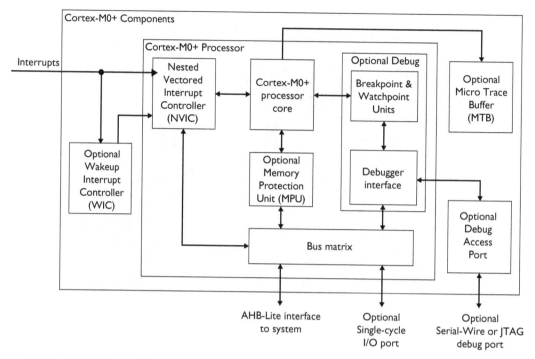

Figure 1.16   ARM Cortex-M0+ processor and its associated components. Courtesy of ARM Ltd.

memory, setting break points to control program execution, and tracing the sequence of instructions actually executed.

Microcontroller

The microcontroller augments the ARM Cortex-M0+ processor by adding memory and supporting circuitry and peripheral devices (Figure 1.17). There are typically two types of memory provided. The flash memory retains its contents even without power, so it holds the program and fixed data. The SRAM does not retain its contents if there is no power and is used for temporary data storage.

The MCU used here (KL25Z128VLK4) features a Cortex-M0+ processor capable of running up to 48 MHz and contains 128 KB of flash ROM, 16 KB of RAM, and a wide range of peripherals [1], [2].

The support circuitry is required to make the processor operate. For example, the processor requires a clock signal, and the MCU adds multiple clock generators. These clocks have different levels of accuracy, speed, power consumption, and configurability.

Peripheral devices off-load work from the program (which executes on the processor) and perform it in hardware. For example, **timer** peripherals allow precise time measurement of events or input signals. They also enable generation of repetitive signals without software overhead. **Communication interfaces** translate digital data between the processor's format and the formats which external devices use. **Analog interfaces** translate data between the processor's digital format and the analog domain, in which signals vary across a continuous

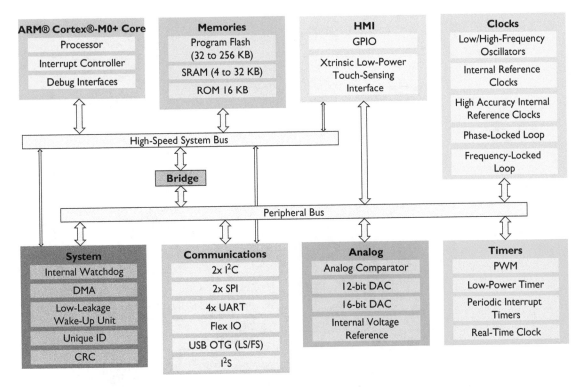

Figure 1.17 NXP Kinetis KL25Z family microcontroller (MCU).

range of voltages, rather than the binary 1/0 of digital electronics. Finally, other peripherals are used to reset an out-of-control program (watchdog), accelerate and automate memory transfers (DMA), and perform other tasks.

Development Board

As shown in Figures 1.15 and 1.18, the microcontroller is mounted on an FRDM-KL25Z development board [3]. This board adds power supplies, a debug interface, and various input and output devices. An 8-MHz clock source provides a stable, accurate timing reference.

The board is normally powered by the 5 V supplied by the USB connection. A voltage regulator drops this to 3.3 V in order to operate the board's components. There is space to mount a small 3 V coin cell and holder, allowing the board to operate without a connection to USB power.

A separate **debug microcontroller** (in the green box labeled OpenSDA) translates commands and data between the development PC (via a USB connection) and the KL25Z MCU (the **target microcontroller**).

Two input devices are provided. A three-axis inertial sensor (accelerometer) is used to detect motion. Because it also senses the force of gravity, it can be used to determine the inclination (tilt) of the board. A touch-pad slider measures the position of a fingertip using a capacitive sensor.

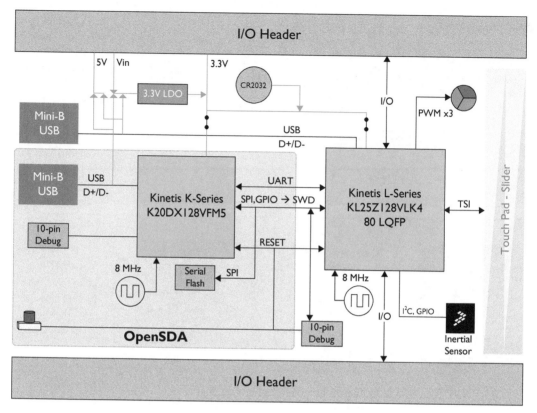

Figure 1.18   NXP FRDM-KL25Z development board. Courtesy of NXP Semiconductors N.V.

A three-in-one output device is included: three high-brightness LEDs (red, green, and blue). These LEDs can be lit with varying levels of brightness to produce a full range of colors.

Summary

Embedding a computer to control a system can provide benefits such as better performance and sophisticated features. We have seen three examples of applications: a hot plate for cooking food, a toy quadcopter aircraft, and a refrigerator. The embedded computer is typically made from a microcontroller that runs specialized control software which monitors the critical aspects of the system and its environment and then adjusts its outputs so the system behaves as needed. The computer uses special hardware to interface with the inputs and outputs. To meet application requirements, embedded systems must provide sufficient concurrency, responsiveness, reliability, fault handling, and diagnostic help while meeting constraints on cost, size, weight, power, energy, and temperature. Finally, we have seen the target platform for this textbook: the ARM Cortex-M0+ processor core within the KL25Z128VKL4 MCU on the NXP FRDM-KL25Z development board.

Exercises

1. You have been asked to add an "automatic power-off" controller to a flashlight. The flashlight should turn off automatically after 3 minutes if it is not being used any more. The controller must be small, inexpensive, and use little power.
   a. Can you think of a way to do this with electronics but without an embedded computer?
   b. Can you think of a way to do this with a mechanical approach?
   c. Now, really thinking outside the box, can you think of a way to do this with a pneumatic approach (using air)?
2. Consider embedding a computer in a flashlight. List three benefits or new useful features that are now possible. How much more would you be willing to pay for each feature?
3. A modern automobile has dozens of embedded computers. However, the auto industry is extremely cost-sensitive, so there must be a compelling reason to add computers. Give five examples of features enabled by embedded computers, and explain what major benefit(s) they provide.
4. Look around and find five devices that are likely to have embedded computer control systems. Answer these questions for each device:
   a. What does the device do?
   b. What are the device's inputs?
   c. What are the device's outputs?
   d. How does the embedded computer improve the device? Does it provide more features? Does it improve performance?
   e. What are the biggest constraints on the device (size, cost, power, etc.)?
   f. Would it be possible to build the device using a different kind of controller (e.g. mechanical)? How would that affect the device's features, performance, cost, size, and weight?

References

[1] *KL25 Sub-Family Reference Manual*, KL25P80M48SF0RM, rev. 3rd ed., NXP Semiconductor, B.V., 2016.
[2] *Kinetis KL25 Sub-Family Data Sheet*, KL25P80M48SF0, rev. 5th ed., NXP Semiconductor, B.V., 2016.
[3] *FRDM-KL25Z User's Manual*, rev. 2.0, NXP Semiconductor, B.V., 2016.
[4] P. Koopman, *Better embedded system software*, Pittsburgh: Drumnadrochit Education LLC, 2010.
[5] J. Ganssle, *The art of designing embedded systems*, 2nd ed. Elsevier Inc., 2008.
[6] J. K. Peckol, *Embedded systems: A contemporary design tool*, John Wiley & Sons, Inc., 2008.
[7] L. Simone, *If I only changed the software, why is the phone on fire? Embedded debugging methods revealed: technical mysteries for engineers*, Elsevier Inc., 2007.

2

General Purpose Input/Output

Chapter Contents

Overview

Embedded computers typically need to sense their environment and then control devices in response. Let's start with the basics by learning how to make an embedded computer flash lights and read a switch by using a *general purpose input/output (GPIO) port*.

A microcontroller unit (MCU) contains a central processing unit (CPU) that executes instructions. The CPU is surrounded by specialized hardware circuits called peripherals that interface with external devices or perform other functions for the MCU. Some of these peripherals are integrated into the MCU, whereas others may be added externally on the printed circuit board.

> general purpose input/output (GPIO) port
> *Peripheral with digital input and output bits*

In this chapter we introduce the GPIO port. We show how to create a C program to communicate with basic devices such as switches and light-emitting diodes (LEDs) as shown in Figure 2.1. An *input GPIO port bit* lets us read a single bit digital value on an MCU pin. If we connect the pin to a switch (as with the signal SWITCH_IN), then the program can tell if the switch is open or closed. An *output GPIO port bit* enables the program to set an MCU pin to one of two voltage levels (e.g. either 3.3 V or 0 V). A program can light or extinguish an LED that is connected to this output pin (e.g. LED1_OUT or LED2_OUT).

> input GPIO port bit
> *Portion of GPIO port which enables program to read a single-bit input signal*

> output GPIO port bit
> *Portion of GPIO port which enables program to write a single-bit output signal*

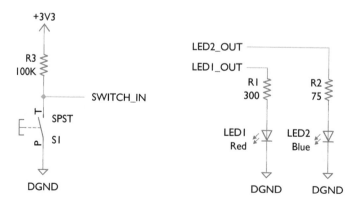

Figure 2.1 A basic digital input and output circuit.

Throughout this chapter we will follow an example of how to interface a C program with the circuit shown in Figure 2.1, which consists of one input (a switch) and two outputs (LEDs).

Some of the implementation details in this chapter are specific to the Kinetis series of MCUs. For further details, consult the reference manual [1] or data sheet [2].

Outside the MCU: Ones and Zeros, Voltages, and Currents

We will start outside the MCU and work our way in. An MCU is a digital computer, so it operates on ones and zeros. How do we present a one or a zero to an input? What does a one or zero look like on an MCU output?

These values are represented by voltages within specific ranges relative to the MCU's power supply voltage, V_{DD}. The actual voltages do not matter much to an embedded system developer when they are inside the MCU, but they do matter when we want to interface with external devices.

Input Signals

Digital inputs are interpreted based on their voltage levels. How do we supply a one or a zero to a digital input? The supply voltage V_{DD} sets the thresholds for determining whether an input voltage will be considered a one or a zero. For example, the MCU's data sheet might specify that an input voltage between 0 V and $0.35 \times V_{DD}$ will be interpreted as a logic zero, whereas an input voltage between $0.7 \times V_{DD}$ and V_{DD} will be interpreted as a logic one. Figure 2.2 shows how input voltages are interpreted based on the supply voltage V_{DD}. For example, if V_{DD} is 3.3 V, then input values between 0 and 1.155 V will be a logic zero and those between 2.31 and 3.3 V will be a logic one. An input voltage between $0.35 \times V_{DD}$ and $0.7 \times V_{DD}$ is **undefined**, and may be read as a one or a zero. This is useless so we design external circuits to keep the voltage out of that range except when switching.

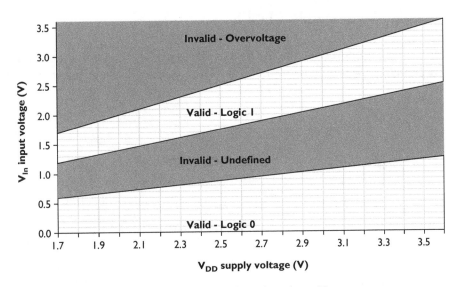

Figure 2.2 Valid input voltage ranges as a function of supply voltage V_{DD}.

Digital inputs do not draw much current from the signal source; they have high input impedance. Typically each GPIO pin will draw no more than 1 μA over the MCU's entire operating temperature range. At room temperature (25°C), the input current will be much smaller (e.g. no more than 25 nA).

Output Signals

Output voltages for digital ports are typically specified as being within a certain voltage range from a supply rail. For common MCUs, a normal output generating a logic one will produce a voltage of $V_{OH\ (out\ high)}$, which is between V_{DD} and $V_{DD} - 0.5$ V. A logic zero will produce a voltage of $V_{OL\ (out\ low)}$ between 0 and 0.5 V.

This specification only holds true if a limited amount of current is drawn from the output. As that current increases, the output circuit's voltage drop increases, pulling the output voltage away from the supply rails (V_{DD} and ground). If the output circuit draws enough current, it will overload and destroy the output *transistor*. So be careful not to exceed the specified ratings.

For many MCUs, the output current I_{OH} or I_{OL} must not exceed 5 mA. Some MCUs include output drivers with more powerful transistors, allowing greater output currents. "High drive" pads may be able to source or sink up more current (e.g. up to 18 mA) and still meet the output voltage specifications.

> transistor
> *Basic electronic component which operates as switch or amplifier*

The drive current capability also depends on the supply voltage V_{DD}. As V_{DD} falls, the transistors have a higher output resistance, increasing the voltage drop. So at lower operating voltages, the maximum output current available falls. Lowering V_{DD} from 3.3 to 2.0 V might cut I_{OH} and I_{OL} from 5 to 1.5 mA.

Interfacing with a Switch and LED Lights

Let's consider the switch and LED example shown in Figure 2.3. A switch and a pull-up resistor are connected to signal SWITCH_IN. When the switch is pressed, the signal is pulled low (logic

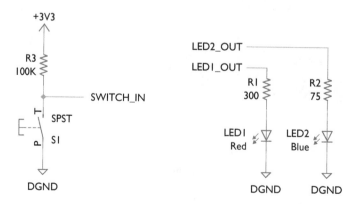

Figure 2.3 A switch and two LEDs.

zero); otherwise it is high (logic one). The input port's current draw I_{In} is so small that we can use a high value pull-up resistor (e.g. 100 kΩ) to minimize current consumption when the switch is pressed.

Each LED has its *anode* (positive end, base of triangle) connected to an MCU output signal (either LED1_OUT or LED2_OUT) through a resistor. The LED's *cathode* (negative end, bar) is connected to ground. An LED's brightness is roughly proportional to the current flowing through it. This current is nearly zero for low voltages, and then rises quickly as the voltage exceeds a threshold. The exact relationship between the voltage and current depends on the type of LED and its temperature. Applying 1.6 V may not light a red LED at all, but 2.0 V will make it bright (with 20 mA of current). Raising the voltage slightly to 2.3 V brightens it more and makes the current shoot up to 43 mA. Raising it further will cause the LED to overheat and fail.

anode
Positive terminal of a polarized component (LED, battery, etc.)

cathode
Negative terminal of a polarized component (LED, battery, etc.)

The GPIO port outputs are digital and do not offer such fine-grain voltage control. They can provide two levels: and almost ground, and almost V_{DD} (e.g. 3.3 V). The first will correctly keep the LED off, but the second will probably burn out the LED. We need to include resistors R2 and R3 to limit the current through the LED and MCU driver output to a safe value.

We can calculate the value R of a current-limiting resistor based on the supply voltage V_{DD}, the LED forward voltage V_F, and the desired LED current I_{LED}:

$$R = \frac{V_{DD} - V_F}{I_{LED}}$$

We start by picking a value of I_{LED} which is safe for both the LED and the MCU output. In this case let's set I_{LED} = 4 mA, and assume V_{DD} = 3.0 V. V_F is 1.8 V for the red LED and 2.7 V for the blue LED. We can now solve for the resistor values. For the red LED, a 300 Ω resistor is needed. For the blue LED, a 75 Ω resistor is needed.

Inside the MCU

Now that we know how to connect these simple devices to the MCU pins, let's look into how to let the program running on the CPU talk with those pins. First the program needs to configure the hardware within the MCU to set up the path between the CPU and the pins. Then the program can read from or write to those pins. Different MCU families use different approaches; here we cover the NXP Kinetis MCU family.

Preliminaries: Control Registers and C Code

Peripherals are built with *control registers* to allow us to configure them, determine their status and transfer data. Figure 2.4 shows some of the control registers for one peripheral module, the System Integration Module (SIM). These control registers appear as special locations in memory, as indicated by the column marked "Absolute address (hex)". The term "hex" indicates the address is in *hexadecimal* format (base 16). We also can see the width of the register, whether we can read from or write to the register, and what its value is after the MCU is reset (e.g. on power-up).

> control register
> *Register used to configure operation of hardware in CPU or peripheral*

> hexadecimal
> *Base-sixteen numbering system. Each digit can have one of sixteen values (0 through 9, A, B, C, D, E and F). Symbols A through F represent values of ten through fifteen.*

SIM memory map

Absolute address (hex)	Register name	Width (in bits)	Access	Reset value	Section/ page
4004_7000	System Options Register 1 (SIM_SOPT1)	32	R/W	See section	12.2.1/183
4004_7004	SOPT1 Configuration Register (SIM_SOPT1CFG)	32	R/W	0000_0000h	12.2.2/184
4004_8004	System Options Register 2 (SIM_SOPT2)	32	R/W	0000_0000h	12.2.3/185
4004_800C	System Options Register 4 (SIM_SOPT4)	32	R/W	0000_0000h	12.2.4/187
4004_8010	System Options Register 5 (SIM_SOPT5)	32	R/W	0000_0000h	12.2.5/189
4004_8018	System Options Register 7 (SIM_SOPT7)	32	R/W	0000_0000h	12.2.6/190
4004_8024	System Device Identification Register (SIM_SDID)	32	R	Undefined	12.2.7/192
4004_8034	System Clock Gating Control Register 4 (SIM_SCGC4)	32	R/W	F000_0030h	12.2.8/193
4004_8038	System Clock Gating Control Register 5 (SIM_SCGC5)	32	R/W	0000_0180h	12.2.9/195
4004_803C	System Clock Gating Control Register 6 (SIM_SCGC6)	32	R/W	0000_0001h	12.2.10/197
4004_8040	System Clock Gating Control Register 7 (SIM_SCGC7)	32	R/W	0000_0100h	12.2.11/199

Figure 2.4 A portion of registers for the System Integration Module (SIM) peripheral [1, p. 182].

Using CMSIS to Access Hardware Registers with C Code

It would be tedious to have to look up and remember the addresses for the hardware control registers. Instead we use special C-language support. The Cortex Microcontroller Software Interface Standard (CMSIS) is a hardware abstraction layer for Cortex-M processors. The CMSIS-CORE component provides a C-language interface to the processor core and peripherals. This consists of macros and functions to perform various operations, and C data structures that map directly to registers.

Consider the SIM_SCGC5 control register. It is one of the SIM peripheral's control registers. CMSIS-CORE lets us access the SIM control registers using a C-language data structure with a useful name (SIM). The data structure for the SIM peripheral contains 32-bit fields called SOPT1, SOPT1CFG, SOPT2, and so forth. To access the SIM_SCGC5 register, we simply write SIM->SCGC5. Note that SIM is defined as a pointer to a data structure, which is why we use the "->" to select the control register within.

There are similar data structures for all of the MCU's peripherals and their control registers. The file **MKL25Z4.h** defines the peripheral access layer for CMSIS-CORE for KL25Z4-type MCUs. We need to be sure that all of our C source files contain the directive **#include <MKL25Z4.h>** before we try to use these features.

Coding Style for Accessing Bits

A control register may hold one item of information (e.g. a count of how many pulses have been received) or several items. Each item is called a "field". Consider the register SIM_SCGC5 shown in Figure 2.5. This is a 32-bit register although only 16 bits are shown here. Bit 0 is a field labeled LPTMR. Bits 1 through 4 are not used and will always be read as zeros. Bit 5 is a field labeled TSI. Bits 9 through 13 are five separate fields labeled PORTA through PORTE.

How can we access fields in these control registers using C code? We often need to access one or more specific bits in a control register to set them to specific values. For example, we might need to set the fields PORTA and PORTE to 1 in SIM_CGC5.

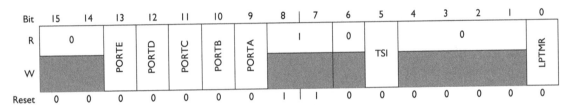

Figure 2.5 SIM_SCGC5 register controls clock gating for ports and two other peripherals [1, p. 206].

The fields are located at bits 9 and 13, respectively. We could write a 32-bit value with those bits set: the binary representation is 0000 0000 0000 0000 0010 0010 0000 0000. In decimal this is $2^9 + 2^{13}$ = 512 + 8192 = 8704. However, it is slow and tedious counting zeros and we are likely to make errors. Furthermore, the meaning of the code (shown below) is not at all clear.

```
n = 8704;
```

We can make the code somewhat easier to write and maintain by forming the value as a sum of shifted one bits. We'll use the left shift operation "$a << b$," which shifts operand a to the left by b bit positions. We will also use the bitwise or operator "$|$" rather than addition.

```
n = (1UL << 9) | (1UL << 13);
```

Why is there "UL" after the 1? To write to a 32-bit register we need for the compiler to generate a 32-bit unsigned integer. To ensure the compiler does not use a signed or short integer and introduce possible errors, we use the suffix UL to specify that a numeric literal (e.g. 1) should be represented as an unsigned long integer, which is 32 bits long for an ARM Cortex-M processor.

We can make the code even easier to understand if we define and use meaningful names for the bit positions. When we use them, our code now becomes much easier to read:

```
#define MY_PORTA_SHIFT (9)
#define MY_PORTE_SHIFT (13)
```

```
n = (1UL << MY_PORTA_SHIFT) | (1UL << MY_PORTE_SHIFT);
```

Let's further simplify things by making a macro to create a mask value by shifting a 1 to the proper position:

```
#define MY_PORTA_SHIFT (9)
#define MY_PORTE_SHIFT (13)
#define MASK(x) (1UL << (x))
n = MASK(MY_PORTA_SHIFT) | MASK(MY_PORTE_SHIFT);
```

CMSIS-CORE specifies macros for inserting and extracting bit fields into and from control registers. Each bit field is described by a shift value and a mask. The shift value indicates the field's position in the register, measured as the offset between the field's bit 0 and the control register's bit 0. The mask value is all zeros except for ones, which indicate the bit field's location. For example, Listing 2.1 shows the definitions related to the SCGC5 bit fields.

Reading, Modifying, and Writing Fields in Control Registers

Now we can see how to use these pieces to access the fields in the control registers:

- How do we find the current value of the PORTE field? We read the control register SCGC5, AND it (using &) with the mask, and then shift it right (using >>) by the shift value:

```
n = (SIM->SCGC5 & SIM_SCGC5_PORTE_MASK) >> SIM_SCGC5_PORTE_SHIFT;
```

- How do we set fields PORTA and PORTE in that register, leaving everything else as zero? We use the = assignment operator:

```
SIM->SCGC5 = SIM_SCGC5_PORTA_MASK | SIM_SCGC5_PORTE_MASK;
```

- How do we *set* fields PORTA and PORTE in that register without modifying anything else? This means we need to perform a read/modify/write operation. We read the initial control

```
/* SCGC5 Bit Fields */
#define SIM_SCGC5_LPTMR_MASK        0x1u
#define SIM_SCGC5_LPTMR_SHIFT       0
#define SIM_SCGC5_TSI_MASK          0x20u
#define SIM_SCGC5_TSI_SHIFT         5
#define SIM_SCGC5_PORTA_MASK        0x200u
#define SIM_SCGC5_PORTA_SHIFT       9
#define SIM_SCGC5_PORTB_MASK        0x400u
#define SIM_SCGC5_PORTB_SHIFT       10
#define SIM_SCGC5_PORTC_MASK        0x800u
#define SIM_SCGC5_PORTC_SHIFT       11
#define SIM_SCGC5_PORTD_MASK        0x1000u
#define SIM_SCGC5_PORTD_SHIFT       12
#define SIM_SCGC5_PORTE_MASK        0x2000u
#define SIM_SCGC5_PORTE_SHIFT       13
```

Listing 2.1 An example of bit field definitions for CMSIS-CORE hardware abstraction layer [2].

register value, modify the value, and then write the result back to the register. The OR read/modify/write operator | = does this:

```
SIM->SCGC5 |= SIM_SCGC5_PORTA_MASK | SIM_SCGC5_PORTE_MASK;
```

- How do we *clear* field PORTA in that register without modifying anything else? Again we need to perform a read/modify/write operation. However, the modification involves zeroing out the bit for PORTA. We do this by first complementing the mask for PORTA using the ~ operator. This flips all of its ones to zeros and zeros to ones. Using the AND read/modify/write operator &= will zero out the control register's bits for Port A's field:

```
SIM->SCGC5 &= ~SIM_SCGC5_PORTA_MASK;
```

set
To change a bit to one

clear
To change a bit to zero

Configuring the I/O Path

Figure 2.6 shows an overview of the hardware circuits between an I/O pin and the CPU for a Kinetis MCU. The PORTA module selects which peripheral modules (e.g. GPIO, UART0, TPM2) will use port A's pins. Pins can be assigned individually to different peripherals. The MCU configures the peripheral module and exchanges data with it. The block labeled SIM provides a clock signal to only the active modules, reducing power consumption.

In order to use the GPIO peripheral, we need to do a little preparation. First, we need to ensure that a clock signal is provided to the port module or else it will not operate. Second, we need to ensure that the GPIO signals inside the integrated circuit are routed to the outside world through an I/O pin (or pad).

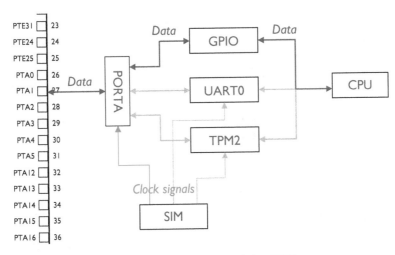

Figure 2.6 An overview of hardware between pin PTA1 and the CPU.

Clock Gating

In Kinetis MCUs, the SIM controls system *clock gating* using control registers SCGC4 through SCGC7 to control the peripherals. The MCU reference manual provides full information ([1] Chapter 12). Figure 2.5 shows an excerpt from the manual. SCGC5 allows individual control of the clock signals to PORTA, PORTB, PORTC, PORTD, and PORTE. Setting a port's bit in this register to one will supply the clock, allowing the port to operate. A zero will disable (gate) the clock signal to reduce power consumption by preventing circuit switching. We use the CMSIS-CORE support in the MKL25Z4.h header file:

```
SIM->SCGC5 |= SIM_SCGC5_PORTA_MASK;
```

clock gating
Method to disable circuit by blocking clock signal, reducing power consumption

Connecting a Pin to a Peripheral Module

The PORTA through PORTE modules provide control for each port's pins. Each bit n of each I/O port x has its own 32-bit pin control register (PCR) called PORTx_PCRn to allow individual bit configuration. Figure 2.7 shows a few of the PCRs for Port A.

MCUs often include a *multiplexer*, which is an electronic selector switch. As shown in Figure 2.8, this allows a specific pin on the IC package to be connected to one of several possible peripheral modules. This provides greater flexibility to PCB designers and reduces MCU package size, circuit board size, and costs.

multiplexer
Electronic selector switch which routes one of N inputs signals to the output. MCU pin multiplexer is bidirectional (includes demultiplexer).

Absolute address (hex)	Register name	Width (in bits)	Access
4004_9000	Pin Control Register n (PORTA_PCR0)	32	R/W
4004_9004	Pin Control Register n (PORTA_PCR1)	32	R/W
4004_9008	Pin Control Register n (PORTA_PCR2)	32	R/W
4004_900C	Pin Control Register n (PORTA_PCR3)	32	R/W
4004_9010	Pin Control Register n (PORTA_PCR4)	32	R/W
4004_9014	Pin Control Register n (PORTA_PCR5)	32	R/W
4004_9018	Pin Control Register n (PORTA_PCR6)	32	R/W
4004_901C	Pin Control Register n (PORTA_PCR7)	32	R/W

Figure 2.7 An example of several pin control registers for a KL25Z microcontroller [1, p. 177].

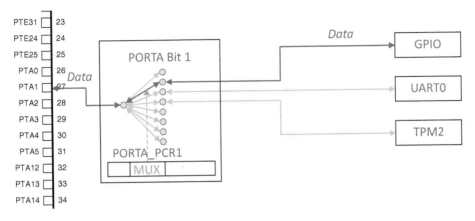

Figure 2.8 A detailed view of a pin multiplexer.

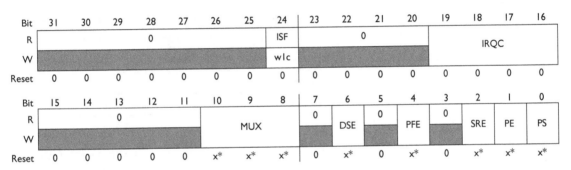

* Notes:
• x = Undefined at reset.

Figure 2.9 Pin control register contents [1, p. 183].

The Kinetis PORT modules provide such a multiplexer for each pin. There is one default position (DEFAULT) and seven alternate positions (ALT1 through ALT7) available for each pin. These are selected through the PCR's MUX bits, shown in Figure 2.9.

In order to access a PCR in C, we will use the CMSIS-CORE support from MKL25Z4.h. For example, the variable PORTA points to an array called PCR, made of 32 PCRs. To specify the PCR for bit 6 of PORTA, we would write PORTA->PCR[6].

The MUX control bits specify multiplexer behavior as shown in Table 2.1. Before writing to any PCR, be sure that the clock signal is provided to the port (using the SIM_SCGC5 register described above). Otherwise, accessing a PCR may trigger a fault and cause the processor to execute error handling code (e.g. for a hard fault).

A value of 000 will disable the digital GPIO functionality to allow the connected analog peripheral device to use the pin. A nonzero value will provide a variety of alternatives. 001 will always enable GPIO whereas the remaining values (010 to 111) will have different effects for different types of chips. For details refer to the MCU's reference manual ([1] Chapter 11).

The CMSIS-CORE support from MKL25Z4.h includes these macros for accessing the MUX field in the PCR. We can use the PORT_PCR_MUX macro to shift the desired value for the MUX bit field leftward to the field's position within the control register:

```
#define PORT_PCR_MUX_MASK  0x700u
#define PORT_PCR_MUX_SHIFT 8
#define PORT_PCR_MUX(x)  (((uint32_t)(((uint32_t)(x))<<PORT_PCR_MUX_SHIFT))&PORT_
  PCR_MUX_MASK)
```

Table 2.1 Pin Multiplexing Control Field Settings with Examples for Selected Pins

MUX field value (bits 10–8)	Configuration	Pin PTA1	Pin PTA2	Pin PTA5
000	Pin disabled (analog)	Touch Sense Input TSI0_CH2	Touch Sense Input TSI_CH3	No connection
001	Alternative 1: GPIO	PTA1	PTA2	PTA5
010	Alternative 2	Serial Communication UART0_RX	Serial Communication UART0_TX	USB_CLKIN
011	Alternative 3	Timer TPM2_CH0	Timer TPM2_CH1	Timer TPM0_CH2
100	Alternative 4	No connection	No connection	No connection
101	Alternative 5	No connection	No connection	No connection
110	Alternative 6	No connection	No connection	No connection
111	Alternative 7	No connection	No connection	No connection

PORT_PCR_MUX_SHIFT indicates the starting position of the least significant bit of the field. We will use this to specify the shift value needed to position the bit field within the register. PORT_PCR_MUX_MASK contains a one in each bit which makes up the field. ANDing this mask with a data value we can ensure that none of the bits for the other fields are set to one. This eliminates our accesses from having side effects.

Our switch and LED example system needs one input (the switch on PTA5) and two outputs (LEDs 1 and 2 on PTA1 and PTA2). We use the MUX field of the PCRs to connect the pins to the GPIO module. As seen in Table 2.1, a value of 1 will select the GPIO module for each of these pins.

```
#define LED1_SHIFT (1) // on port A
#define LED2_SHIFT (2) // on port A
#define SW1_SHIFT (5)  // on port A

PORTA->PCR[LED1_SHIFT]  &= ~PORT_PCR_MUX_MASK;
PORTA->PCR[LED1_SHIFT]  |= PORT_PCR_MUX(1);
PORTA->PCR[LED2_SHIFT]  &= ~PORT_PCR_MUX_MASK;
PORTA->PCR[LED2_SHIFT]  |= PORT_PCR_MUX(1);
PORTA->PCR[SW1_SHIFT]   &= ~PORT_PCR_MUX_MASK;
PORTA->PCR[SW1_SHIFT]   |= PORT_PCR_MUX(1);
```

Listing 2.2 Using read-modify-write operations to configure port control register multiplexer.

In order to preserve the other fields within the control register, we will use two read–modify–write operations: first we zero out the bits for the MUX field by ANDing with the complement (~) of the mask, then we OR in the new values for the MUX field. The code in listing 2.2 will accomplish this.

GPIO Peripheral

The KL25Z GPIO peripheral module has five ports (GPIOA through GPIOE). Although each port could be up to 32 bits wide, there are not enough pins on the MCU package to support all bits. The MCU's data sheet pin-out section describes which port bits are implemented [2].

An input GPIO port bit lets us read a single bit digital value on an MCU pin. For example, if we connect the pin to a switch, then the program can tell if the switch is open or closed. An output GPIO port bit enables the program to set an MCU pin to be a logic one or zero. For example, a program can light or extinguish an LED that is connected to an output pin.

The main logic hardware for a single GPIO port bit is simple and built around registers, as shown in Figure 2.10. Each GPIO port bit has its own version of this hardware. A register stores one bit of data, which is visible on the output signal (marked Q). A register will read its data input (marked D) and store that value every time its clock signal (marked with a triangle) is triggered. These signals are triggered when the CPU writes to or reads from the register's address, as labeled in Figure 2.10. The GPIO port bit has three main registers:

- Input data is held in the **data in register**. The MCU's I/O clock automatically updates this register (e.g. 24 million times per second). To read this register, the CPU reads from the Port Data Input Register address (GPIOx_PDIR), which enables the buffer (triangle to the right of the register) to transmit its contents to the CPU over the data bus.
- Output data is held in the **data out register**. The CPU writes data to this register by putting the data on the data bus and writing to the Port Data Output Register address (GPIOx_PDOR), which triggers the register's clock signal.
- The pin's direction is controlled by the **data direction register**. The CPU writes data to this register by putting the data on the data bus and writing to the Port Data Direction Register (PDDR) address (GPIOx_PDDR), which triggers the register's clock signal. The value of the data direction bit controls whether a pin is an input or an output by enabling or disabling the buffer from the data out register to the pin driver.

Multiple GPIO bits are grouped together to create a port of one or more bytes that can be accessed in parallel for efficiency. MCU designers often make ports as wide as the processor's native data word size, so a 32-bit processor may have 32-bit wide ports.

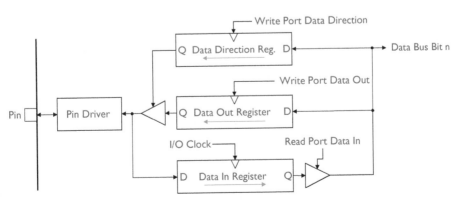

Figure 2.10   The main logic components of a GPIO port.

GPIO Module Configuration

The direction of most GPIO port bits can be configured. The PDDR GPIOx_PDDR controls data direction. A zero in the PDDR register bit makes the corresponding port bit an input, while a one makes it an output. When the MCU is powered up or reset, all PDDRs are cleared to zero, making them inputs. This is done to protect the hardware against conflicts.

The CMSIS-CORE hardware abstraction layer in MKL25Z4.h provides C-language names and data structures for the GPIO control registers. Note that they are named PTA through PTE (rather than GPIOA through GPIOE).

Our switch and LED example system needs PTA5 as an input for the switch, and PTA1 and PTA2 as outputs for LED1 and LED2. We initialize the PDDR by setting the output bits (Port A bits 1 and 2) to one and the input bit (Port A bit 5) to zero. We'll perform a read/modify/write operation to preserve the other bits:

```
// set LED bits to outputs
PTA->PDDR |= MASK(LED1_SHIFT) | MASK(LED2_SHIFT);
// clear switch bit to input
PTA->PDDR &= ~MASK(SW1_SHIFT);
```

GPIO Module Use

In order to use the GPIO module, we need to read or write data:

- Input values are read from the GPIOx_PDIR register.
- Output values are written to the GPIOx_PDOR register.

In order to simplify the software for manipulating individual output bits in a port, the hardware provides several special registers that can change specific output bits without affecting the others. These are shown in Figure 2.11.

- Writing a value *n* to GPIOx_PSOR (Port Set Output Register) will set all the bits that are one in *n*. For example, to set the least significant byte of Port A to all ones, write 0x000000ff to GPIOA_PSOR (PTA->PSOR).
- Writing a value *n* to GPIOx_PCOR (Port Clear Output Register) will clear all the bits that are one in *n*. For example, to clear the least significant byte of Port A to all zeros, write 0x000000ff to GPIOA_PCOR (PTA->PCOR).

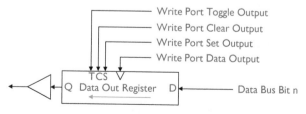

Figure 2.11   Additional control signals to toggle, clear, and set output bits without read/modify/write operations.

- Writing a value *n* to GPIOx_PTOR (Port Toggle Output Register) will invert all the bits that are one in *n*. For example, to *invert* the least significant byte of Port A to all Zeros, write 0x000000ff to GPIOA_PTOR (PTA->PTOR).

> invert
> *To change a bit to the opposite value. Also called toggle.*

```
// turn on LED1, turn off LED2
PTA->PSOR = MASK(LED1_SHIFT);
PTA->PCOR = MASK(LED2_SHIFT);

while (1) {
if (PTA->PDIR & MASK(SW1_SHIFT)) {
    // switch is not pressed, so light only LED 2
    PTA->PSOR = MASK(LED2_SHIFT);
    PTA->PCOR = MASK(LED1_SHIFT);
  } else {
    // switch is pressed, so light only LED 1
    PTA->PSOR = MASK(LED1_SHIFT);
    PTA->PCOR = MASK(LED2_SHIFT);
  }
}
```

Listing 2.3 Code uses PSOR and PCOR to eliminate read-modify-write operations.

Listing 2.3 shows the code for the switch and LED example. We first initialize the output data values so LED 1 is off and LED 2 is on. Then we add a loop that reads whether the switch is pressed and lights the LEDs appropriately using the port set and port clear control registers. This simplifies the code, eliminating the need for a read/modify/write instructions for each port access.

Faster GPIO Access

If we examined the timing of this code, we would find that it takes several extra cycles for each access to the GPIO controller and its ports. Communication between the CPU and GPIO controller is delayed because the information must pass through several stages, including a crossbar switch and a peripheral bridge, as shown in Figure 2.12. The Kinetis KL25Z MCU includes a second path between the CPU and the GPIO controller which bypasses these stages.

To use this faster path, we need to access the GPIO controller and the port data registers through a different set of addresses. The CMSIS-CORE hardware abstraction layer provides the names FPTA for PTA, FPTB for PTB, and so forth.

Putting the C Code Together

Now we can assemble the complete program, shown in Listing 2.4. We use regular GPIO access, leaving the fast GPIO access for a homework exercise.

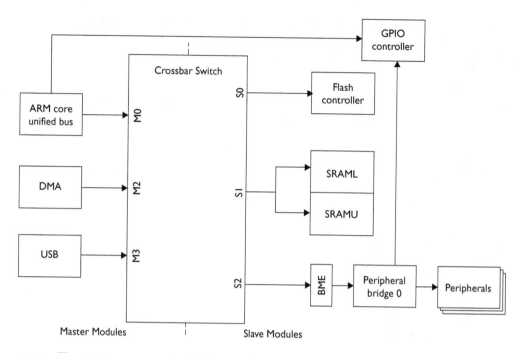

Figure 2.12   The CPU can access the GPIO peripheral directly, avoiding delay of a crossbar switch.

```
#include <MKL25Z4.h>

#define LED1_SHIFT (1) // on port A
#define LED2_SHIFT (2) // on port A
#define SW1_SHIFT (5) // on port A

#define MASK(x) (1UL << (x))

void Basic_Light_Switching_Example(void) {
    // Enable Clock to Port A
    SIM->SCGC5 |= SIM_SCGC5_PORTA_MASK;

    // Make 3 pins GPIO
    PORTA->PCR[LED1_SHIFT] &= ~PORT_PCR_MUX_MASK;
    PORTA->PCR[LED1_SHIFT] |= PORT_PCR_MUX(1);
    PORTA->PCR[LED2_SHIFT] &= ~PORT_PCR_MUX_MASK;
    PORTA->PCR[LED2_SHIFT] |= PORT_PCR_MUX(1);
    PORTA->PCR[SW1_SHIFT] &= ~PORT_PCR_MUX_MASK;
    PORTA->PCR[SW1_SHIFT] |= PORT_PCR_MUX(1);

    // set LED bits to outputs
    PTA->PDDR |= MASK(LED1_SHIFT) | MASK(LED2_SHIFT);
    // clear switch bit to input
    PTA->PDDR &= ~MASK(SW1_SHIFT);

    // turn on LED1, turn off LED2
    PTA->PSOR = MASK(LED1_SHIFT);
    PTA->PCOR = MASK(LED2_SHIFT);
```

```
while (1) {
  if (PTA->PDIR & MASK(SW1_SHIFT)) {
      // switch is not pressed, so light only LED 2
      PTA->PSOR = MASK(LED2_SHIFT);
      PTA->PCOR = MASK(LED1_SHIFT);
    } else {
      // switch is pressed, so light only LED 1
      PTA->PSOR = MASK(LED1_SHIFT);
      PTA->PCOR = MASK(LED2_SHIFT);
    }
  }
}
```

Listing 2.4 Completed program for LED and switch example.

More Interfacing Examples

Let's examine some more examples of interfacing.

Freedom KL25Z Example: Driving a Three-Color LED

Let's see how to use a GPIO port bit to drive the three-color LED on the Freedom board. The schematic in Figure 2.13 shows that the three-color (red, green, blue or RGB) LED D3 has its cathodes connected to the MCU through ports PTB18 (red), PTB19 (green), and PTD1 (blue).

Note that this is different from our previous example in Figure 2.3, in which the LED anode is connected to the MCU. Because of this difference, clearing the output bit to zero will light the LED, and setting the output bit to one will turn off the LED. This configuration is used because many MCU output drivers can handle more current this way.

Let's write a program to configure the port, lighting all possible combinations of the LEDs in a repeating sequence. We will follow these steps:

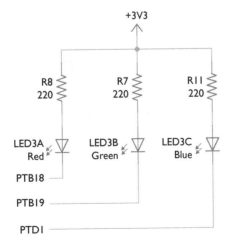

Figure 2.13 FREEDOM-KL25Z RGB LED connections.

- Define symbolic names for our LED port bits:

```
#define RED_LED_SHIFT   (18)    // on port B
#define GREEN_LED_SHIFT (19)    // on port B
#define BLUE_LED_SHIFT  (1)     // on port D
```

- Declare the function and enable the clock signal to PORTB and PORTD by setting bits 10 and 12 in the SIM's SCGC5 register. A bitwise OR operation (| =) is used to set the bits as it leaves the other bits unchanged:

```
void KL25Z_RGB_Flasher(void) {
    // Enable clock to Port B and Port D
    SIM->SCGC5 |= SIM_SCGC5_PORTB_MASK | SIM_SCGC5_PORTD_MASK;
```

- Select pin MUX mode to GPIO by setting the MUX field of PORTB_PCR18, PORTB_PCR19, and PORTD_PCR1 to 001:

```
    // Make 3 pins GPIO
    PORTB->PCR[RED_LED_SHIFT] &= ~PORT_PCR_MUX_MASK;
    PORTB->PCR[RED_LED_SHIFT] |= PORT_PCR_MUX(1);
    PORTB->PCR[GREEN_LED_SHIFT] &= ~PORT_PCR_MUX_MASK;
    PORTB->PCR[GREEN_LED_SHIFT] |= PORT_PCR_MUX(1);
    PORTD->PCR[BLUE_LED_SHIFT] &= ~PORT_PCR_MUX_MASK;
    PORTD->PCR[BLUE_LED_SHIFT] |= PORT_PCR_MUX(1);
```

- Define appropriate port bits to be outputs. We will do this by setting bits 18 and 19 in Port B's PDDR register and bit 1 in Port D's PDDR:

```
    // Set ports to outputs
    PTB->PDDR |= MASK(RED_LED_SHIFT) | MASK(GREEN_LED_SHIFT);
    PTD->PDDR |= MASK(BLUE_LED_SHIFT);
```

- Turn on the LEDs by clearing the port bits to zeros:

```
    // Turn on LEDs
    PTB->PCOR |= MASK(RED_LED_SHIFT) | MASK(GREEN_LED_SHIFT);
    PTD->PCOR |= MASK(BLUE_LED_SHIFT);
```

- Now we are ready for the code to light the different LEDs. Note that the last brace ends the function KL25Z_RGB_Flasher:

```
    while (1) {
      for (num = 0; num < 8; num++) {
        if (num & 1)
          PTB->PSOR = MASK(RED_LED_SHIFT);
```

```
    else
      PTB->PCOR = MASK(RED_LED_SHIFT);
    if (num & 2)
      PTB->PSOR = MASK(GREEN_LED_SHIFT);
    else
      PTB->PCOR = MASK(GREEN_LED_SHIFT);
    if (num & 4)
      PTD->PSOR = MASK(BLUE_LED_SHIFT);
    else
      PTD->PCOR = MASK(BLUE_LED_SHIFT);
    Delay(2000000);
    }
  }
}
```

- Notice the Delay function that was added at the end. It slows down the code to make the different LED colors visible:

```
void Delay(volatile unsigned int time_del) {
    while (time_del--) {
      ;
    }
}
```

Driving a Speaker

We can generate a simple tone with a speaker using the circuit shown in Figure 2.14. We use the MCU to toggle to an output (labeled AUDIO) to create a square wave that is filtered by a resistor and capacitor to drive a speaker. The frequency of the signal determines the pitch of the sound. In this example, we use software and a delay loop to generate the square wave. The code in Listing 2.5 toggles the output by writing to the toggle output register (PTOR), and then delays for half of the period before repeating the process.

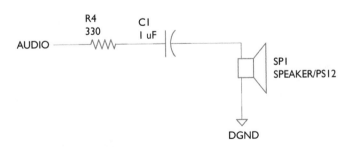

Figure 2.14 Driving a speaker with a digital output.

```
#define SPKR_SHIFT (0)

void Init_Speaker( void ) {
    SIM->SCGC5 |= SIM_SCGC5_PORTC_MASK; // enable clock for port C
    PORTC->PCR[SPKR_SHIFT] |= PORT_PCR_MUX(1); // select GPIO
    PTC->PDDR |= MASK(SPKR_SHIFT); // set I/O bit direction to output
    PTC->PDOR |= MASK(SPKR_SHIFT); // set to 1 initially
}

void Beep(void) {
    Init_Speaker();
    while (1) {
      PTC->PTOR = MASK(SPKR_SHIFT);
      Delay(20000);
    }
}
```

Listing 2.5 Code to initialize speaker output and drive it with square wave.

We use the same time delay function as in the previous example, but use a shorter time delay:

```
void Delay(volatile unsigned int time_del) {
    while (time_del--) {
      ;
    }
}
```

The output waveforms are shown in Figure 2.15. The upper trace shows the digital output of the GPIO pin, toggling about every 2 ms. The lower trace shows the filtered voltage after the capacitor.

Note that this software-based approach does not share the processor with the other processing tasks, so it limits what else the system can do during tone generation. Microcontrollers have a variety of other methods (peripherals such as timers and interrupt service routines) that can generate a square wave in hardware with minimal software overhead. We will be learning more about this in Chapter 3.

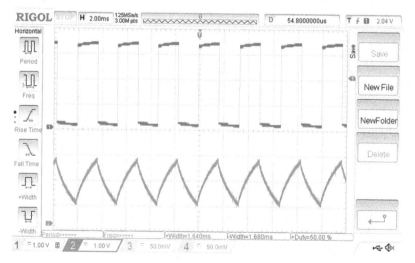

Figure 2.15 Waveforms generated by a beep function and speaker circuit.

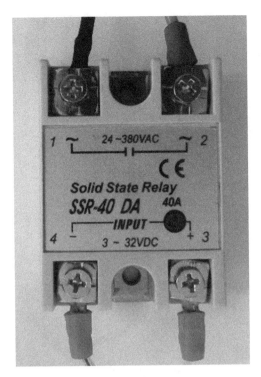

Figure 2.16   A solid-state relay allows the MCU to switch devices powered by up to 380 V AC.

Driving the Hot Plate's Heating Element

In the first chapter we looked at how to use an embedded computer as a hot plate controller. The circuit requires a driver to switch the heating element and indicator light on and off. These devices require much more power and higher voltages than the MCU can provide. The heating element operates at 120 V, drawing about 8 A of current. This is far more than the MCU's digital output can provide. We need a driver circuit that uses a logic-level control signal (3.3 V, a few mA) to switch a mains-voltage level signal (120 V, 8 A).

There are various circuits and devices that can be used. One convenient option is called a solid-state relay (SSR, Figure 2.16). When a logic-level one is present on the input (terminals 3 and 4), the internal circuit will connect the output terminals (1 and 2) electrically. The input and output circuits in the SSR are completely electrically isolated to make the circuit safer, reducing the risk of circuit damage or user injury from voltage surges on the mains or circuit malfunctions.

Additional Pin Configuration Options

The MCU may offer additional options for the circuits driving each pin. These can determine an output signal's strength, rate of change (to reduce generated noise), and other characteristics.

The inputs may be configurable to support different voltage thresholds or provide pull-up or pull-down resistors.

The Kinetis KL25Z MCU uses Pin Control Registers to control these configuration options as well as pin multiplexing described previously. Shown in Figure 2.17, the Pin Control Register n (PORTx_PCRn) also controls drive strength (DSE), noise filtering (PFE), slew rate control (SRE), and pull resistor behavior (direction (PS) and enablement (PE)) for each I/O pin. The PCR also configures event generation (e.g. interrupt and direct memory access requests (IRQC)), which will be discussed in Chapters 4 and 9. We examine the most common options below.

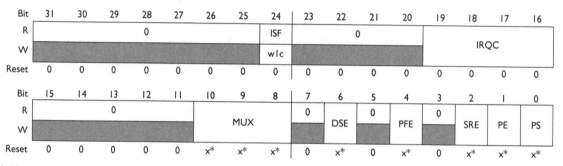

* Notes:
* x = Undefined at reset.

Figure 2.17   KL25Z pin control register contents [1, p. 183].

Pull-Up Resistors for Inputs

Some types of input signals will not swing the full voltage range from valid logic zero to valid logic one. For example, the switch in Figure 2.3 can only pull the input signal to ground. If the switch is not pressed, the input signal will be disconnected ("floating") and sensitive to noise and even static electricity. The resistor R1 was added to pull the signal up to V_{DD} when the switch is open.

This pull-up functionality is so useful that most microcontrollers include built-in pull-up support. The Kinetis MCUs are no exception. The typical value of the internal pull-up and pull-down resistors is between 20 and 50 kΩ.

We configure the pull functionality using the PCR (see Figure 2.17). Bit 1 (Pull Enable, or PE) controls whether the pull circuitry is enabled (one) or disabled (zero). Some MCUs (but not the KL25Z) have GPIO bits that can be pulled up or pulled down. For these devices, bit 0 (Pull Select) controls whether the input signal is pulled up (one) or down (zero).

Using this feature, we could simplify the circuit of Figure 2.3 by eliminating the external pull-up resistor. This would reduce parts and assembly costs, as well as circuit size. The code would need to enable the pull-up resistor by setting PE = 1 and PS = 1 in the PCR corresponding to the input pin.

High Current Drive Outputs

A normal digital output can drive a limited amount of current: KL25 MCU output can handle up to 5 mA (at $V_{DD} \geq 2.7$ V) or 1.5 mA (at $V_{DD} < 2.7$ V). This current may not be sufficient for an application (e.g. lighting an LED in a bright environment). In this case an external buffer is typically used to supply more current. To avoid the need for external circuitry, MCUs often include some outputs with a higher drive current capability.

In the KL25 MCUs, there are several outputs with a high drive capability (18 mA at $V_{DD} \geq$ 2.7 V, or 6 mA at $V_{DD} < 2.7$ V). The Drive Strength Enable (DSE) bit controls drive strength. A zero specifies a low drive strength, while a one specifies a high drive strength. Which particular outputs have high drive capability are described in the reference manual (GPIO Instantiation Information in the chapter on Chip Configuration [1]), and in the data sheet (Voltage and Current Operating Behaviors [2]).

Summary

This chapter has introduced the concepts of general purpose I/O ports and how to use them in a Freescale Kinetis KL25Z MCU using C code and the CMSIS-CORE hardware abstraction layer. Input and output interfacing was introduced with examples using LEDs, a switch, and a speaker.

Exercises

1. What are the valid input voltage ranges for a KL25Z MCU with $V_{DD} = 3$ V? With 2 V?
2. What is the actual value of V_{DD} on your MCU board? Use a multimeter to measure this voltage.
3. Examine the schematic for your Freedom KL25Z board:
   a. How many GPIO port bits are available for Port A?
   b. Port B?
   c. Port C?
   d. Port D?
   e. Port E?
4. Which digital outputs on the KL25 subfamily support high drive capability? Refer to the MCU's data sheet or reference manual.
5. Calculate the resistor values needed to limit current through the blue and red LEDs of Figure 2.3 to 18 mA each. Assume that the supply voltage V_{DD} is 3.0 V.
6. Convert the program from the section "Putting the C Code Together" to use fast GPIO access rather than regular GPIO.
7. Consider a program that uses bits 0 through 5 on Port E as GPIO inputs, and bits 16 through 20 as GPIO outputs:
   a. What control register settings are needed?
   b. Write a C code to implement these control register settings.
8. Consider a system with a KL25Z128VLK4 MCU, one switch, and four LEDs. As long as the switch is not pressed, all lights shall be turned off. When the switch is pressed, the LEDs shall start to turn on one at a time (starting with LED 0), with a delay of roughly ½ second per LED. After all the LEDs are turned on, they shall remain on until the switch is released. The selection of port bits for the switch and the LEDs is your choice. The following table shows the required sequence of LED activity, assuming the switch is pressed at time T_1 and released at time T_2.

Time (sec)	Switch	LED0	LED1	LED2	LED3
$< T_1$	Not pressed	off	off	off	off
T_1	Pressed	on	off	off	off
$T_1 + 0.5$	Pressed	on	on	off	off
$T_1 + 1.0$	Pressed	on	on	on	off
$T_1 + 1.5$	Pressed	on	on	on	on
T_2	Not pressed	off	off	off	off

a. What control register settings are needed?
b. Write a C program to implement this system.

References

[1] *KL25 Sub-Family Reference Manual*, KL25P80M48SF0RM, rev. 3rd ed., NXP Semiconductor, B.V., 2016.

[2] *Kinetis KL25 Sub-Family Data Sheet*, KL25P80M48SF0, rev. 5th ed., NXP Semiconductor, B.V., 2016.

[3] NXP Semiconductor, B.V., "MKL25Z4.h."

[4] J. Ganssle, *The art of designing embedded systems*, 2nd ed., Elsevier Inc., 2008.

[5] P. Koopman, *Better embedded system software*, Pittsburgh: Drumnadrochit Education LLC, 2010.

[6] L. Simone, *If I only changed the software, why is the phone on fire? Embedded debugging methods revealed: Technical mysteries for engineers*, Elsevier Inc., 2007.

[7] J. K. Peckol, *Embedded systems: A contemporary design tool*, John Wiley & Sons, Inc., 2008.

3

Basics of Software Concurrency

Chapter Contents

Overview

In this chapter, we explore the basic concepts of how to make a microcontroller unit (MCU) perform multiple software activities apparently simultaneously, providing the illusion of concurrent execution. Embedded systems use peripheral hardware to perform some activities, while other activities are performed in software on the central processing unit (CPU). In order to get everything done on time and provide the illusion of concurrent processing, the processor's time needs to be shared among these activities. We demonstrate these processor **scheduling** concepts by starting with a basic program and then enhancing it to improve its *modularity*, *responsiveness*, and *CPU overhead*. Figure 3.1 presents an overview of how these topics are related.

> modularity
> *Measure of how program is structured to group related portions and separate independent portions*

> responsiveness
> *Measure of how quickly a system responds to an input event*

> CPU overhead
> *Portion of time CPU spends executing code which does not perform useful work for the application*

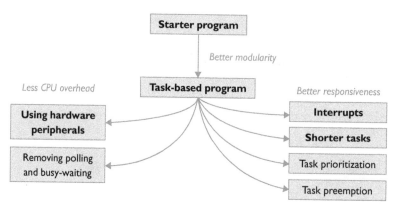

Figure 3.1 An overview of concurrency concepts presented in this chapter. Topics in bold are examined in detail.

Concepts

In order to investigate the concepts of concurrency, we will consider a system with an MCU, two switches, and an RGB (red, green, blue) LED.[1]

- When switch 1 is not pressed, the system displays a repeating sequence of colors (red, then green, then blue).
- When switch 1 is pressed, the system makes the LED flash white (all LEDs on) and off (all LEDs off) until the switch is released.

---

[1] This LED can create a wide range of colors by changing the brightness of each LED. White is created by lighting all three LED colors simultaneously.

• As long as switch 2 is pressed, faster timing is used for the flashing and RGB sequences.

The time delay between the user pressing the switch and seeing the LED flash white is the system's response time for switch 1. A shorter response time is better. How we share the processor's time among the tasks is one of the main factors determining the system's responsiveness.

Starter Program

Let's start with a simple program for the LED flasher. We will put everything into one loop that reads the switches and lights the LEDs accordingly. This loop will use functions to control the LEDs (Control_RGB_LEDs) and delay program execution (Delay). It will use a macro to read the switches (SWITCH_PRESSED).

Program Structure

```
#define W_DELAY_SLOW 400
#define W_DELAY_FAST 200
#define RGB_DELAY_SLOW 4000
#define RGB_DELAY_FAST 1000
void Flasher(void) {
        uint32_t w_delay = W_DELAY_SLOW;
        uint32_t RGB_delay = RGB_DELAY_SLOW;
        while (1) {
                if (SWITCH_PRESSED(SW1_POS)) { // flash white
                        Control_RGB_LEDs(1, 1, 1);
                        Delay(w_delay);
                        Control_RGB_LEDs(0, 0, 0);
                        Delay(w_delay);
                } else { // sequence R, G, B
                        Control_RGB_LEDs(1, 0, 0);
                        Delay(RGB_delay);
                        Control_RGB_LEDs(0, 1, 0);
                        Delay(RGB_delay);
                        Control_RGB_LEDs(0, 0, 1);
                        Delay(RGB_delay);
                }
                if (SWITCH_PRESSED(SW2_POS)) {
                        w_delay = W_DELAY_FAST;
                        RGB_delay = RGB_DELAY_FAST;
                } else {
                        w_delay = W_DELAY_SLOW;
                        RGB_delay = RGB_DELAY_SLOW;
                }
        }
}
```

Listing 3.1 Initial LED flasher code.

The core of the program is shown in Listing 3.1. The program will first check to see if switch 1 is pressed. If so, the code will make the LED white, delay for some time, turn off the LED, and delay for some time again.

If switch 1 is not pressed, the program will first light the red LED (turning off the others) and then wait for a fixed time. It will then light the green LED (turning off the others) and then wait for a fixed time. Finally, it will turn on the blue LED (turning off the others) and wait for a fixed time.

After flashing the LEDs, the code updates the time delays based on whether switch 2 is pressed or not. The program will then repeat.

```
void Delay(unsigned int time_del) {
    volatile int n;
    while (time_del--) {
        n = 1000;
        while (n--)
            ;
    }
}

void Control_RGB_LEDs(int r_on, int g_on, int b_on) {
    if (r_on)
        PTB->PCOR = MASK(RED_LED_POS);
    else
        PTB->PSOR = MASK(RED_LED_POS);
    if (g_on)
        PTB->PCOR = MASK(GREEN_LED_POS);
    else
        PTB->PSOR = MASK(GREEN_LED_POS);
    if (b_on)
        PTD->PCOR = MASK(BLUE_LED_POS);
    else
        PTD->PSOR = MASK(BLUE_LED_POS);
}
```

Listing 3.2 Support functions for starter program. Delay uses busy-waiting in a loop. Control_RGB_LEDs target LEDs in active-low configuration (output pin connected to LED cathode).

The support functions Delay and Control_RGB_LEDs are presented in Listing 3.2. Initialization code and header files are not included here, but are essentially the same as shown in Chapter 2.

Analysis

How responsive is our system to switch 1 being pressed and released? Figure 3.2 shows that if we press the switch when the green LED is lit, the system does not start flashing until the green turns off, the blue turns on, and then turns off. The program only polls the switch between full red/green/blue color cycles, or white flash cycles.

So we must hold the switch until the cycle ends. In fact, if we press the switch briefly during the color cycle and release it before the end, the program will not detect it, missing the input event. Input events shorter than the red/green/blue color cycle may be lost. The longer the code takes to run, the slower the cycle, and the greater the chance of missing an input.

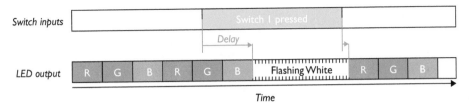

Figure 3.2 The response of an LED initial flasher program to switch press and release.

Similarly, the sooner the code finishes running, the more responsive the system is. Notice in Figure 3.2 how releasing the switch results in a very short delay until the LED begins color cycling. This short delay results from the short duration of the white flash, which enables the program to check the switch more frequently.

Another disadvantage of this code is that the processor wastes quite a bit of time in its delay function. This kind of waiting is called *busy-waiting* and should be avoided except for certain special cases. We will see how later.

> busy-waiting
> *Wasteful method of making a program wait for an event or delay. Program executes test code repeatedly in a tight loop, not sharing time with other parts of program.*

Finally, the program mixes together different activities in a single function. As the program grows larger, it will be more difficult to maintain and enhance because of these interdependencies. Poorly structured code is often called *spaghetti code* because so many different parts are tangled together.

> spaghetti code
> *Code which is poorly structured because it entangles unrelated features, complicating development and maintenance.*

To summarize, the system is sluggish and inefficient, may ignore brief inputs, and is structured badly.

Creating and Using Tasks

Let's restructure the code into three separate tasks. This will make it easier to develop and maintain the code. A task is a subroutine that performs a specific activity (or a closely related set of activities). Tasks simplify code development by grouping related features and processing together, and separating unrelated parts. Each task has a *root function*, which may call other functions as subroutines as needed.

> root function
> *A task's main software function, which may call other functions as subroutines.*

Program Structure

```
#define W_DELAY_SLOW 400
#define W_DELAY_FAST 200
#define RGB_DELAY_SLOW 4000
#define RGB_DELAY_FAST 1000

uint8_t g_flash_LED = 0;                        // initially just do RGB sequence
uint32_t g_w_delay = W_DELAY_SLOW;              // delay for white flash
uint32_t g_RGB_delay = RGB_DELAY_SLOW;          // delay for RGB sequence

void Task_Read_Switches(void) {
        if (SWITCH_PRESSED(SW1_POS)) {          // flash white
                g_flash_LED = 1;
        } else {
                g_flash_LED = 0;                // RGB sequence
        }
        if (SWITCH_PRESSED(SW2_POS)) {
                w_delay = W_DELAY_FAST;
                RGB_delay = RGB_DELAY_FAST;
        } else {
                w_delay = W_DELAY_SLOW;
                RGB_delay = RGB_DELAY_SLOW;
        }
}
```

Listing 3.3 Task_Read_Switches is responsible for updating the global variables to share information based on switches.

The first task has a root function called Task_Read_Switches, shown in Listing 3.3. It will determine which switches are pressed and share that information with the other tasks. We will use global variables to do this in this example, but later we will learn why global variables are dangerous and how to use other mechanisms to share information. We use the g_ prefix in their names to indicate that these are global variables. This is helpful but not essential; it will help us and other code developers in the future by making this information obvious. Many aspects of coding style come from the desire to prevent misunderstandings and the resulting mistakes.

The code reads switch 1 to determine whether the LED should flash white or sequence through the RGB colors, and sets variable g_flash_LED to one (to request flashing) or zero (to request the color sequence). The code then reads switch 2 to determine the time delays for the LED flashing and RGB sequencing tasks, setting g_w_delay and g_RGB_delay accordingly.

```
void Task_Flash(void) {
        if (g_flash_LED == 1) {             // Only run task when in flash mode
                Control_RGB_LEDs(1, 1, 1);
                Delay(g_w_delay);
                Control_RGB_LEDs(0, 0, 0);
                Delay(g_w_delay);
        }
}
```

Listing 3.4 Task_Flash is responsible for flashing the LED white and off once.

The second task has a root function called Task_Flash, shown in Listing 3.4. This function first checks to see if it has any work to do. If g_flash_LED is equal to one, this indicates the LED needs to flash white. The code will flash the LED white, delay for a time based on g_w_delay, turn off the LED, delay again, and then return. Otherwise, the code will return immediately.

```
void Task_RGB(void) {
        if (g_flash_LED == 0) {              // only run task when NOT in flash mode
                Control_RGB_LEDs(1, 0, 0);
                Delay(g_RGB_delay);
                Control_RGB_LEDs(0, 1, 0);
                Delay(g_RGB_delay);
                Control_RGB_LEDs(0, 0, 1);
                Delay(g_RGB_delay);
        }
}
```

Listing 3.5 Task_RGB is responsible for lighting the LEDs once in the sequence red, green, blue.

The third task has a root function called Task_RGB , shown in Listing 3.5. This task also first checks to see if it has any work to do. If g_flash_LED is equal to zero, this indicates that the LED needs to sequence through the RGB colors. The code will cycle the LED though the colors with appropriate delays (determined by g_RGB_delay), turn off the LEDs, and then return. Otherwise, the code will return immediately.

Figure 3.3 shows the overview of how the tasks (in ovals) communicate with each other through the global variables (rectangles), with the direction of the arrow indicating the flow of information from writer to reader. Note that Task_Read_Switches writes to all three global variables, whereas the other tasks read from just two of them.

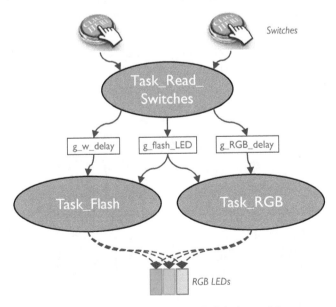

Figure 3.3 Tasks communicate information through shared global variables.

```
void Flasher(void) {
        while (1) {
                Task_Read_Switches();
                Task_Flash();
                Task_RGB();
        }
}
```

Listing 3.6 Flasher function acts as a scheduler that is responsible for running each task.

Finally, we need the scheduler function (Flasher) in Listing 3.6 that simply calls the three tasks in order and then repeats. Notice how simple the scheduler is, calling each function repeatedly in order. This approach is called *cooperative multitasking*: multiple tasks can run on the CPU because they **cooperate** by yielding the processor to other tasks when they have finished their work. If one task takes a long time to run, then it will delay the other tasks by that much time.

cooperative multitasking
Scheduling approach where tasks share CPU by voluntarily yielding it to other tasks

We could speed up the code slightly by moving the tests of the variable g_flash_LED into the scheduler, but this would defeat our goal of keeping as much task-related code in the task itself, coupling the scheduler more closely to the tasks. However, we will examine this idea later in this chapter.

Analysis

The program is now structured much better because it isolates the three tasks from each other. However, the responsiveness is no better than the first program. In fact, it is slightly worse because of the overhead of the scheduler calling the task functions.

Figure 3.4 shows how the switch press is only recognized when Task_Read_Switches can run, which occurs after Task_RGB completes. The switch release is detected more quickly because Task_Flash completes sooner.

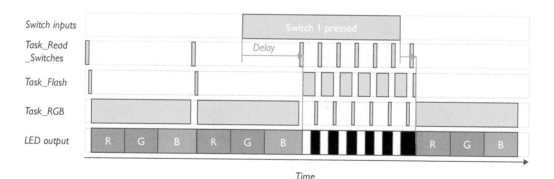

Figure 3.4 Response of task-based LED flasher program to switch press and release.

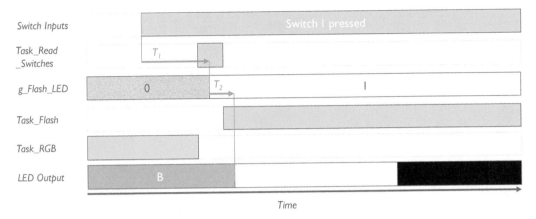

Figure 3.5 Delay between pressing the switch and the LED flashing differently has two parts.

In order to improve the responsiveness, let's first examine the delay between our **changing the switch** (pressing or releasing it) and the **LEDs flashing differently**. As shown in Figure 3.5, this delay has two parts:

- First, there is a delay T_1 between when the switch is pressed (or released) and when the variable g_Flash_LED is updated (by Task_Read_Switches).
- Second, there is a delay T_2 between when the variable g_Flash_LED is updated (by Task_Read_Switches) and the LED starts flashing (in Task_Flash).

T_1 is large in Figure 3.4 because the switch is pressed while Task_RGB is running. Task_Read_Switches can run only after Task_RGB completes (and it is a long task). A task that takes a long time to complete will increase T_1 significantly, especially if an event (e.g. switch press) occurs early in the task. If there are other tasks that run after Task_RGB but before Task_Read_Switches, they will also increase T_1.

T_2 is small in Figure 3.5 because Task_Flash runs immediately after Task_Read_Switches (and it is short). If instead we changed the loop so that the task order was Task_Read_Switches, Task_RGB, and then Task_Flash, T_2 would be increased by the time taken to run Task_RGB. In this case it would be short, since Task_RGB would return after determining that g_Flash_LED was one. If there are other tasks that run after Task_Read_Switches but before Task_Flash, they will increase T_2.

Improving Responsiveness

So how can we reduce these times?

A very bad approach would be to have Task_RGB call Task_Read_Switches (and maybe even Task_Flash) after lighting each LED. This tangles the tasks together, complicating future code development.

There are much better ways to improve responsiveness that do not make a mess of the code. In this section, we will discuss the following approaches:

- Using interrupts to provide event-triggered processing

- Restructuring tasks to complete earlier
- Using hardware so tasks complete earlier

We will also introduce the following advanced topics but will not cover them in detail:

- Prioritizing tasks that the scheduler will run first
- Enabling tasks to preempt each other
- Moving waiting out of tasks into the scheduler

Interrupts and Event Triggering

Our code explicitly checks to see if processing is needed, for example, to determine if the timer has expired yet. This is called *polling*. There is an alternative approach called *event-triggering*, in which the processor gets notifications from hardware that a specific event has occurred and processing is needed.

> polling
> *Scheduling approach in which software repeatedly tests a condition to determine whether to run task code*

> event-triggering
> *Scheduling approach in which task software runs only when triggered by an event*

Software that uses event-triggering runs much more efficiently than polling, since no time needs to be wasted checking to see if processing is needed. Even better, the event-triggered approach leads to a much more responsive system since events are detected much sooner. This may allow a much slower processor to be used, saving money, power, and energy.

Peripheral hardware on microcontrollers explicitly supports this event-triggered approach through the *interrupt* system. A peripheral can generate an *interrupt request (IRQ)* to the processor to indicate that an event has occurred. The processor will finish executing the current instruction in the program, save the program's current information, and then start to execute a special part of the program called an *interrupt service routine (ISR)* (or *handler*) in order to service that interrupt request. After completing the ISR, the processor reloads the program's saved information and then resumes its execution at the next instruction.

> interrupt request (IRQ)
> *Hardware signal indicating that an interrupt is requested*

> interrupt service routine (ISR)
> *Software routine which runs in response to interrupt request. Also called a handler.*

> handler
> *Software routine which runs in response to interrupt or exception request.*

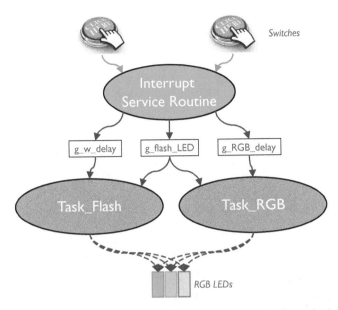

Figure 3.6 Interrupt service routine communicates information to tasks through shared global variables.

For many embedded systems, a combination of polling and ISRs is enough to meet requirements quickly and inexpensively. Event-driven processing in ISRs handles the urgent processing activities, while less-urgent work is performed on a polling basis in the background. Often an ISR will do the initial urgent processing and then save partial results for later, more time-consuming processing.

Program Structure

Let's modify our system by using interrupts to detect when a switch has been pressed or released. As shown in Figure 3.6, we replace Task_Read_Switches with an ISR. The ISR updates the shared variables, which in turn are read by the tasks.

```
#define W_DELAY_SLOW 400
#define W_DELAY_FAST 200
#define RGB_DELAY_SLOW 4000
#define RGB_DELAY_FAST 1000

volatile uint8_t g_flash_LED = 0; // initially don't flash LED, just do RGB sequence
volatile uint32_t g_w_delay = W_DELAY_SLOW; // delay for white flash
volatile uint32_t g_RGB_delay = RGB_DELAY_SLOW; // delay for RGB sequence

void PORTD_IRQHandler(void) {
    // Read switches
    if ((PORTD->ISFR & MASK(SW1_POS))) {
        if (SWITCH_PRESSED(SW1_POS)) { // flash white
            g_flash_LED = 1;
        } else {
            g_flash_LED = 0;
        }
    }
```

```
    if ((PORTD->ISFR & MASK(SW2_POS))) {
        if (SWITCH_PRESSED(SW2_POS)) { // short delays
            g_w_delay = W_DELAY_FAST;
            g_RGB_delay = RGB_DELAY_FAST;
        } else {
            g_w_delay = W_DELAY_SLOW;
            g_RGB_delay = RGB_DELAY_SLOW;
        }
    }
    // clear status flags
    PORTD->ISFR = 0xffffffff;
}
```

Listing 3.7 Source code for shared variables and interrupt service routine (handler).

The source code is shown in Listing 3.7. Note that the shared variables are now defined as volatile, which indicates to the compiler that they may change unexpectedly (e.g. an ISR may change them). We omit the code needed to configure the port peripheral to request an interrupt, and to enable interrupts. We will cover these details in Chapter 4.

```
void Flasher(void) {
    while (1) {
        Task_Flash();
        Task_RGB();
    }
}
```

Listing 3.8 New scheduler function for LED flasher does not read switches.

Finally, the scheduler function no longer calls Task_Read_Switches, as shown in Listing 3.8

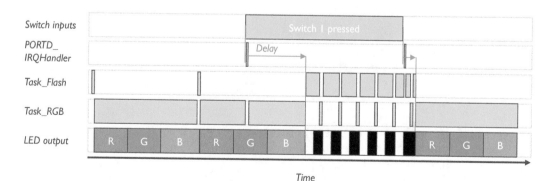

Figure 3.7 Response with switches read by interrupt service routine. Switch-reading code in PORTD_IRQ_Handler runs only when needed.

Analysis

Figure 3.7 shows the resulting behavior. First, the code to read switches (in PORTD_IRQHandler) now executes only when needed, freeing up time for other tasks to run. Second, the delay between pressing the switch and the LED changing its flashing pattern has been reduced. The first component of the delay (from switch press to updating the variable g_Flash_LED) has been reduced significantly. Microcontrollers can respond to interrupts very quickly. For the ARM Cortex-M0+ CPUs, there is a delay of fifteen clock cycles from interrupt request to the start of the handler execution. With a 48-MHz CPU clock rate, this is a fast 312.5 ns.

Using an interrupt has improved the responsiveness somewhat. But it has not addressed the second delay, which depends on the task switching. The scheduler that we are using cannot switch to a different task until after the currently running task has completed. It is called a *non-preemptive scheduler*. In this example, the RGB task takes a long time to run and hence limits the responsiveness.

> non-preemptive scheduler
> *Scheduler which does not allow tasks to preempt each other*

One way to address the second delay is to move more code from the task into the interrupt handler, so it runs without any task scheduling delay. When this approach is possible, the developer needs to be careful to keep the handler from growing too long, which will reduce the responsiveness of all other code (and interrupt handlers). It is also surprisingly easy to turn interrupt handlers into spaghetti code, which is hard to understand, maintain, and enhance.

Consider the example in Figure 3.7. We can speed up the response to switch presses by making the interrupt handler light all LEDs (making white). But as soon as the handler finishes, Task_RGB resumes execution. It completes its delay, then lights the blue LED, waits for another delay, and then finishes. Task_Flash finally runs and flashes the LED correctly. How can the interrupt handler make Task_RGB stop running? Since the handler changes g_Flash_LED based on the switch position, an obvious way is to test that variable's value more often.

```c
void Task_Flash(void) {
    if (g_flash_LED == 1) {        // Only run task when in flash mode
        Control_RGB_LEDs(1, 1, 1);
    }
    if (g_flash_LED == 1) {        // Only run task when in flash mode
        Delay(g_w_delay);
    }
    if (g_flash_LED == 1) {        // Only run task when in flash mode
        Control_RGB_LEDs(0, 0, 0);
    }
    if (g_flash_LED == 1) {        // Only run task when in flash mode
        Delay(g_w_delay);
    }
}
```

```
void Task_RGB(void) {
    if (g_flash_LED == 0) {        // only run task when NOT in flash mode
        Control_RGB_LEDs(1, 0, 0);
    }
    if (g_flash_LED == 0) {        // only run task when NOT in flash mode
        Delay(g_RGB_delay);
    }
    if (g_flash_LED == 0) {        // only run task when NOT in flash mode
        Control_RGB_LEDs(0, 1, 0);
    }
    if (g_flash_LED == 0) {        // only run task when NOT in flash mode
        Delay(g_RGB_delay);
    }
    if (g_flash_LED == 0) {        // only run task when NOT in flash mode
        Control_RGB_LEDs(0, 0, 1);
    }
    if (g_flash_LED == 0) {        // only run task when NOT in flash mode
        Delay(g_RGB_delay);
    }
}
```

Listing 3.9 A very bad idea: adding more tests to help the tasks stop running earlier if not needed.

The resulting code in Listing 3.9 is messy and inefficient. And it doesn't work that well. If the switch is pressed while the Delay function is running, the task won't finish until Delay completes. To get a better responsiveness, we would have to test g_Flash_LED in the function Delay. But remember that both Task_Flash and Task_RGB call Delay, so we would need two versions of Delay, or a way of tracking which function called it (e.g. by passing a parameter).

```
void Delay(unsigned int time_del, int called_by_Task_Flash) {
    volatile int n;
    while (time_del--) {
        if ( ((called_by_Task_Flash == 1) && (g_Flash_LED == 1)) ||
             ((called_by_Task_Flash == 0) && (g_Flash_LED == 0))) {
            n = 1000;
            while (n--)
                ;
        }
    }
}
```

Listing 3.10 More of a bad thing: adding tests and a caller parameter to the Delay function.

One possible version of a new delay function is shown in Listing 3.10. Note that we now need to change the task codes to call Delay with a parameter indicating the caller task. This is a wonderful example of spaghetti code and how not to do things!

Reducing Task Completion Times with Finite State Machines

We wish to modify a task so it returns before it has finished all of its work. This gives the scheduler more frequent opportunities to run other tasks, improving its responsiveness. We will use a structure called the *finite state machine (FSM)*, rather than the spaghetti code of Listing 3.9 and Listing 3.10.

> state machine
> *State-based system model with rules for transitions between states*

> finite state machine (FSM)
> *A type of state machine with all states and transitions defined.*

To make the task work correctly, we will need to make some changes to the task's source code. We may need to call the task several times to complete all of its work. We will also need to keep track of the task's progress so it completes all the work necessary in the correct order and without duplication.

We could combine this approach with using an interrupt to further improve responsiveness. To simplify the explanation, we do not do so here.

Program Structure

```
void Task_RGB(void) {
        if (g_flash_LED == 0) {              // only run task when NOT in flash mode
                // Red state
                Control_RGB_LEDs(1, 0, 0);
                Delay(g_RGB_delay);

                // Green state
                Control_RGB_LEDs(0, 1, 0);
                Delay(g_RGB_delay);

                // Blue state
                Control_RGB_LEDs(0, 0, 1);
                Delay(g_RGB_delay);
        }
}
```

Listing 3.11 Identifying code for different states in Task_RGB.

Consider the code for Task_RGB, shown in Listing 3.11. We will convert the body of the task into a state machine to make this all work.

A state machine executes the code of one state each time it is called, and then returns. We break up the code into separate states after each long-running operation (delay functions, in this case). If we had conditionals or loops in the code, we could still create states, but would need to ensure each state starts and ends at the same level of conditional nesting or looping.

We can create a state transition diagram (as in Figure 3.8) to describe how the state machine operates. Circles represent states, and the lines between them represent possible transitions.

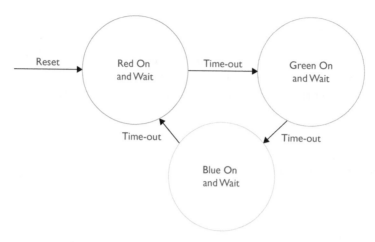

Figure 3.8   State transition diagram for Task_RGB.

A transition is labeled with text to indicate the trigger event or the condition under which it occurs. An unlabeled transition will execute automatically after the state completes.

The system is initialized to the red state, as indicated by the transition labeled "reset". The system stays in the red state until a time-out occurs, when it exits the red state and enters the green state. After another time-out, the system exits the green state and enters the blue state. Yet another time-out later, the system exits the blue state and enters the red state. The cycle then repeats.

We can also represent this information with a state transition table, as shown in Table 3.1. In this example, there is only one type of input event (the time-out), but other FSMs may have more types. In that case, there would be a next state column for each event. Note that a state may have several next states, based on conditions within the FSM or which input event occurred.

Table 3.1 Task_RGB Finite State Machine

State	Action	Next state (time-out event)
ST_RED	Light red LED	ST_GREEN
ST_GREEN	Light green LED	ST_BLUE
ST_BLUE	Light blue LED	ST_RED

```
void Task_RGB_FSM(void) {
    static enum {ST_RED, ST_GREEN, ST_BLUE, ST_OFF} next_state;

    if (g_flash_LED == 0) { // only run task when NOT in flash mode
        switch (next_state) {
            case ST_RED:
                Control_RGB_LEDs(1, 0, 0);
                Delay(g_RGB_delay);
                next_state = ST_GREEN;
                break;
```

```
            case ST_GREEN:
                Control_RGB_LEDs(0, 1, 0);
                Delay(g_RGB_delay);
                next_state = ST_BLUE;
                break;
            case ST_BLUE:
                Control_RGB_LEDs(0, 0, 1);
                Delay(g_RGB_delay);
                next_state = ST_RED;
                break;
            default:
                next_state = ST_RED;
                break;
        }
    }
}
```

Listing 3.12 Source code for the finite state machine version of Task_RGB.

The source code for Task_RGB_FSM (our state machine version of Task_RGB) appears in Listing 3.12.

We use a state variable called next_state to track the next state to execute. Note that this variable must be declared as static so that it retains its value from one subroutine call to the next. In order to make the code easier to understand, we make next_state an enumerated type. These use names (e.g. ST_RED) to represent integer values (e.g. 0). The enum keyword is followed by a list of names, and then the name of the variable.

A switch statement selects which code to execute based on the value of next_state. Each case statement contains the code for one state and may update the state variable for future calls to Task_RGB_FSM.

```
void Task_Flash_FSM(void) {
    static enum {ST_WHITE, ST_BLACK} next_state = ST_WHITE;

    if (g_flash_LED == 1) { // Only run task when in flash mode
        switch (next_state) {
            case ST_WHITE:
                Control_RGB_LEDs(1, 1, 1);
                Delay(g_w_delay);
                next_state = ST_BLACK;
                break;
            case ST_BLACK:
                Control_RGB_LEDs(0, 0, 0);
                Delay(g_w_delay);
                next_state = ST_WHITE;
                break;
            default:
                next_state = ST_WHITE;
                break;
        }
    }
}
```

Listing 3.13 Source code for the finite state machine version of Task_Flash.

The source code for Task_Flash_FSM is similarly modified and appears in Listing 3.13. Note that the two variables named next_state declared in Task_Flash_FSM and Task_Flash_RGB are separate variables. They are called local variables because they are only visible and accessible to code in the function where they are declared. Other functions cannot access Task_Flash_FSM's version of next_state. Finally, the scheduler function does not need to be modified beyond calling the FSM versions of the tasks. It continues to call them repeatedly.

Analysis

Figure 3.9 shows the system's behavior, and we see that the responsiveness is much better. The flashing starts after the current stage of the sequence (green here), rather than the last stage (blue). If this is still not responsive enough, we could split up the delay into two or more states to reduce the response time.

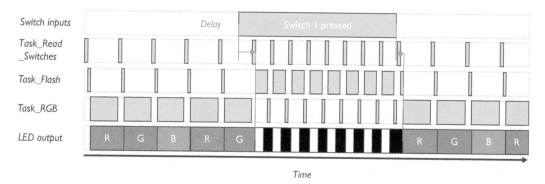

Figure 3.9 Response of task-based LED flasher program with RGB task implemented as finite state machine.

Using Hardware to Save CPU Time

As mentioned in the introduction, the microcontrollers used in embedded systems include specialized hardware circuits called peripherals. These devices offload and accelerate specific types of work from the processor or perform activities that the CPU core is not capable of performing. This peripheral hardware is able to execute essentially independently of the processor. Embedded system designers use the peripherals to reduce the computational load on the processor, reducing the need for a high-speed processor and saving costs.

One common peripheral is called a timer or a counter. At its heart, a timer is a counter circuit that counts how many pulses it receives. Using a pulse source with a known frequency allows us to measure time. The peripheral can generate an event after a specified time delay, measure pulse width, generate pulse outputs, and measure pulse counts. We will study timer/counter peripherals more closely in Chapter 7.

Note that the processor may be capable of doing these operations in software, but with much greater complexity and less accuracy. Furthermore, the processor may need to spend all of its time on this single activity to get adequate timing precision.

Program Structure

We will use a timer to replace the call to the function called Delay, which performs busy-waiting to incur a time delay. We will introduce a new state in the FSM to wait for the delay to complete. The FSM does not advance past this state until the delay has completed. If there are multiple such delays, each will have a new state. Figure 3.10 shows the modified state machine with three wait states added (for red, green, and blue delays).

In this example, we are using a particular type of timer called the periodic interrupt timer (PIT). We load the timer with a starting count value (using Init_PIT) and then start it running (using Start_PIT). The timer receives periodic pulses from a clock source (24 MHz in this case). With each pulse, the timer decrements the timer's count value by one. When the count value reaches zero, the timer will set a flag in one of its control registers to indicate that the timer has expired. We will use the software function PIT_Expired to read this flag and stop the timer using Stop_PIT.

Figure 3.11 is a sequence diagram that shows the interactions between software and hardware in this approach. It is a vertical timeline that starts at the top. Each hardware or software component (called an actor) has its own column. Here, the software components are labeled Scheduler and Task_Flash_FSM_Timer and the hardware components are labeled PIT_TIMER and LED.

The arrows in Figure 3.11 show communication between specific actors. For example, Scheduler starts Task_Flash_FSM_Timer running. That task then turns on the LEDs to make the LED white, and starts the timer (PIT_TIMER) running.

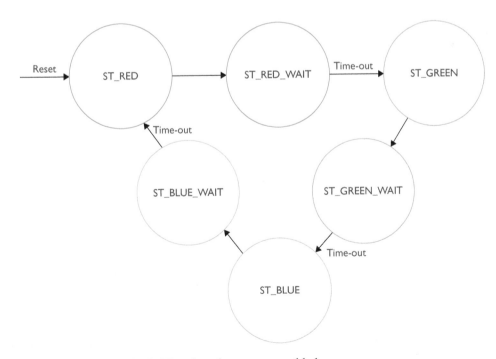

Figure 3.10   State machine for RGB task with wait states added.

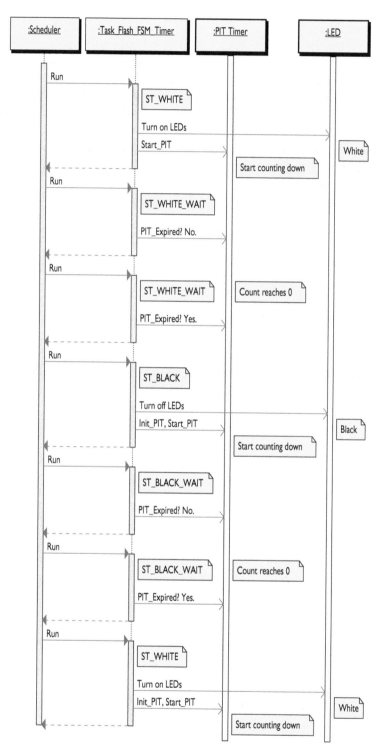

Figure 3.11   Sequence diagram showing interactions between the software (scheduler and task) and the hardware (timer and LED).

```
void Task_Flash_FSM_Timer(void) {
    static enum {ST_WHITE, ST_WHITE_WAIT, ST_BLACK, ST_BLACK_WAIT} next_state =
    ST_WHITE;

    if (g_flash_LED == 1) {          // Only run task when in flash mode
        switch (next_state) {
            case ST_WHITE:
                Control_RGB_LEDs(1, 1, 1);
                Init_PIT(0, g_w_delay);
                Start_PIT(0);
                next_state = ST_WHITE_WAIT;
                break;
            case ST_WHITE_WAIT:
                if (PIT_Expired(0)) {
                    Stop_PIT(0);
                    next_state = ST_BLACK;
                }
                break;
            case ST_BLACK:
                Control_RGB_LEDs(0, 0, 0);
                Init_PIT(0, g_w_delay);
                Start_PIT(0);
                next_state = ST_BLACK_WAIT;
                break;
            case ST_BLACK_WAIT:
                if (PIT_Expired(0)) {
                    Stop_PIT(0);
                    next_state = ST_WHITE;
                }
                break;
            default:
                next_state = ST_WHITE;
                break;
        }
    } else {
        next_state = ST_WHITE;
    }
}
```

Listing 3.14 Source code for a Flash task using a finite state machine and a hardware timer.

We will apply this modification to both Task_Flash_FSM and Task_RGB_FSM, as they both use the delay function. The updated task source code for Task_Flash_FSM_Timer appears in Listing 3.14. Let's examine the code in the white state (ST_WHITE):

- Turn on all LEDS to make white light
- Initialize the timer with a time delay (g_w_delay)
- Start the timer
- Set next_state to ST_WHITE_WAIT

Now let's examine the code in the white wait state (ST_WHITE_WAIT):

- Check whether the timer has expired yet
- If it has not expired, exit without changing next_state
- If it has expired, stop the timer and advance next_state to ST_BLACK

Notice that the state machine won't advance past ST_WHITE_WAIT until the timer expires. The function Task_Flash_FSM_Timer may be called once or one million times, but it won't advance past ST_WHITE_WAIT until enough time has passed. This allows different FSMs in the program to make progress at different speeds without slowing each other down excessively.

Analysis

Figure 3.12 shows the resulting system behavior. The delays are very small because all calls to an FSM function complete very quickly. Because a hardware timer tracks the delay (rather than a software function executing on the CPU), even calls to FSMs in a WAIT state will return quickly.

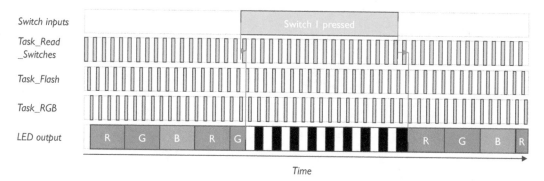

Figure 3.12 Response with tasks implemented as finite state machines using timer peripheral for delays.

Advanced Scheduling Topics

Our scheduling improvements have improved performance, but some issues remain:

- First, the CPU wastes quite a bit of time trying to run tasks that do not have any work to do. Currently it is up to the task to determine whether to run or not. Can we use the scheduler to make this decision? And can the scheduler make it easier for us to use the processor efficiently (e.g. periodic task execution)?
- Second, the tasks always run in the same order. Can we change the scheduler to run more time-critical tasks before others, improving responsiveness by prioritizing the work?

- Third, if an important event occurs just after a long-running task starts, we will need to wait for it to finish, or else restructure the task as an FSM. Is there a different way to reduce this task running time which does not require so much code modification?

Addressing these questions fully is beyond the scope of this introductory embedded systems textbook, but it is good to be aware of them. So we will cover them briefly in the remainder of this chapter.

You may wonder about the differences between a scheduler, a kernel, and an operating system. A task scheduler grows more complex when we add support to address the issues listed above. The result is a *kernel*, which supplements the scheduler with task-oriented features, such as synchronization, signaling, communication, and time delays. Many embedded systems use a kernel to share the processor's time among multiple tasks. The fundamental role of the kernel is to execute the highest priority task that is ready (i.e. is not waiting for any event or resource). Such kernels are typically preemptive (described later) so that tasks are responsive without having to be broken into state machines. The kernel also provides support for efficient time delays, signaling between tasks, sharing data safely, managing tasks, and other useful features.

> kernel
> *Scheduler with support for task features such as communication, delays, and synchronization*

An *operating system* enhances the kernel with application-oriented features, such as a file system, a graphical user interface, and networking support. However, there is always a task scheduler at the heart.

> operating system
> *Kernel with support for application-oriented features such as file systems, networking support, etc.*

Waiting

Who determines if a task has no work to do? The task or the scheduler? Earlier we left the question up to the task in order to simplify the scheduler. For some systems that is reasonable, but systems with tight timing requirements or many tasks will waste quite a bit of time.

For example, the system shown in Figure 3.12 is wasting a tremendous amount of the CPU's time by polling the task frequently to determine if it needs to run.

The program only does useful work when the switch changes or when an LED needs to change, as shown in Figure 3.13. We would like a scheduling approach that behaves this way by using an event-driven approach.

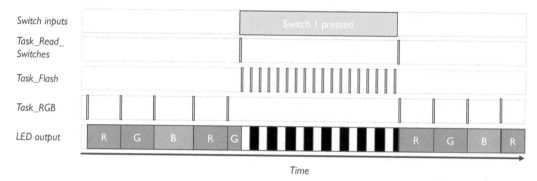

Figure 3.13   Useful work performed by the program.

In the scheduling approaches we've seen so far, there are two possible states for a task: running and ready to run. There can only be one running task per processor core,[2] but there can be many ready tasks. Let's introduce a new task state: *waiting* (also called *blocking*). A task in that state is waiting for a particular event to happen: a time delay to expire, a message to be received, a resource to be made available, etc. The kernel does not waste any time trying to schedule tasks that are waiting. Instead, the kernel only schedules tasks that are ready or running. When an event occurs, the kernel checks to see if any tasks are waiting for it. If so, those tasks are moved to the ready state and will be able to run.

> waiting
> *A state in which a task is waiting for an event to occur. Also called blocking.*

> blocking
> *A state in which a task is waiting for an event to occur. Also called waiting.*

Compare this with our waiting in the FSM. When we restructured our code, we broke out the waiting portions. By using kernel support for waiting, we do not need to restructure the code, but instead call a kernel function that will manage the waiting. From the point of view of the task, it is just a call to a wait function that does not return until the desired event has occurred.

Task Prioritization

Task **prioritization** can be used in deciding which processing activity to perform next. We may decide, for instance, that when tasks A and C are ready to execute, we always run C first since it needs a shorter response time. Task A will run after C finishes since it is of lower priority.

---

[2] We do not consider hardware multithreading support here, but these scheduling concepts are easily extended and applied for such processors.

```
void Flasher(void) {
        while (1) {
                Task_Read_Switches();
                Task_Flash();
                Task_RGB();
        }
}
```

Listing 3.15 Flasher function acts as a scheduler with fixed task priorities.

Consider the early version of the task scheduler, reproduced here in Listing 3.15. It always runs the tasks in the same order: Task_Read_Switches, Task_Flash, and then Task_RGB. Consider how to minimize the response time when we **press** the switch. Since we want to start flashing the LEDs, we want Task_Flash to run **before** Task_RGB (have a higher priority). If we want to minimize the response time when we **release** the switch, we want the LEDs to follow the RGB sequence, so Task_Flash should run **after** Task_RGB (have a lower priority).

Task priorities may be assigned so they are fixed (task A always has the lowest priority) or dynamically (based on some condition that may change at run time). Embedded system kernels typically provide only fixed priorities, though some allow a task's priority to be changed as the system runs.

Task Preemption

The cooperative multitasking approach we have been examining does not switch to running a different task until the currently running task yields the processor. This delays the system's response. A preemptive multitasking approach uses *task preemption* so that an urgent task is not delayed by a currently running task of lower urgency. Consider that task A is already running, and task C becomes ready to run, perhaps due to an ISR executing and saving some deferred work for C. A *preemptive scheduler* can temporarily halt the processing of task A, run task C, and then resume the processing of task A.

> task preemption
> *Scheduling approach in which a task is paused to allow a different task to run. Eventually the first task resumes execution where it was paused.*

> preemptive scheduler
> *Scheduler which supports task preemption*

The LED flasher with two tasks and an interrupt handler is shown in Figure 3.14. Pressing or releasing the switch triggers an interrupt event. The interrupt support hardware forces the CPU to preempt the currently running Task_RGB, execute the code of PORTD_IRQHandler (the ISR), and then resume Task_RGB where it left off. However, we still have to wait for Task_RGB to complete.

With task preemption in Figure 3.15, we can use kernel features so that Task_Flash (not Task_RGB) runs after PORTD_IRQHandler. Once Task_Flash completes its work and waits, then Task_RGB can run.

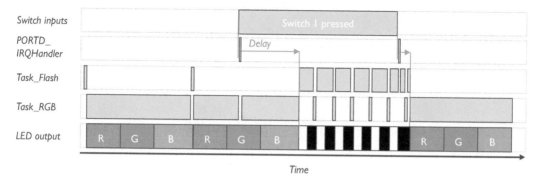

Figure 3.14   An LED flasher with two tasks and an interrupt handler is still delayed by Task_RGB after interrupt.

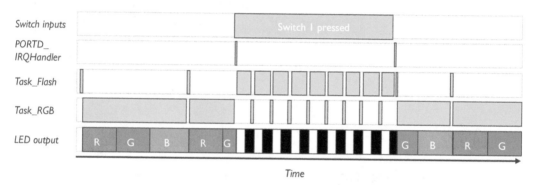

Figure 3.15   An LED flasher with task preemption. Task_Flash prempts Task_RGB in the green cycle when the switch is pressed.

Real-Time Systems

A *real-time system* is one in which tasks have **deadlines**. If the software and hardware are not sufficiently responsive, then the task will not complete before its deadline, leading to a system failure. **Real-time scheduling analysis** gives us the mathematical methods to calculate the **worst-case response time** for each task in such a software system. We can compare these response times to our system's deadlines in order to verify whether the system is **schedulable** (will always meet its deadlines).

> real-time system
> *System which must respond to events before given deadlines*

If the system is not schedulable, then we have several options to make it schedulable. We could change the **hardware** (use a faster processor) if the customer budget allows it. We could improve the **application software** by speeding up the code or by reducing the amount of processing needed. We could also improve the **scheduling approach** by changing the balance of work performed in ISRs versus deferred activities, adding or changing task priorities, or adding preemption.

A real-time kernel (RTK) or a real-time operating system (RTOS) is designed to make it easier to create real-time systems. Preemptive scheduling is typically used to provide short response times. Prioritized task scheduling also reduces response times. The kernel is designed and built to execute with consistent and predictable timing, rather than with widely varying behavior. One example of an RTK is Keil's RTX, which is included with the Keil MDK-ARM integrated development environment [1].

Summary

This chapter has presented various approaches to sharing a CPU among multiple software activities. We began with a starter program with all of the activities mixed together (spaghetti code). We then saw how to improve it in several important ways:

- **Modularity** is improved by dividing the activities into separate tasks.
- **Responsiveness** is improved by allowing preemption of tasks (by interrupts or other tasks), by shortening task run-times using FSMs, and by prioritizing tasks.
- **CPU overhead** is reduced by using hardware peripherals and by introducing a task wait state.

Exercises

1. Consider the scheduling approach described in the section "Creating and Using Tasks". See Figure 3.4. Assume there is no time taken to switch between tasks, and that the tasks have the following execution times:

Task or handler	Execution time when in flash mode	Execution time when in RGB mode
Task_Read_Switches	1 ms	1 ms
Task_Flash	100 ms	1 ms
Task_RGB	1 ms	1000 ms

a. Describe the sequence of events that leads to maximum delay between pressing the switch and seeing the LED flash. Calculate the value of that delay.

b. Describe the sequence of events that leads to maximum delay between pressing the switch and seeing the LED sequence through RGB colors. Calculate the value of that delay.

c. What is the minimum amount of time the switch must be pressed to change the LED flashing pattern?

d. Would changing the scheduler to call Task_RGB **before** Task_Flash change the delays in (a) and (b)? If so, determine the new delays and explain why they changed.

2. Another developer wants to add two more tasks (Task_X and Task_Y) to the system of the previous question. Each task can take up to 80 ms to complete.
   a. When will there be maximum delay between pressing the switch and seeing the LED flash? Calculate the value of that delay.
   b. When will there be maximum delay between releasing the switch and seeing the LED sequence through RGB colors? Calculate the value of that delay.
   c. What is the minimum amount of time the switch must be pressed to change the LED flashing pattern?

3. Consider the scheduling approach of the section "Interrupts and Event Triggering". See Figure 3.7. Assume that PORTD_IRQHandler starts executing as soon as the switch changes from pressed to released or from released to pressed. Also assume there is no time taken to switch between tasks or the handler, and that the tasks and handler have the following execution times:

Task or handler	Execution time when in flash mode	Execution time when in RGB mode
PORTD_IRQ_Handler	0.01 ms	0.01 ms
Task_Flash	100 ms	1 ms
Task_RGB	1 ms	1000 ms

   a. Describe the sequence of events that leads to maximum delay between pressing the switch and seeing the LED flash. Calculate the value of that delay.
   b. Describe the sequence of events that leads to maximum delay between pressing the switch and seeing the LED sequence through RGB colors. Calculate the value of that delay.
   c. What is the minimum amount of time the switch must be pressed to change the LED flashing pattern?

4. Consider the scheduling approach of the section "Reducing Task Completion Times with Finite State Machines". See Figure 3.9. Assume there is no time taken to switch between tasks, and that the tasks have the following execution times:

Task	Execution time when in flash mode	Execution time when in RGB mode
Task_Read_Switches	1 ms	1 ms
Task_Flash	34 ms	1 ms
Task_RGB	1 ms	334 ms

   a. Describe the sequence of events that leads to maximum delay between pressing the switch and seeing the LED flash. Calculate the value of that delay.
   b. Describe the sequence of events that leads to maximum delay between pressing the switch and seeing the LED sequence through RGB colors. Calculate the value of that delay.
   c. What is the minimum amount of time the switch must be pressed to change the LED flashing pattern?

5. Consider using the approaches from both the previous two problems. Use an interrupt to reduce switch detection latency (from section "Interrupts and Event Triggering") and FSMs to reduce task

execution time (from section "Reducing Task Completion Times with Finite State Machines"). Assume that PORTD_IRQHandler starts executing as soon as the switch changes from pressed to released or from released to pressed. Also assume there is no time taken to switch between tasks or the handler and that the tasks and the handler have the following execution times:

Task or handler	Execution time when in flash mode	Execution time when in RGB mode
PORTD_IRQ_Handler	0.01 ms	0.01 ms
Task_Flash	34 ms	1 ms
Task_RGB	1 ms	334 ms

a. Describe the sequence of events that leads to maximum delay between pressing the switch and seeing the LED flash. Calculate the value of that delay.

b. Describe the sequence of events that leads to maximum delay between pressing the switch and seeing the LED sequence through RGB colors. Calculate the value of that delay.

c. What is the mlinimum amount of time the switch must be pressed to change the LED flashing pattern?

6. Finally consider the approach of the section "Task Preemption". Assume that the IRQ handler can tell the scheduler to change which task to run, and that tasks can preempt each other. See Figure 3.15. Assume that PORTD_IRQHandler starts executing as soon as the switch changes from pressed to released or from released to pressed. Also assume there is no time taken to switch between tasks or the handler and that the tasks and the handler have the following execution times:

Task or handler	Execution time when in flash mode	Execution time when in RGB mode
PORTD_IRQ_Handler	0.01 ms	0.01 ms
Task_Flash	100 ms	1 ms
Task_RGB	1 ms	1000 ms

a. Describe the sequence of events that leads to maximum delay between pressing the switch and seeing the LED flash. Calculate the value of that delay.

b. Describe the sequence of events that leads to maximum delay between pressing the switch and seeing the LED sequence through RGB colors. Calculate the value of that delay.

c. What is the minimum amount of time the switch must be pressed to change the LED flashing pattern?

References

[1]   ARM Ltd., "RTX Real-Time Operating System" [Online]. Available: http://www.keil.com/rl-arm/kernel.asp. [Accessed 24 May 2016].

[2]   J. Ganssle, *The art of designing embedded systems*, 2nd ed., Elsevier Inc., 2008.

[3]   P. Koopman, *Better embedded system software*, Pittsburgh: Drumnadrochit Education LLC, 2010.

[4]   J. K. Peckol, *Embedded systems: A contemporary design tool*, John Wiley & Sons, Inc., 2008.

[5]   L. Simone, *If I only changed the software, why is the phone on fire? Embedded debugging methods revealed: Technical mysteries for engineers*, Elsevier Inc., 2007.

4

ARM Cortex-M0+ Processor Core and Interrupts

Contents

Overview

In this chapter we examine the processor core, which runs a program by executing its instructions. We learn about the organization of the core, how instructions are executed, how data can be stored and accessed in registers and memory, and what types of operations the processor can perform.

We then examine exceptions and interrupts, which allow a program to respond quickly to events while maintaining a simple software structure. We examine how the processor responds to exceptions and interrupts and then study the hardware support circuits. Finally, we discuss how to write software to configure and use interrupts.

CPU Core

Concepts

Figure 4.1 shows an overview of the components within a microcontroller. These include a processor core (for executing a program), memory (for storing data and instructions), and supporting peripheral components that add functionality or improve performance. In this chapter we study the CPU core, which can be found in the upper left corner in Figure 4.1.

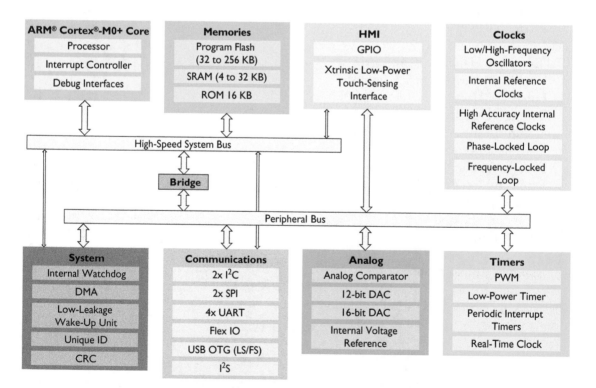

Figure 4.1   Overview of components within an NXP Kinetis KL25Z microcontroller.

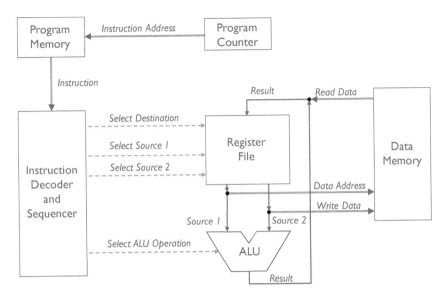

Figure 4.2 Simplified structure of a CPU core.

The processor core executes the *instructions* that make up a program. Figure 4.2 shows the components of a simple CPU core from the instruction-processing point of view. Each instruction specifies an *operation* to perform and which *operands* to use for that operation.

instruction
Command for processor to execute. Consists of an operation and zero or more operands.

operation
Part of an instruction: specifies what work to do

operand
Part of an instruction: parameter used by operation

- The program's instructions are stored in program memory (at the top of the diagram). A *register* called the program counter (PC) specifies the location (address) of the next instruction in that memory to execute.
- The *register file* holds temporary data values before and after the arithmetic/logic unit (ALU) processes them. It is easy to access but is small, holding only a few items.
- The heart of the CPU is the ALU. It performs the actual data processing operations such as addition, subtraction, logic operations (and, or, etc.), comparison, and so on. The ALU gets its operands from the register file (described next) or from within the instruction itself.

- The data memory provides longer-term data storage. It is much larger, holding thousands, millions or more data items. However, it is slower and more complex to access.
- Control logic decodes the instruction into various control and data signal sequences that are sent to other components of the CPU to control their operation.

> register
> *Hardware circuit which can store a data value*

> register file
> *Holds CPU's general purpose registers*

Figure 4.2 highlights three different types of information flowing in the CPU as it executes a program:

- Register and ALU data flow, identified with single lines.
- Memory addresses and data, identified with double lines.
- Control and selection signals, identified with dotted lines.

Instruction processing follows this sequence:

- The CPU reads an instruction from the program memory location specified by the program counter.
- The control logic decodes the instruction and uses the resulting information to control other subsystems in the CPU core. This information specifies:

  o Which registers in the register file to read for the instruction's source operands
  o How to generate any other source operands
  o Whether the ALU will perform an operation (and which one), or whether memory will be accessed
  o Which register in the register file will be written with the result
  o How to update the PC

Programs normally follow a sequential instruction execution, by advancing to the instruction located immediately after the current one. However, a control-flow instruction (e.g. branch, subroutine call, return) or interrupt request will make the flow of control jump to a different location, enabling loops, condition tests, subroutine calls, and other behaviors.

Some CPU cores speed up programs by improving this execution sequence. For example, pipelining involves starting to work on the next instruction before the current instruction has completed.

Architecture

The **architecture** defines several aspects of a processor:

- Programmer's model: operating modes, registers, memory map
- Instruction set architecture: instructions, addressing modes, data type
- Exception model: interrupt handling
- Debug architecture: debug features.

The Cortex-M0+ processors implement the ARMv6-M architecture profile [1], which is a specialized and smaller version of the more general ARMv6 architecture profile. For further information beyond what is presented here, please refer to the existing texts and manuals [2], [3], [4].

In the ARM programming model, only the data located in registers can be processed. Data in memory cannot be processed directly. Instead it must be loaded into registers before processing and perhaps stored back to memory afterward; hence it is called load/store architecture. This type of architecture simplifies the design of hardware, generally increasing speed and reducing power consumption.

The *native data types* for a CPU core are directly supported by the processor's hardware and execute quickly. The ARMv6-M native data types are signed and unsigned 32-bit values. Operations with other data types can be emulated by multiple software instructions, potentially taking more time.

> native data type
> *Primary data type used by ALU and registers. 32-bit integer for ARM Cortex-M CPUs.*

Registers

The ARM programmer's model features multiple 32-bit registers. Some of them are for general use, whereas others have specific purposes and unique characteristics.

- Registers R0 through R12 are general purpose registers for data processing.
- Register R13 is called the stack pointer (SP), and is used to manage a data storage structure called the stack. SP refers to one of two possible stack pointers, the main stack pointer (MSP) or the process stack pointer (PSP). Simple applications typically use the only MSP, although a kernel or operating system may use both.
- Register R14 is called the Link Register, and it holds the return address when a Branch and Link instruction is used.

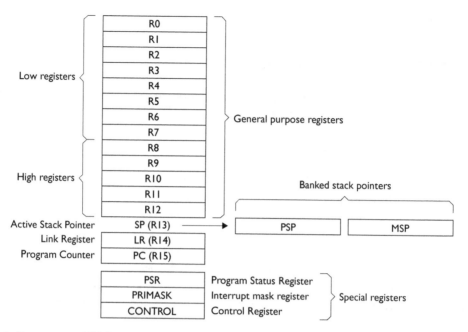

Figure 4.3 Registers in ARM programmer's model.

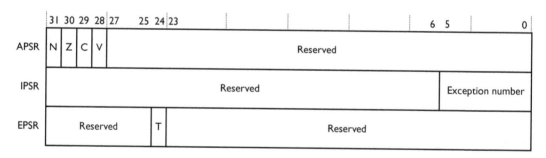

Figure 4.4 Program status register.

- Register R15 is called the program counter (PC), and it holds the address of the next instruction to execute in the program.

There are three special registers:

- The program status register (PSR) is one register but has three different views, as shown in Figure 4.4. The application PSR (APSR) view shows the *condition code flag* bits (Negative, Zero, Carry, and Overflow), which are set by the instructions based on their result. The interrupt PSR (IPSR) view holds the exception number of the currently executing exception handler. The execution PSR (EPSR) view indicates whether the CPU is operating in Thumb mode.

> condition code flag
> *Indicates whether result of instruction is negative (N) or zero (Z), or whether instruction resulted in carry (C) or overflow (V)*

- The PRIMASK register will cause the CPU to ignore some types of exceptions when it is set to one. We will discuss this further in the section on interrupts.
- The CONTROL register has one field (SPSEL) that determines which stack pointer is used if the processor is in Thread mode, and a field that determines if the processor should be running with privileged or unprivileged level when in Thread mode. Support for the unprivileged level is optional in the Cortex-M0+ processor and might not be available in some microcontroller products.

Memory

Memory Map

The ARMv6-M architecture has a 32-bit address space, allowing up to 2^{32} locations to be addressed. An address specifies a particular byte, so the memory is called *byte-addressable*. This address space is divided into various regions for different uses, as shown in Figure 4.5. There is space for code memory, on-chip SRAM for storing data, on-chip peripheral device control and status registers, off-chip RAM for storing data, off-chip peripheral device control and status registers, a private bus with fast access to peripherals, and space for system control and status registers.

> byte-addressable
> *Memory in which each address identifies a single byte*

Code	0x0000 0000
	0x1FFF FFFF
SRAM	0x2000 0000
	0x3FFF FFFF
Peripheral	0x4000 0000
	0x5FFF FFFF
	0x6000 0000
External RAM	
	0x9FFF FFFF
	0xA000 0000
External Device	
	0xDFFF FFFF
	0xE000 0000
Private Peripheral Bus	0xE00F FFFF
	0xE010 0000
System	0xFFFF FFFF

Figure 4.5 Memory map for Cortex-M processors.

In the KL25Z128VLK4, 128 KB of Flash ROM is located in the bottom of the code memory at addresses 0x0000 0000 to 0x0001 FFFF; 16 KB of read/write memory (called SRAM, static RAM) is located straddling the Code and SRAM regions, from 0x1FFF F000 to 0x1FFF FFFF (code region) and 0x2000 0000 to 0x2000 2FFF (SRAM region).

Endianness

Endianness describes the order in which multi-byte values are stored in memory at a range of addresses. For example, a four-byte value (a word) could be stored at addresses A through A+3. For *little-endian* systems, the *least-significant* byte is stored at the lowest address, as in Figure 4.7. For *big-endian* systems, the *most-significant* byte is stored at the lowest address, as in Figure 4.8.

> endianness
> *Property which describes order of bytes in multi-byte structures stored in memory*

> little-endian
> *Describes byte ordering convention in which least-significant byte is stored first in memory*

> least-significant
> *Having the smallest place value. The least-significant byte of a two-byte value represents values of 0 to 255.*

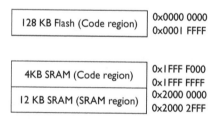

Figure 4.6 Flash ROM and SRAM memories in KL25Z128VLK4 MCU.

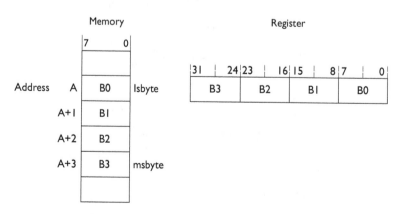

Figure 4.7 With little-endian storage, lowest memory address holds least-significant byte.

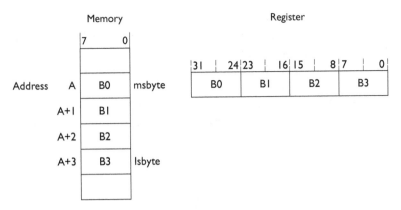

Figure 4.8 With big-endian storage, lowest memory address holds most-significant byte.

> big-endian
> *Describes byte ordering convention in which most-significant byte is stored first in memory*

> most-significant
> *Having the greatest place value. The most-significant byte of a two-byte value represents values of 0 to 65,280 which are multiples of 256.*

For ARMv6-M systems, instructions are always little-endian. Data can be of either endianness, as determined by the CPU implementation. Kinetis microcontrollers built with Cortex-M processors are little-endian for data (and instructions, of course).

Stack

A *stack* is a data structure that helps programs reuse memory safely. Rather than permanently allocate a memory location for a temporary data value, a stack allows the program to allocate a location, use it, and then free it when done, allowing for later reuse of that location for other purposes.

Adding data to a stack is called *pushing* data onto the stack, whereas removing data is called *popping* data. Stacks use a "last-in, first-out" data organization. If item X and then item Y are pushed onto the stack, then the first pop will return Y, and the second pop will return X.

The SP (R13) points to the last item on the stack, not the first free location. Pushing data decreases the SP value by the number of bytes of data added. Popping data increases SP value by the number of bytes removed. This means that the stack grows toward smaller addresses.

> stack
> *Last-in, first-out data structure. Data items are removed (popped) in the opposite order they were inserted (pushed).*

> push
> *Instruction which writes a data item next free stack location in memory and updates the stack pointer*

> pop
> *Instruction which reads a data item from the top of the stack (last used location) in memory and updates the stack pointer*

Let's walk through an example of stack use. We begin with the item D on the top of the stack at address A, as shown in Figure 4.9. We push a data item X (Figure 4.10), and then push another data item Y (Figure 4.11). The first time we pop an item off the stack, we get Y (Figure 4.12) and the next pop results give the value X (Figure 4.13). The push or pop operation adjusts the stack pointer SP to point to the top item of the stack.

For the ARM Cortex-M, all pushes and pops use 32-bit data items; no other size is possible. Since all possible stack pointer values are multiples of four, the hardware is designed so that the two least significant bits of the stack pointer are always zeros.

Memory Address	Contents
0x2000 0000	Free space
0x2000 0004	Free space
0x2000 0008	Free space
0x2000 000c	Free space
0x2000 0010	D (existing data)

SP before pushing data onto stack → (points to 0x2000 0010)

Figure 4.9 Initially stack has one data item (D). SP points to D, the top-of-stack.

Memory Address	Contents
0x2000 0000	Free space
0x2000 0004	Free space
0x2000 0008	Free space
0x2000 000c	X
0x2000 0010	D (existing data)

SP after pushing data onto stack → (points to 0x2000 000c)

Figure 4.10 Stack after pushing item X. SP now points to X, the new top-of-stack.

Memory Address	Contents
0x2000 0000	Free space
0x2000 0004	Free space
0x2000 0008	Y
0x2000 000c	X
0x2000 0010	D (existing data)

SP after pushing data onto stack → (points to 0x2000 0008)

Figure 4.11 Stack after pushing item Y. SP now points to Y.

Memory Address	Contents
0x2000 0000	Free space
0x2000 0004	Free space
0x2000 0008	Free space
0x2000 000c	X
0x2000 0010	D (Existing data)

SP after popping data from stack → (points to 0x2000 000c)

Figure 4.12 Stack after popping one item from stack. Popped value is Y. SP now points to X.

Memory Address	Contents
0x2000 0000	Free space
0x2000 0004	Free space
0x2000 0008	Free space
0x2000 000c	Free space
SP after popping data from stack → 0x2000 0010	D (Existing data)

Figure 4.13 Stack after popping another item from stack. Popped value is X. SP points to D again.

Instructions

```
9800            LDR       r0,[sp,#0]
1900            ADDS      r0,r0,r4
9000            STR       r0,[sp,#0]
```

Listing 4.1 Instructions in machine language (first column) and assembly language (remaining columns).

An instruction must specify which operation to perform, and possibly data and parameters for the operation. The instruction may be written in *machine language* or *assembly language*.

> machine language
> *Code in which each instruction is represented as a numerical value. Processed directly by CPU.*

> assembly language
> *Human-readable representation of machine code*

The machine language form is a number that is stored in program memory and which the CPU can decode quickly and easily. For example, in Listing 4.1, we see three instructions in machine language: 9800, 1900, and 9000.

Assembly language is a text form that is more easily understood than machine language, which is tedious to read, write, and edit. An assembly language instruction uses mnemonics to specify the operation and any operands. The first operand usually specifies the destination of the operation, which will be overwritten with the result. The following operands usually specify the sources of the input values. For some instructions, the destination or source is implied by the instruction itself. A software tool called an *assembler* translates the assembly language code into machine language code for the CPU to execute.

> assembler
> *Software tool which translates assembly language code into machine code*

Listing 4.1 also shows the assembly language forms of the same three instructions:

- LDR r0, [sp, #0] loads register r0 from memory starting at address sp+0.

- ADDS r0, r0, r4 adds the contents of r0 and r4, placing the results in r0.
- STR r0, [sp, #0] saves the contents of r0 to memory starting at address sp+0.

Operands may be located in a general-purpose register (R0 through R12), in the instruction word itself, in a condition code flag or in memory. Most instructions can access operands only in registers, the instruction word, or condition code flags. Some instructions (load, store, push, and pop) are able to access operands in memory.

Table 4.1 provides an overview of the different instructions available for the Cortex-M0+. Some of the instructions have two versions, one that updates the condition code flags in the APSR (indicated with an S suffix after the instruction mnemonic) and one that does not (no S suffix). Full details of the instruction set are presented in the Cortex-M0+ User Guide [3].

Data Movement Instructions

The MOV and MOVS instructions move data to a general-purpose register and have several forms:

- MOV R3, R5 copies the data from register R5 into register R3.
- MOV R2, #151 copies the value 151 into register R2. The value to be moved is called an *immediate value* because it is located in the instruction itself, in an 8-bit field. Unsigned values from 0 to 255 can be loaded into registers in this way. Larger values must be loaded from memory using the LDR instruction, described later.

> immediate value
> *Data value which is stored as part of a machine instruction*

Table 4.1 Summary of Cortex-M0+ Instructions

Category	Instruction type	Instruction mnemonic
Data movement	Move	MOV, MOVS, MRS, MSR
Data processing	Math	ADD, ADDS, ADCS, ADR, MULS, RSBS, SBCS, SUB, SUBS
	Logic	ANDS, EORS, ORRS, BICS, MVNS, TST
	Compare	CMP, CMN, TST
	Shift and rotate	ASRS, LSLS, LSRS, RORS
	Extend	SXTB, SXTH, UXTB, UXTH
	Reverse	REV, REV16, REVSH
Memory access	Load	LDR, LDRB, LDRH, LDRSH, LDRSB, LDM
	Store	STR, STRB, STRH, STM
	Stack	PUSH, POP
Control flow	Branch	B, BL, BX, BLX, Bcc
Miscellaneous		BKPT, CPSID, CPSIE, WFE, WFI, SVC, DMB, DSB, ISB, SEV, NOP

The special registers (such as CONTROL, PRIMASK, xPSR) are accessed using MSR and MRS instructions. MRS moves the data from a special register into a general-purpose register, whereas MSR does the opposite.

Data Processing Instructions

Data processing instructions include both math and logic operations. These are performed on one or more 32-bit data values, typically two registers or one register and an immediate constant.

Math operations include addition (with and without carry), subtraction (with and without borrow), subtraction with reversed operands, and multiplication:

- ADDS R0, R1, R2 adds the contents of R1 and R2, writing the result to R0 and updating the condition code flags in the APSR.

Logic operations include bitwise and, bitwise and with complement, exclusive or complement, and test.

- ANDS R4, R3, R7 computes the bitwise and of registers R3 and R7, writing the result to R4 and updating the condition code flags in the APSR.

Compare instructions calculate the difference between two operands, set the condition code flags accordingly, but discard the calculated difference. A **test** instruction performs a logical AND on two operands and then sets the condition code flags. Condition code flags are explained in depth in the instruction set reference [3].

- CMP R3, R5 computes R3 – R5 and sets the flags according to the difference. For example, if R3 holds 61 and R5 holds 29, then the comparison results in a value of 61–29 = 32. This will clear all flags: N, Z, C, and V, as the result is not negative, not zero, no carry occurred, and no overflow occurred.

Shift and **rotate** instructions shift a word left or right by the specified number of bits. Both logical and arithmetic operations are supported.

- LSRS R1, #1 shifts register R1 to the right by one bit position. Because this is a logical shift, the MSB is loaded with zero. Bit 0 is shifted into the carry flag.

Extend instructions convert an 8- or 16-bit value to fill a 32-bit register. The upper bits can be filled in one of two ways, depending on whether the original value is signed or unsigned. An *unsigned* extend instruction (UXTB or UXTH) will fill the upper bits with zeros, preserving the value of unsigned data. A *signed* extend instruction (SXTB or SXTH) will fill the upper bits with the most significant bit of the original value, preserving the value of the signed data.

---

unsigned
Numbering system which is able to represent positive values and zero

signed
Numbering system which is able to represent positive and negative values and zero

Reverse instructions can reverse the byte order in a 32-bit word or two 16-bit half-words, providing conversion between little-endian and big-endian data.

Memory Access Instructions
Recall that in the ARM programming model, data in memory must be loaded into registers before it can be processed, and then may need to be stored back into memory.

Memory Addressing
Memory accesses use offset addressing, in which a base register Rn and an offset are added together to create the actual address for the memory access. The offset can be another register or an immediate constant value (which is stored in the instruction word). The base register is not modified by the address calculation.

The assembly code syntax for addressing memory is a bracketed expression. For example:

- [R0] indicates the memory location starting at the address which is the sum of the values in R0 and R3. If R0 has a value of 4000, then this indicates the memory value starting at address 4000.
- [R0, #22] indicates the memory location starting at the address which is the sum of the values in R0 and R3. If R0 has a value of 4000, then this indicates the memory value starting at address 4022.
- [R0, R3] indicates the memory location starting at the address in register R0. If R0 has a value of 4000 and R3 has a value of −80, then this indicates the memory value starting at address 3920.

Load/Store Instructions
The LDR instruction loads a register with a 32-bit word from the four memory locations starting at the source address. The STR instruction stores the 32-bit contents of a register to the four memory locations starting at the destination address.

- LDR R0, [R4, #8] will load register R0 with the contents of the memory word (4 bytes) starting at location R4 + 8.
- STR R1, [R4, R5] will store register R1 to the memory word (4 bytes) starting at location R4 + R5.

Data smaller than 32 bits can be loaded or stored from memory as well. Byte (8 bits) and half-word (16 bits) loads and stores are supported. The STRB operation stores the least-significant byte of a register at the destination memory address, whereas STRH stores the least-significant half-word in the two bytes starting at the destination address.

Loads are more complex because an 8- or 16-bit value from memory does not completely fill a 32-bit register. This is similar to the signed and unsigned extension instructions described earlier. A load register unsigned instruction (LDRB or LDRH) will fill the upper bits with zeros, preserving the value of the unsigned data. A load register signed instruction (LDRSB or LDRSH) will fill the upper bits with the most significant bit of the value loaded from memory, preserving the value of signed data.

The ARMv6-M architecture does not support unaligned data accesses to memory. When accessing a word (which is four bytes) in memory, the starting address must be a multiple of four. When accessing a half-word (two bytes), the starting address must be a multiple of two.

The instruction set also offers load/store multiple instructions to reduce the amount of code and time needed by the program. The LDM operation will load the registers specified in an operand list from memory starting at the given address. STM will store multiple registers to memory starting at the given address.

Stack Instructions

The ARM ISA supports a stack in memory to simplify subroutine calls and returns. The SP register points to the last data item on the stack.

The PUSH operation pushes (writes) selected registers onto the stack and updates the stack pointer. Source registers R0 through R7 and the link register (LR) can be specified in the instruction. With each register pushed to memory, the CPU decrements the stack pointer by four bytes. Registers are always pushed in the same order, regardless of the operand ordering.

- PUSH {R0, R5–R7} will push registers R0, R5, R6, and R7 onto the stack, and subtract 16 from SP.

The POP operation pops (reads) selected registers from the stack and updates the stack pointer. Destination registers R0 through R7 and the PC can be specified in the instruction. With each register popped from memory, the CPU increments the stack pointer by four bytes. Registers are always pushed in the same order (which is opposite to the push order), regardless of the operand ordering.

- POP {R2, R4} will load registers R2 and R4 from the stack and add 8 to SP.

Popping a value into the PC will change the program's flow of control. This can be used to make the CPU return from a subroutine to the calling routine, which will be discussed later.

Control Flow Instructons

Control flow instructions allow programs to repeat code in a loop or execute a selected section of the code based on a conditional test. This is done by changing the PC to a different value.

An unconditional branch always transfers program execution to the specified destination address.

- B Target_label will cause the program to start executing code at (**branch to**) the program location called Target_label.

A conditional branch will transfer program execution to the specified destination address if a given condition is true. The operation consists of a B followed by a condition code suffix (e.g. BEQ, BNE). This suffix specifies which particular combination of the condition code flags (N, Z, C, V) to evaluate. The conditional branch instruction executes if the condition code flags match the specified condition. Figure 4.14 shows the meanings of the different condition code suffixes.

Suffix	Flags	Meaning
EQ	Z = 1	Equal, last flag setting result was zero.
NE	Z = 0	Not equal, last flag setting result was non-zero.
CS or HS	C = 1	Higher or same, unsigned.
CC or L0	C = 0	Lower, unsigned.
MI	N = 1	Negative.
PL	N = 0	Positive or zero.
VS	V = 1	Overflow.
VC	V = 0	No overflow.
HI	C = 1 and Z = 0	Higher, unsigned.
LS	C = 0 or Z = 1	Lower or same, unsigned.
GE	N = V	Greater than or equal, signed.
LT	N != V	Less than, signed.
GT	Z = 0 and N = V	Greater than, signed.
LE	Z = 1 or N != V	Less than or equal, signed.
AL	Can have any value	Always. This is the default when no suffix is specified.

Figure 4.14 Condition code suffixes indicate which flags to test [3].

The condition suffixes correspond to the flag settings after a compare instruction has been executed. Earlier we presented the instruction CMP R3, R5. If R3 holds 61 and R5 holds 29, then the comparison results in a value of 61–29 = 32. This will clear the flags N, Z, V, and C. Let's see how different types of conditional branch would behave:

- Branch if equal: BEQ Target_label will not branch to the target, since Z is not one. This is correct; 61 is not equal to 29.
- Branch if not equal: BNE Target_label will branch to the target, since Z is zero. This is correct; 61 is not equal to 29.
- Branch if greater than: BGT Target_label will branch to the target, since Z is zero and both N and V have the same value (zero in this case). This is correct; 61 is greater than 29.
- Branch if greater than or equal: BGE Target_label will branch to the target, since both N and V have the same value (zero in this case). This is correct; 61 is greater than or equal to 29.
- Branch if less than: BLT Target_label will not branch to the target, since N and V do not have different values. This is correct; 61 is not less than 29.

Note that the conditional branch can be performed after any instruction, not just a compare. It will evaluate the current values of the condition code flags. Remember that some instructions do not update the condition code flags.

Another useful control flow concept is the subroutine. Multiple functions may need to perform similar work. Rather than duplicate the instructions for that work in each function, the instructions may be placed into a subroutine that may be called by different functions as needed. Only one version of the instructions needs to be stored (reducing code size) and maintained (reducing development time). Software developers use subroutines to create building blocks, enabling them to think at a higher level when developing a system.

When a function calls the subroutine, the subroutine executes, and then the calling function resumes execution at the instruction following the subroutine call. Subroutine calls are performed using a branch and link (BL) or a branch and link with exchange (BLX). These are similar to the unconditional branch (B) with one major difference. When a function calls a subroutine, it expects to resume execution after the subroutine completes. The *return address* indicates the location of the next instruction in that function to execute after the subroutine completes. The return address is stored in the LR when a BL or BLX instruction is executed.

> return address
> *Address of next instruction to execute after completing a subroutine*

- BL Subroutine1 will call Subroutine1 and save the return address in the link register.
- BLX R0 will call the code with the address specified by R0 and save the return address in the link register. R0 needs to have been loaded already with the address of the subroutine.

Returning from the subroutine requires copying the return address to the program counter. When LR holds the return address, this can be done with BX LR. If this subroutine (Sub_1) may call another subroutine (Sub_2), then Sub_1 will save the LR onto the stack before calling Sub_2. Sub_1 returns by popping the saved LR value from the stack into the PC using the POP {PC} instruction.

Miscellaneous Instructions

The CPSID and CPSIE instructions are used to control the PRIMASK register, which determines whether the CPU responds to interrupts and certain other exceptions. CPSIE enables the response, whereas CPSID disables the response.

NOP is an instruction that does nothing (no operation). It can be used to align instructions in memory or delay program execution.

There are additional instructions that support debugging, exceptions, sleep modes, complex memory systems, and signaling, but we do not discuss them here.

Operating Behaviors

A CPU may have several operating modes with different capabilities to provide better performance, more safety, or additional features.

Thread and Handler Modes

The processor normally runs in Thread mode, but enters Handler mode when servicing exceptions and interrupts. The Thread mode simplifies the creation of multitasking systems. Thread and Handler modes differ in stack pointer use, which is described in the section "Handler Mode and Stack Pointers" below.

Instruction Execution versus Debugging

Normally the CPU runs non-stop, executing a program instruction by instruction unless it is in sleep mode or halted. However, there is a debug state in which the CPU does not execute instructions, but is instead controlled by a debugger circuit. Because this debugger hardware has full access to registers and memory, the target program does not need to be modified, simplifying the development tools.

Thumb Instructions

The full ARM instruction set uses 32 bits to represent each instruction, but this makes programs larger and raises costs, which are often crucial for embedded systems. The ARMv6-M profile only supports the Thumb instruction set, a subset of the full ARM instruction set in which most instructions are represented as 16-bit half-words. This reduces program memory requirements significantly and usually allows instructions to be fetched faster. The main limitation of the 16-bit instruction is that there are fewer bits available to represent the operation and operands. As a result, some 32-bit ARM instructions and advanced features are not available. For example, most 16-bit Thumb instructions can access only registers R0 through R7, but not R8 through R13. As a result, a program using 16-bit Thumb instructions may require more instructions (and likely execution cycles), but it will still be much smaller than a program with 32-bit ARM instructions.

Exceptions and Interrupts

Exceptions and interrupts are critical tools for making an embedded system responsive while supporting concurrent operation of hardware and software. In the ARM programmer's model, interrupts are a type of exception.

Events such as hardware signals or anomalous program conditions can trigger exceptions. A peripheral or external device sends a hardware signal to the exception controller hardware to indicate that an event has occurred. The processor then services (handles) the exception with these steps:

- Pauses the program.
- Saves context information, such as registers and which instruction to execute next in the current program.
- Determines which handler (also called a service routine) to run. Each type of exception or interrupt can have a separate handler.
- Runs the code for the handler.
- Restores the context information that was saved previously. The processor then resumes executing the current program where it left off.

The CPU performs most of this work automatically in hardware, making the system more responsive. The only work performed in software is running the handler.

Exceptions provide efficient event-based processing, unlike polling that can waste many CPU cycles. Exceptions provide a quick response to events regardless of program complexity, location, or processor state. They enable many multitasking embedded systems to be responsive without needing to use a task scheduler or kernel.

Most interrupts and exceptions are *asynchronous*, meaning they can occur almost anywhere in the program. Note that parts of the program may disable interrupts temporarily, which will keep the ISR from running until after interrupts are enabled. Although there are methods to trigger an interrupt or an exception in software, we will not cover them here.

asynchronous
Activities which are not synchronized with each other, or a protocol which does not send clocking information

CPU Exception Handling Behavior

Handler Mode and Stack Pointers

The CPU can operate in one of two modes. It normally operates in Thread mode, but switches to Handler mode when performing exception processing. The mode determines which stack pointer (MSP or PSP) is used.

- When the CPU is in the Handler mode, SP refers to the MSP.
- When the CPU is in Thread mode, SP can refer to either MSP or PSP. The special CPU register called CONTROL has a flag field called SPSEL that selects which stack pointer to use. If SPSEL is zero, SP refers to the main stack pointer. This is the value after the CPU is reset. If SPSEL is one, SP refers to the process stack pointer.

In systems with a kernel or operating system, threads will use the PSP and the OS, and exception handlers will use the MSP. In systems without such support, only the MSP is used.

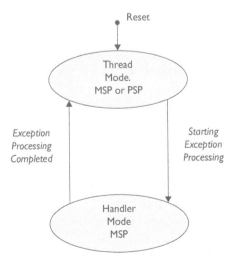

Figure 4.15 CPU operating mode changes when handling exceptions and interrupts.

Entering a Handler

The CPU performs the following steps in hardware in order when an enabled exception is requested. This takes fifteen cycles (unless memory is slow enough to require wait states).

1. Complete executing the current instruction; otherwise it will take many cycles to complete. Such an instruction (LDM, STM, PUSH, POP, and MULS) would delay the exception handling significantly. These instructions are abandoned to allow prompt exception handling, and then restarted after the exception handling completes.
2. Push part of the processor's context onto the current stack (either MSP or PSP). Eight 32-bit registers are pushed: the program status register (xPSR), the program counter (the return address), the LR (or R14), R12, R3, R2, R1, and R0. Recall that the stack grows toward smaller addresses. Figure 4.16 shows how critical processor registers that hold execution context for the interrupted code are stored on the stack after performing these steps.
3. Switch the processor to Handler mode and start using MSP.
4. Load the PC with the address of exception handler from the vector table, based on the type of exception. We will examine this shortly.
5. Load LR with EXC_RETURN code to select which mode and stack to use after completing the exception processing. The codes are listed in Table 4.2.
6. Load the IPSR with the number of the exception being processed. For an IRQ, the exception number is 16 + the IRQ number.

The CPU can now start executing the code of exception handler.

	Memory Address	Contents
	0x2000 0ffc	Free space
SP upon entering exception handler →	0x2000 1000	Saved R0
	0x2000 1004	Saved R1
	0x2000 1008	Saved R2
	0x2000 100c	Saved R3
	0x2000 1010	Saved R12
	0x2000 1014	Saved LR
	0x2000 1018	Saved PC
	0x2000 101c	Saved xPSR
SP before entering exception handler →	0x2000 1020	Data

Figure 4.16 Stack changes upon preparing to enter an exception handler.

Table 4.2 Descriptions of Exception Return Codes

EXC_RETURN Code	Return stack	Description
0xFFFF_FFF1	0 (MSP)	Return to Handler mode with MSP
0xFFFF_FFF9	0 (MSP)	Return to Thread mode with MSP
0xFFFF_FFFD	1 (PSP)	Return to Thread mode with PSP

Memory Address	Contents
0x2000 0ffc	Free space
SP before exiting exception handler → 0x2000 1000	Saved R0
0x2000 1004	Saved R1
0x2000 1008	Saved R2
0x2000 100c	Saved R3
0x2000 1010	Saved R12
0x2000 1014	Saved LR
0x2000 1018	Saved PC
0x2000 101c	Saved xPSR
SP after exiting exception handler → 0x2000 1020	Data

Figure 4.17 Stack changes upon preparing to exit an exception handler.

Exiting a Handler

The CPU performs these steps in order when exiting an exception handler. The first step is a software instruction, while the remainder are hardware operations.

1. Execute an instruction that triggers exception return processing. There is no "return from interrupt" instruction for ARMv6-M processors. Instead, we use an instruction to update the PC with a special exception return code (EXC_RETURN) that triggers the CPU's exception processing hardware. One option is a branch indirect to the link register (BX LR). Another option is to pop the exception return code from the stack into the PC.
2. On the basis of the exception return code, the CPU selects either the main or process stack pointer, and also selects either Handler or Thread mode.
3. The CPU restores the context from that stack, as shown in Figure 4.17. This consists of the registers that were saved previously: the xPSR, the program counter (the return address), the LR (or R14), R12, R3, R2, R1, and R0.
4. The CPU has now restored the processor context and will resume execution of code at the address that has been restored to the PC.

Hardware for Interrupts and Exceptions

Hardware Overview

Figure 4.18 shows an overview of the hardware involved in recognizing interrupts. At the left are peripherals that can generate interrupt requests. These peripherals contain control registers to configure the peripheral's interrupt generation behavior.

In the center is the nested vectored interrupt controller (NVIC). If any enabled interrupts have been requested, the NVIC selects the one with the highest priority and directs the CPU to start executing its ISR. The NVIC contains control registers to enable and prioritize interrupts.

Between the peripherals and NVIC there may be an optional wakeup interrupt controller (WIC). The WIC duplicates the interrupt masking of the NVIC, which enables the NVIC to be turned off to reduce power use when the system is idle or sleeping. The WIC will wake up the

NVIC if interrupts are requested, ensuring they are processed and not lost. The Kinetis KL25Z MCU features a WIC called the asynchronous WIC (AWIC).

Finally, on the right is the processor core, which can be directed to respond to an IRQ and execute an ISR. Within the control register PRIMASK, the PM flag determines whether interrupts (and certain other exceptions) are recognized or ignored. Setting PM to one will cause the CPU to ignore these interrupts. PM is cleared to Zero when the processor is reset.

Exception Sources, Vectors, and Handlers

Each possible exception source has a *vector* to specify its handler routine. The starting addresses for these handlers are stored in a *vector table*. Table 4.3 shows information (including the vector address) for Cortex-M system exceptions, and Table 4.4 shows similar information for microcontroller-specific interrupts. Each vector is four bytes long in order to hold the 32-bit address of the corresponding handler routine. Each vector starts on an address that is a multiple of four, starting with address 0x0000_0004.

vector
Address of an exception handler

Vector Table
Table of vectors used to process different exceptions

Cortex-M0+ Exception Sources

The Cortex-M0+ CPU core can generate several types of exceptions, which are listed in Table 4.3. These exceptions occur when the CPU starts up, when errors occur, and when system services are requested. Two critical exceptions are **Reset**, which occurs when the processor first starts running (after being powered up or reset) and **HardFault**, which occurs when software tries to perform an illegal operation. If you find your program stuck in the HardFault handler, your code may have tried accessing a peripheral that hadn't been enabled yet through clock gating.

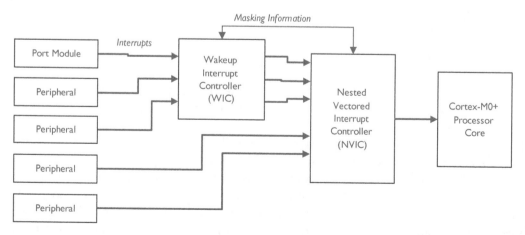

Figure 4.18 Overview of hardware for interrupt system in KL25Z MCU.

Table 4.3 Selected Cortex-M0+ Exception Sources and Descriptions

Vector Address	Vector #	Name	Description
0x0000_0004	1	Reset	CPU reset
0x0000_0008	2	NMI	Nonmaskable interrupt
0x0000_000C	3	HardFault	Hard fault error
0x0000_002C	11	SVCall	Call to supervisor with SVC instruction
0x0000_0038	14	PendSV	System-level service request
0x0000_003C	15	SysTick	System timer tick

Table 4.4 KL25Z Interrupt Sources and Descriptions

Vector address	Vector #	IRQ	Description
0x0000_0040, 44, 48, 4C	16–19	0–3	Direct memory access controller
0x0000_0058	22	6	Power management controller
0x0000_005C	23	7	Low leakage wake up
0x0000_0060, 64	24–25	8–9	I²C communications
0x0000_0068, 6C	26–27	10–11	SPI communications
0x0000_0070, 74, 78	28–30	12–14	UART communications
0x0000_007C	31	15	Analog to digital converter
0x0000_0080	32	16	Comparator
0x0000_0084, 88, 8C	33–35	17–19	Timers and pulse-width modulation
0x0000_0090, 94	36–37	20–21	Real-time clock alarm and seconds
0x0000_0098	38	22	Programmable interval timer
0x0000_00A0	40	24	USB on-the-go
0x0000_00A4	41	25	Digital to analog converter
0x0000_00A8	42	26	Touch sense interface
0x0000_00AC	43	27	Main clock generator
0x0000_00B0	44	28	Low power timer
0x0000_00B8	46	30	Port control module, Port A pin detect
0x0000_00BC	47	31	Port control module, Port D pin detect

KL25Z Interrupt Sources

Many of the KL25Z MCU peripherals can request interrupts, and are shown in Table 4.4. Vectors for interrupts start with IRQ0 at address 0x0000_0040. Further details can be found in the MCU reference manual [5].

In our example system, the two switches are connected to PORTD. When a switch changes, the port control module signals the NVIC, which will issue interrupt request #31 to the CPU. The CPU will read the vector table to find the location of the ISR for IRQ #31 (vector #47). In particular, it will read the word starting at address 0x0000_00BC and load it into the PC so the ISR will execute.

Vector Table Definition and Handler Names

CMSIS-CORE specifies standard names for system exception handlers. Different micro-controllers will have different peripherals, so the interrupt handler's names and vectors are defined in the MCU-specific startup code. The KL25Z4 MCUs use the assembly language file startup_MKL25Z4.s, shown in Listing 4.2. The DCD symbol tells the assembler to define a constant data word with the value specified, in this case the address of the specified handler.

```
__Vectors
        DCD     __initial_sp ; Top of Stack
        DCD     Reset_Handler  ; Reset Handler
        DCD     NMI_Handler  ; NMI Handler
        DCD     HardFault_Handler  ; Hard Fault Handler
        DCD     0 ; Reserved
        DCD     0 ; Reserved
        DCD     0 ; Reserved
        DCD     0 ; Reserved
        DCD     0 ; Reserved
        DCD     0 ; Reserved
        DCD     0 ; Reserved
        DCD     SVC_Handler  ; SVCall Handler
        DCD     0 ; Reserved
        DCD     0 ; Reserved
        DCD     PendSV_Handler  ; PendSV Handler
        DCD     SysTick_Handler  ; SysTick Handler
; External Interrupts
        DCD     DMA0_IRQHandler  ; DMA channel 0 transfer complete interrupt
        DCD     DMA1_IRQHandler  ; DMA channel 1 transfer complete interrupt
        DCD     DMA2_IRQHandler  ; DMA channel 2 transfer complete interrupt
        DCD     DMA3_IRQHandler  ; DMA channel 3 transfer complete interrupt
        DCD     Reserved20_IRQHandler  ; Reserved interrupt 20
        DCD     FTFA_IRQHandler  ; FTFA interrupt
        DCD     LVD_LVW_IRQHandler  ; Low Voltage Detect, Low Voltage Warning
        DCD     LLW_IRQHandler  ; Low Leakage Wakeup
        DCD     I2C0_IRQHandler  ; I2C0 interrupt
        DCD     I2C1_IRQHandler  ; I2C0 interrupt 25
        DCD     SPI0_IRQHandler  ; SPI0 interrupt
        DCD     SPI1_IRQHandler  ; SPI1 interrupt
        DCD     UART0_IRQHandler  ; UART0 status/error interrupt
        DCD     UART1_IRQHandler  ; UART1 status/error interrupt
        DCD     UART2_IRQHandler  ; UART2 status/error interrupt
        DCD     ADC0_IRQHandler  ; ADC0 interrupt
        DCD     CMP0_IRQHandler  ; CMP0 interrupt
        DCD     TPM0_IRQHandler  ; TPM0 fault, overflow and channels interrupt
        DCD     TPM1_IRQHandler  ; TPM1 fault, overflow and channels interrupt
        DCD     TPM2_IRQHandler  ; TPM2 fault, overflow and channels interrupt
        DCD     RTC_IRQHandler  ; RTC interrupt
        DCD     RTC_Seconds_IRQHandler  ; RTC seconds interrupt
        DCD     PIT_IRQHandler  ; PIT timer interrupt
```

```
DCD    Reserved39_IRQHandler  ; Reserved interrupt 39
DCD    USB0_IRQHandler   ; USB0 interrupt
DCD    DAC0_IRQHandler   ; DAC interrupt
DCD    TSI0_IRQHandler   ; TSI0 interrupt
DCD    MCG_IRQHandler   ; MCG interrupt
DCD    LPTimer_IRQHandler  ; LPTimer interrupt
DCD    Reserved45_IRQHandler  ; Reserved interrupt 45
DCD    PORTA_IRQHandler  ; Port A interrupt
DCD    PORTD_IRQHandler  ; Port D interrupt
```

Listing 4.2 Vector table for KL25Z MCU in startup_MKL25Z4.s.

Peripheral Interrupt Configuration

We must configure the peripheral and the NVIC in order to use interrupts, as shown in Figure 4.19. After reset, the processor core is already set up to accept interrupts, since the PM bit is cleared to zero. We first examine how to configure a peripheral to generate an interrupt request. Different types of peripherals have interrupt configuration options. Here we will examine the Kinetis KL25Z's PORT module as it is used in our example system. We will examine interrupt configuration for other peripherals in later chapters.

The IRQC field in the pin control register (PCR), shown in Figure 4.20, controls the conditions under which an interrupt will be generated. Interrupts can be generated when the input is

Figure 4.19 Configure peripheral to generate interrupts.

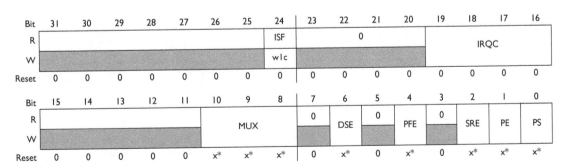

* Notes:
• x = Undefined at reset.

Figure 4.20 Pin control register contents [1] p. 183.

logic zero, logic one, a rising edge, a falling edge, or either edge, as selected by the code in Table 4.5. Full details are presented in the reference manual [5].

Listing 4.3 shows how to set the IRQC field using the Kinetis-specific macro PORT_PCR_IRQC from the CMSIS-compliant device driver.

```
PORTD->PCR[SW1_POS] = PORT_PCR_IRQC(9) | PORT_PCR_MUX(1);
```

Listing 4.3 Configuring Port D bit SW1_POS to generate an interrupt on the rising edge of input signal.

The port module interrupt status flag register (ISFR) indicates which interrupts have been detected for this port. A bit value of one indicates the corresponding interrupt has been detected. The ISR needs to write a one to a bit to clear it to zero, with CMSIS-CORE, the ISFR is accessed as PORTD->ISFR.

NVIC Operation and Configuration

Next we examine how to configure the NVIC (Figure 4.21), which selects the highest-priority-enabled interrupt request and directs the CPU to execute its ISR. The NVIC supports up to 32 interrupt sources, called IRQ0 through IRQ31. Each source can be configured. Each interrupt source can be enabled, disabled, and prioritized. Pending interrupt processing status can be read and modified.

Table 4.5 Interrupt Generation Condition Codes

Code	Condition Selected
0	Interrupt/DMA request disabled
8	Interrupt when logic zero
9	Interrupt on rising edge
10	Interrupt on falling edge
11	Interrupt on either edge
12	Interrupt when logic one
Other	Reserved, or for DMA

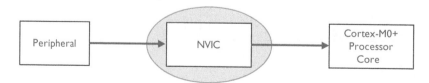

Figure 4.21 Configure NVIC to manage interrupt requests.

Enable

Each interrupt source can be enabled or disabled separately using the NVIC registers ISER and ICER. Each is 32 bits, with each bit corresponding to an interrupt source. To enable an interrupt source N, write a 1 to bit N in ISER. To disable an interrupt source N, write a 1 to bit N in ICER. Reading ISER or ICER will return the enabled or disabled state for all 32 interrupt sources.

The CMSIS-CORE API provides this interface:

```
void NVIC_EnableIRQ(IRQnum) - Enable interrupts of type IRQnum
void NVIC_DisableIRQ(IRQnum) - Disable interrupts of type IRQnum
```

Values for IRQnum are defined by the CMSIS-compliant device driver, and are listed in the MKL25Z4.h file in the section called "Interrupt Number Definitions". Examples are TMP0_IRQn, LPTimer_IRQn, and PORTD_IRQn.

Priority

Each exception source has a priority that determines the order in which simultaneous exception requests are handled. The requested exception with the lowest priority number will be handled first. Some exceptions have fixed priorities, such as reset, NMI, and hard fault. Other exceptions (including interrupts) have configurable priorities.

The NVIC contains multiple interrupt priority registers (IPR0 through IPR7). Each IPR has an 8-bit field for each of four interrupt sources. Each field specifies one of four possible priority levels (0, 64, 128, and 192) for that source. Multiple interrupt sources can have the same priority. The CMSIS-CORE API provides the interface here. Note that the prio parameter should be set to 0, 1, 2, or 3, as the code shifts the value 6 bits to the left before saving it to the priority field:

```
void NVIC_SetPriority(IRQnum, prio) - Set interrupt source IRQnum to priority prio
uint32_t NVIC_SetPriority(IRQnum) - Get priority of interrupt source IRQnum
```

Pending

An interrupt is *pending* if it has been requested but has not yet been serviced. The flag is set by hardware when the interrupt is requested. Software can also set the flag to request the interrupt. An interrupt handler that runs must clear its source's pending IRQ flag or else the handler will run repeatedly.

> *pending*
> *Requested but not yet serviced (e.g. interrupt)*

The CMSIS-CORE API provides this interface:

```
uint32_t NVIC_GetPendingIRQ(IRQnum) - Returns 1 if interrupt from IRQnum is
pending
void NVIC_SetPendingIRQ(IRQnum) - Sets interrupt pending flag for IRQnum
void NVIC_ClearPendingIRQ(IRQnum) - Clears interrupt pending flag for IRQnum
```

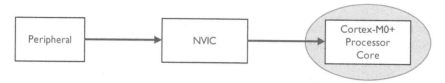

Figure 4.22 Configure processor core to process exceptions.

Exception Masking

Finally the processor core can be configured to accept or ignore certain types of exceptions, as shown in Figure 4.22. The CPU core's PRIMASK register controls whether interrupts and other exceptions of configurable priority are recognized or not. The PM flag is stored in bit zero of PRIMASK. A PM value of zero allows those exceptions to be recognized by the CPU, whereas a one prevents it. The PM bit is accessed using the CPSID and CPSIE instructions. Note that when the CPU is reset or powers up, PM is set to zero, so these exceptions are not ignored.

The CMSIS-CORE API provides these interfaces for accessing the PM flag:

```
void __enable_irq() - clears PM flag
void __disable_irq() - sets PM flag
uint32_t __get_PRIMASK() - returns value of PRIMASK
void __set_PRIMASK(uint32_t x) - sets PRIMASK to x
```

Safely Masking Interrupts
A function may need to ensure no interrupts are handled during a certain sequence of operations (called a critical section). One approach is to call __disable_irq() before the sequence of operations and __enable_irq() after. However, if interrupts were already disabled (for some other reason) before executing the sequence of operations, then it is incorrect to enable them afterward.

The correct approach is shown in Listing 4.4. The code must save the masking state (using __get_PRIMASK()) before disabling interrupts (using __disable_IRQ()). After performing the critical section operations, the saved masking state is restored (using __set_PRIMASK()).

```
void my_function(void) {
    uint32_t masking_state;
    // Perform non-critical processing
    // ...
    masking_state = __get_PRIMASK();    // Get current interrupt masking state
    __disable_irq();                    // disable interrupts
    // Perform critical section operations
    // ...
    __set_PRIMASK(masking_state);       // Restore previous interrupt masking state
    // Perform more non-critical processing
    // ...
}
```

Listing 4.4 Correct method to prevent interrupts during critical section of code saves and restores interrupt masking state.

Software for Interrupts

When creating software for a system that uses interrupts, we design the system first and then implement it by writing the code. We design the system by identifying which interrupts to use and then deciding how to divide (partition) the work between ISRs and main-line code. We can then write the code to configure hardware to generate and handle interrupts, and finally write the code for the ISRs themselves.

Program Design

Selecting which interrupts to use is generally simple because they are peripheral-specific. Some peripherals have flexible interrupt generation capabilities that can simplify the software design significantly when used appropriately. We will examine these features in later chapters.

Determining how to structure the code in response to the interrupt depends on two major issues: How should we partition work between the ISR and the main-line code? How will the ISR communicate the remaining work to the main-line code? We discuss these next. These topics are covered further in other texts [6], [7], [8].

Partitioning

The ISR should perform only quick, urgent work related to the interrupt. Other work should be deferred to the main-line code when feasible. This keeps each ISR quick and doesn't delay other ISRs unnecessarily. Keeping ISRs short also makes the code much easier to debug.

Consider the flashing LED example from the previous chapter. Pressing or releasing a switch will trigger an interrupt. Figure 4.23 shows the work involved in response. Software must identify which switch changed, determine the new value of the switch, update the variables g_w_delay, g_RGB_delay, and g_flash_LED, and light the LEDs.

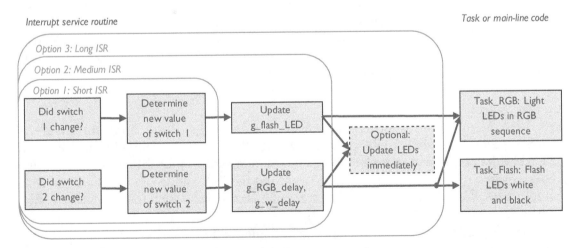

Figure 4.23 Three options for partitioning work between ISR and task code for the flashing LED example.

How much of this work should be done in the ISR, and how much should be left in the main-line code? Let's consider three options:

- Option 1: Short ISR. The ISR simply signals which switch changed and how (whether pressed or released). A task in the main-line program needs to update the delay and flash mode variables based on this switch information. This could be done by Task_RGB and Task_Flash, which would reduce the code's modularity. The variables could be updated by a new task, which would add the overhead of creating and running another task.
- Option 2: Medium ISR. The ISR directly updates the delay and flash mode variables. This is a quick, low overhead approach.
- Option 3: Long ISR: The ISR directly updates the delay and flash mode variables, and immediately updates the LED based on the new delay or flash mode. This approach is much more responsive than the first two, but we have a problem when the ISR completes and the previously executing task resumes. That task will light the LEDs with the wrong colors or the wrong delays. We need a way to disable or restart that task, and this is not simple.

Communication

When work is split up between the ISR and the main-line code, we need a way to communicate the intermediate results between the pieces.

In Options 2 and 3 above, the ISR directly updates the delay and flash mode variables. These can be shared variables which the ISR writes and the task code reads. This is a straightforward and simple solution.

The first option is more complex. The ISR writes to shared variables that indicate which switch changed and how. The task code reads the switch variables and then updates the delay and flash mode variables. However, how do we keep the task code from reusing the switch variables the next time it runs? Should the ISR use a flag to tell the task to run once? Or should the task erase the switch variables when it is done with them?

There are more questions to consider. What should the system do if the ISR runs more than once before the main-line task code can run? Should the task code process the data from just the first ISR instance, or just the last? If the task code must process all the data, then it must be saved somehow. For example, a system with serial communication should not lose any incoming or outgoing data. The ISR and the task code will need to coordinate on how to store the data and reuse space effectively. We will see how to do this with queues in a later chapter. Kernels and RTOSs also provide queues for application programs to use.

Example System Design

We choose the intermediate partitioning approach to create the design shown in Figure 4.24. The ISR updates the shared variables g_w_delay, g_RGB_delay, and g_flash_LED, which in turn are read by the tasks. We do not need to buffer or accumulate data for this example. If the user presses a switch multiple times before a task can run, the ISR will update the shared variables multiple times. We only care about the last value of each variable, which the task uses to control the flashing.

The developer should consider the range of partitioning options to find a good balance between performance (responsiveness) and complexity. More partitioning improves responsiveness for the rest of the system, but increases the communication complexity and reduces responsiveness for the interrupt in question.

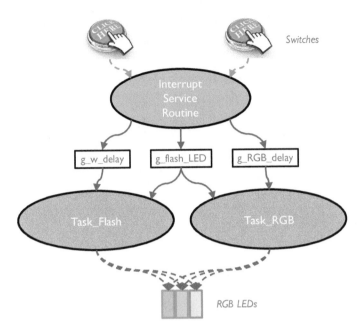

Figure 4.24 Communication and control paths among hardware and software components in example LED flashing system.

Interrupt Configuration

Let's write the code to configure the hardware. As shown in Figure 4.25, the code must configure three parts of the system to use interrupts: the peripheral, the NVIC, and the CPU core.

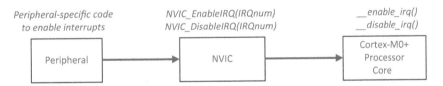

Figure 4.25 Interrupts must be enabled in peripheral, NVIC, and processor core.

The code to initialize interrupts for our example is shown in Listing 4.5. First, the code configures the peripheral to generate interrupts. This step is peripheral-specific. In our example with the KL25Z port module, we need to specify which port input bits should generate interrupts and under what circumstances. The port module is described earlier in this chapter, in the section "Peripheral Interrupt Configuration" below. The two switches are connected to port D bits SW1_POS (bit 7) and SW2_POS (bit 6), so we will access the PCR for each bit. If we want any input change to generate an input, referring to Table 4.5, we find that we will need to set IRQC for these bits to binary 11 (decimal 3).

Second, the code configures the NVIC to recognize this interrupt and with a given priority. Both switches are connected to the PORTD module, so we will use the PORTD_IRQn name from CMSIS-CORE. We first set the priority using a call to NVIC_SetPriority, then clear any pending interrupts using a call to NVIC_ClearPendingIRQ, and then finally enable the interrupt using NVIC_EnableIRQ.

```c
#define SW1_POS (7)    // on port D
#define SW2_POS (6)    // on port D

#define MASK(x) (1UL << (x))

void Initialize_Interrupts(void) {
    /* Configure PORT peripheral. Select GPIO and enable pull-up
    resistors and interrupts on all edges for pins connected to switches */
    PORTD->PCR[SW1_POS] = PORT_PCR_MUX(1) | PORT_PCR_PS_MASK |
        PORT_PCR_PE_MASK | PORT_PCR_IRQC(11);
    PORTD->PCR[SW2_POS] = PORT_PCR_MUX(1) | PORT_PCR_PS_MASK |
        PORT_PCR_PE_MASK | PORT_PCR_IRQC(11);

    /* Configure NVIC */
    NVIC_SetPriority(PORTD_IRQn, 2);
    NVIC_ClearPendingIRQ(PORTD_IRQn);
    NVIC_EnableIRQ(PORTD_IRQn);

    /* Optional: Configure PRIMASK in case interrupts were disabled. */
    __enable_irq();
}
```

Listing 4.5 Code to initialize interrupts.

Third, the code may ensure that interrupts are not disabled. When the processor comes out of reset, the PM bit in the CPU's PRIMASK register will be zero, so interrupts will be enabled and the PM bit will not need to be modified. However, if other code has run and set the PM bit, then it is necessary to call __enable_irq.

Writing ISRs in C

Let's move on to writing the actual ISR. The ISR function takes no arguments and has no return values (e.g. void PORTD_IRQHandler (void)). An ISR must be named according to the CMSIS-CORE exception handler names shown in Listing 4.2 (e.g. PORTD_IRQHandler, RTC_IRQHandler). This ensures that the software toolchain places ISR addresses in the vector table correctly. The source code for the ISR for our example system is shown in Listing 4.6.

```c
volatile uint8_t g_flash_LED = 0;   // initially don't flash LED, just do RGB sequence
volatile uint32_t g_w_delay = W_DELAY_SLOW;       // delay for white flash
volatile uint32_t g_RGB_delay = RGB_DELAY_SLOW;  // delay for RGB sequence
void PORTD_IRQHandler(void) {
    // Read switches
    if ((PORTD->ISFR & MASK(SW1_POS))) {
        if (SWITCH_PRESSED(SW1_POS)) { // flash white
            g_flash_LED = 1;
        } else {
            g_flash_LED = 0;
        }
    }
    if ((PORTD->ISFR & MASK(SW2_POS))) {
```

```
        if (SWITCH_PRESSED(SW2_POS)) { // short delays
            g_w_delay = W_DELAY_FAST;
            g_RGB_delay = RGB_DELAY_FAST;
        } else {
            g_w_delay = W_DELAY_SLOW;
            g_RGB_delay = RGB_DELAY_SLOW;
        }
    }
    // clear status flags
    PORTD->ISFR = 0xffffffff;
}
```

Listing 4.6 Source code for shared variables and interrupt service routine (handler).

Both switches are connected to Port D, so we name the ISR PORTD_IRQHandler to match the entry in the vector table.

Our ISR needs to determine which switch changed, and what the switch's new value is. To do this, the ISR needs to read the interrupt status flag register (ISFR) in PORTD to determine which bit triggered the interrupt. The new value of the switch is determined by reading the port input data bit with the macro SWITCH_PRESSED.

After determining which switch changed and how, the code can update the shared variables g_flash_LED, g_w_delay, and g_RGB_delay.

Finally, we clear the interrupt status flag register by writing all ones to PORTD->ISFR.

Sharing Data Safely Given Preemption

Sharing data in a system with preemption introduces possible problems. Note that both interrupts and preemptive task scheduling (e.g. with a kernel) can cause preemption. Interrupts can preempt tasks. In a system with preemptive scheduling, tasks can preempt other tasks.

Volatile Data Objects

The first problem comes from the fact that shared data objects are stored in memory. When creating a function that uses the shared data, the compiler generates instructions to copy the data into a register to process it. This occurs each time the variable appears in the source code. However, if the shared data is used multiple times in the function, the compiler may optimize the code by reusing the value that was loaded the first time, rather than generating more instructions to reload it for successive uses.

```
void Task_RGB(void) {
  if (g_flash_LED == 0) {      // Only run task when NOT in flash mode
      Control_RGB_LEDs(1, 0, 0);
      Delay(g_RGB_delay); // Code reads g_RGB_delay from memory into register
      // If switch 2 changes now, the ISR will run and update g_RGB_delay in memory
      Control_RGB_LEDs(0, 1, 0);
      Delay(g_RGB_delay);   // Error: using old value of g_RGB_delay in register
      Control_RGB_LEDs(0, 0, 1);
      Delay(g_RGB_delay);   // Error: using old value of g_RGB_delay in register
  }
}
```

Listing 4.7 Task_RGB might reuse first value of g_RGB_delay.

Consider the code in Listing 4.7. The shared variable g_RGB_delay is used three times. The compiler generates code to load g_RGB_delay from memory into a register for the first call to the subroutine called Delay. For optimization reasons, the compiler may reuse the value that was read the first time in the second and third calls to Delay. Consider the case shown in the code listing, in which switch 2 changes after the first use of g_RGB_delay. The ISR will run and change the value of g_RGB_delay in memory. However, the code is still using the old value of g_RGB_delay, causing a program error.

In other cases the source code may specify writing the result back to memory. To speed up the program, the compiler may not save the updated values back to memory until necessary (e.g. the end of the function). Imagine that such a function is executing. It has already loaded the value and updated the value, but the code is optimized so that it does not save the updated value back to memory until the end of the function. An interrupt is requested, causing an ISR to run that changes the shared variable in memory. When the function resumes executing, it will be using the old value of the shared variable, not the new value. When the function completes, it will overwrite the new value with the updated old value, causing an error.

We call this shared data volatile because it can change outside a program's normal flow of control. If an ISR may change a variable used by main-line code, then that data is volatile. Similarly, a hardware register (e.g. a counter) that may change on its own is also volatile.

```
volatile uint8_t g_flash_LED = 0;    // initially don't flash LED, just do RGB
volatile uint32_t g_w_delay = W_DELAY_SLOW;    // delay for white flash
volatile uint32_t g_RGB_delay = RGB_DELAY_SLOW;  // delay for RGB sequence
```

Listing 4.8 Variables shared between ISR and mainline code must be defined as volatile.

We tell the compiler that a variable may change outside of its control by using the volatile keyword before the data type in the variable's definition. This forces the compiler to reload the variable from memory each time it is used in the source code. In Listing 4.8 the shared variables g_Flash_LED, g_w_delay, and g_RGB_delay are defined as volatile. This indicates to the compiler that they may change unexpectedly (e.g. an ISR may change them).

Atomic Object Access

The second problem comes from the fact that some data objects take multiple operations to modify. This means they do not have *atomic* (i.e. indivisible) access. If the program is preempted in the middle of these operations, then the data object is only partially updated and is incorrect. If the preempting code accesses the data object, it will get incorrect data, causing an error.

> atomic
> *Indivisible, cannot be interrupted or preempted*

Consider our example LED flasher system. Let's consider changing the size of g_RGB_delay from one word (uint32_t, which is 32 bits) to two words (uint64_t, which is 64 bits) to allow longer time delays. The code will now need to perform two load operations to read g_RGB_delay from memory: LDR r0, [g_RGB_delay] for the low word and LDR r1, [g_RGB_delay+4] for the high word. Similarly, two store operations are needed to write the two words back.

Consider the case in which switch 2 changes, while the first load instruction is executing. The CPU will complete that first load (low word) and then execute the ISR. The ISR will update the two words of g_RGB_delay in memory. The task code will then resume by loading r1 with the second (high) word from memory. The registers now hold corrupted data: r0 holds the old low word, and r1 holds the new high word. This is called a *data race* situation, as it depends on the specific timing relationship between the program execution and the interrupt request. The sequence of instructions that should not be interrupted is called a *critical section*.

> data race
> *Situation in which the ill-timed preemption of a code critical section can result in an incorrect program result*

> critical section
> *Section of code which may execute incorrectly if not executed atomically*

```
volatile uint64_t g_RGB_delay_64;

void my_function(void) {
    uint32_t masking_state;
    uint64_t temp_delay;

    // Perform non-critical section processing
    // ...

    // Disable interrupts before critical section
    masking_state = __get_PRIMASK();   // Get current interrupt masking state
    __disable_irq();                   // disable interrupts

    // Execute critical section
    temp_delay = g_RGB_delay_64;       // load delay safely into temporary variable

    // Restore interrupt masking state after critical section
    __set_PRIMASK(masking_state);      // Restore previous interrupt masking state

    // Resume non-critical section processing
    Delay(temp_delay);                 // Use temporary variable
    // ...
}
```

Listing 4.9 Disabling interrupts to make a critical section atomic.

We solve this problem by disabling preemption during the critical section. For example, we can disable interrupts during the critical section as shown in Listing 4.9. As described in the section "Safely Masking Interrupts" above, we need to save the interrupt masking state, mask interrupts, and then restore the previous interrupt masking state. Preemptive kernels offer this and related methods to prevent preemption during critical sections of code.

Summary

In this chapter, we explored the basic organization and programmer's model of a Cortex-M0+ CPU core. We learned about general-purpose registers and special control registers in the core. We saw how memory is addressed and how a stack works. We examined the available instructions, including data movement, data processing, memory access, control flow, and miscellaneous instructions. We learned about different processor operating modes and how Thumb instructions differ from standard ARM instructions.

We then examined exceptions and interrupts. We saw the steps the CPU follows to handle exceptions: looking up a handler's address in the vector table, entering the exception handler and then exiting it. We then covered the path that interrupts follow: from generation by a peripheral, through the NVIC, and finally through the CPU masking hardware. Finally we discussed how to design software for interrupts: how to partition work between the ISR and main-line code, how to write software which configures the hardware to generate and recognize interrupts, and how to write the ISR. We also discussed how to handle volatile data and provide atomic object access.

Exercises

1. How does the word 0xdec0ded1 appear in memory in a little-endian memory system as well as in a big-endian memory system? Specify the relative address for each byte.
2. Does the stack in ARM processors grow toward larger or smaller addresses?
3. Assuming that SP is 0x0000_2220 initially, what is its value after executing the instruction PUSH {r0,r2}?
4. Assuming that SP is 0x0000_2010 initially, what is its value after executing the instruction POP {r0-r7,PC}?
5. Write the Thumb code to add number five to the contents of register r6.
6. Write the Thumb code to subtract 1,000 from the contents of register r6, using r3 as a temporary register.
7. Write the Thumb code to multiply the two 32-bit values in memory at addresses 0x1234_5678 and 0x7894_5612, storing the result in address 0x2000_0010.
8. Write the Thumb code to load register r0 with the ASCII code for the letter "E" if the number in r12 is even, or "O" if it is odd.
9. Which modules generate the IRQ0, IRQ10, and IRQ31 interrupt requests, and what are their CMSIS typedef enumeration labels? Examine the interrupt vector assignments (IVA) table in the KL25Z subfamily reference manual and the MKL25Z4.h file (or appropriate device.h file for a different MCU device).
10. We would like to configure a KL25Z MCU so that if interrupts IRQ0, IRQ10, and IRQ31 are requested simultaneously, the CPU responds by servicing IRQ10 first, then IRQ0, and finally IRQ31. Write the C code using CMSIS functions to configure the MCU.
11. We wish to enable IRQ13 but disable IRQ24. What values need to be loaded into which register bits, and what is the sequence of CMSIS calls to accomplish the same?
12. We wish to determine if IRQ7 has been requested. Which register and which bit will indicate this? What is the CMSIS call that will reveal the information?

13. Which register can an exception handler use to determine if it is servicing exception number 0×21? What value will the register have? What is the CMSIS interface code to read the IPSR?
14. The code in Listing 4.6 clears the status flags for *all* bits in Port D's interrupt status flag register. Under what circumstances might this lead to incorrect system operation?

References

[1] *ARMv6-M Architecture Reference Manual*, DDI 0419C, ARM Ltd., 2010.
[2] *Cortex-M0+ Technical Reference Manual*, DDI 0484C, r0p1 ed., ARM Ltd., 2012.
[3] *Cortex-M0+ Devices Generic User Guide*, DUI 0662B, r0p1 ed., ARM Ltd., 2012.
[4] J. Yiu, *The definitive guide to the ARM cortex-M0 and cortex-M0+ processors*, 2nd ed., Newnes, 2015.
[5] *KL25 Sub-Family Reference Manual*, KL25P80M48SF0RM, Rev. 3rd ed., NXP Semiconductor, B.V., 2016.
[6] P. Koopman, *Better embedded system software*, Drumnadrochit Education LLC, 2010.
[7] J. Ganssle, *The art of designing embedded systems*, 2nd ed., Elsevier Inc., 2008.
[8] J. K. Peckol, *Embedded systems: A contemporary design tool*, John Wiley & Sons, Inc., 2008.

5

C in Assembly Language

Contents

Overview

In Chapter 4 we examined the ARM Cortex-M0+ processor core, including the instructions that it can execute, the registers for general-purpose data processing, and methods to access memory. In this chapter we will see the object code that the compiler creates to implement the C-language source code. Understanding this object code will help us debug our programs and write source code that is more efficient in its use of time or memory.

Motivation

We have seen the instructions that the ARM Cortex-M0+ processor core can execute. Each instruction performs simple operations, such as adding two integers, comparing values, or pushing registers onto the stack in memory. Creating a program using these instructions requires the developer to make many small decisions: where to place a data variable in memory, which register to use to process that variable, which kind of conditional branch to use after a comparison, how to share data between functions, and so forth. This complexity slows software development and introduces many opportunities for errors.

High-level programming languages were developed to free the software developer from these issues. C and C++ are the dominant programming languages for embedded systems. We use a language translation tool called a compiler to convert an application program from one high-level language to assembly language, and another tool called an assembler to convert the assembly language to object code. The CPU executes the program by reading each object code instruction and then executing it very quickly (e.g. within one or two CPU clock cycles).

In some programming languages (e.g. Java, Perl, Python), an application program is not converted to the CPU's native executable format. Instead, at runtime the application program is processed by another program (such as an interpreter or virtual machine) to carry out the work specified. Java code can be compiled to an intermediate form called bytecode before the program is run. At runtime the virtual machine program interprets and executes the bytecode. The interpreter or virtual machine program increases the amount of time and memory needed to run an application program. Compiled languages dominate embedded systems development because they do not incur these runtime and memory overheads, and also because they offer more predictable behavior.

A **toolchain** is a set of tools used to build the program (to convert it from source code to executable object code), download it to the MCU's memory, and control its execution for debugging.

The toolchain must be configured to support the specific type of processor we are using and how much memory is in the system.

Using a high-level programming language introduces trade-offs. We expect the toolchain to generate an object code that is correct, and also reasonably fast and small. It may be possible to manually create faster or smaller object code by writing the assembly code ourselves, but we will do this only when necessary.

Software Development Tools

Three major types of tools used for embedded software development are the **program build toolchain**, the **programmer**, and the **debugger**. The program build toolchain translates a program into a format that the MCU can understand, stored in an executable file. The programmer programs that information into the MCU's program memory. This memory is nonvolatile (typically Flash ROM), so it will remain even after power is removed. The debugger enables the developer to control program execution and examine the program state (e.g. current instruction, values of processor registers, and data memory) as it runs on the processor.

These tools are often grouped together in a single integrated development environment (IDE) to simplify development. In this textbook we cover the Keil µVision (microVision) IDE.

Program Build Tools

Figure 5.1 gives an overview of the build tools and the files they process to create the final executable file. Programs are built of modules that are translated through a series of formats and then combined into an executable file. The file my_module.c contains the module's code in the C language format. This is compiled to create an assembly language module in the file my_module.s, which is then assembled to create an object module in the file my_module.o. This module is linked with other modules (also in object format) to create the executable file.

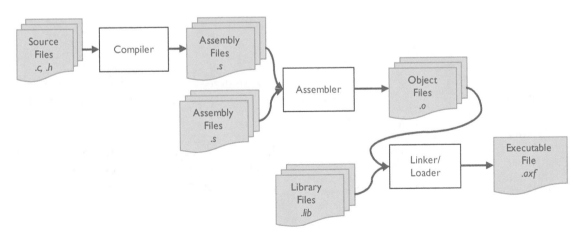

Figure 5.1 Program build tools process different files to create a file holding the executable program.

Compiler

A compiler converts a module from a high-level language such as C into assembly language. Keil µVision uses the armcc compiler [1]. The compiler compiles one source file (e.g. .c) at a time, following these steps:

- Pre-process the.c file by including the text of any included files (e.g. with #include) and performing macro substitution (e.g. #define).
- Verify that the syntax of the program is correct.
- Create intermediate code from the source code.
- Perform high-level optimization of the intermediate code.
- Generate assembly code from the intermediate code and allocate variable uses to registers.
- Perform low-level optimization of the assembly code.
- Generate an output file (.s) containing the assembly code for the module.

Note that the compilation process is not one-to-one. The compiler's primary goal is to create object code that **correctly implements the requirements** specified by the source code. This means that there are many possible correct object code versions of a single C language program. They may differ in the number and type of instructions used, which registers are used, how much data memory is used, how code is laid out, and other aspects as well.

A compiler can generate an assembly language listing file to help understand the code it has generated. The next section has an example in Listing 5.2. The professional version of the Keil MDK-ARM IDE can generate such a listing, but the light version cannot.

A source file may refer to variables and functions defined in other files using external references. Since at this point in the build process the addresses of these variables and functions haven't been defined yet, the output assembly code file uses the symbols (text names) as placeholders.

Commonly used functions are often gathered together in a library to simplify their reuse. The C language defines many standard libraries, including common mathematical functions (math), input and output (stdio), string processing (string), time and date (time).

Assembler

An assembler converts a human-readable assembly language module into an object module that describes the size and contents of the memory sections required for the module. Each memory section may hold instructions, data, or both. The assembler processes one .s file at a time. This file may have been written directly by a developer or created by a compiler. Keil µVision uses the armasm assembler [2].

The assembler steps through the input file one line at a time, though it may make multiple passes through the file. It uses a location counter for each memory section to track where to place (or allocate) the current memory item, and then updates the counter accordingly.

```
Stack_Size                      EQU     0x00000400
                                AREA    STACK, NOINIT, READWRITE, ALIGN=3
Stack_Mem                       SPACE   Stack_Size
__initial_sp


                                THUMB
; Vector Table Mapped to Address 0 at Reset
                                AREA    RESET, DATA, READONLY
                                EXPORT  __Vectors
                                EXPORT  __Vectors_End
                                EXPORT  __Vectors_Size
__Vectors                       DCD     __initial_sp ; Top of Stack
                                DCD     Reset_Handler  ; Reset Handler
                                DCD     NMI_Handler  ; NMI Handler
                                DCD     HardFault_Handler  ; Hard Fault Handler


                                AREA    |.text|, CODE, READONLY
; Reset Handler
Reset_Handler                   PROC
                                EXPORT  Reset_Handler                [WEAK]
                                IMPORT  SystemInit
                                IMPORT  __main
                                LDR     R0, =SystemInit
                                BLX     R0
                                LDR     R0, =__main
                                BX      R0


                                ENDP
```

Listing 5.1   Example of assembly language file (filename suffix is .s).

Listing 5.1 shows part of an assembly language file. An assembly language file is made of several types of elements.

An **instruction** consists of a mnemonic and possibly operands, as described in the previous chapter. Upon seeing instruction CMP r1, #0x14, the assembler will generate the encoded Thumb instruction according to the ARM architecture specification [3] and advance the location counter. The CMP instruction will be encoded into a 16-bit value:

- Bits 15 through 11 (the most-significant bits) are set to 00101 to specify the CMP immediate instruction.
- Bits 10 through 8 are set to 001 to specify register r1.
- Bits 7 through 0 are set to 00010100 to specify an immediate data value of 0x14.

A **directive** directs the assembler to do something.

- AREA tells the assembler to place the next items declared in a given memory area and change to that area's location counter.

- SPACE tells the assembler to allocate space for data but not fill it with any specific data, and then advance the current location counter.
- Define constant data (DCD) tells the assembler to define a 32-bit constant data item, placing that data in the next available memory location.
- EQU tells the assembler to define a temporary symbolic name and assign it a specific value, but not allocate any memory for it.
- Other common assembler directives are IMPORT, EXPORT, THUMB, PROC, ENDP, and DCB.

There are other elements in an assembly language file; some of the most common are these:

- A comment contains text that will be ignored by the assembler. Comments begin with a ; (semicolon).
- A *symbol* is a text name that represents a value. For example, Stack_Size is a symbol.
- A *label* defines a symbol to refer to the current location in memory. For example, Stack_Mem, __initial_sp, __Vectors and Reset_Handler are all labels.

> symbol
> *Text name representing a value (e.g. address, data value) in a program*

> label
> *Symbol in assembly language which represents an address*

The object code created by the assembler is not complete if it has any external references. The assembler will include a list of external references and the instructions that use them. The linker/loader will resolve these references later.

```
;;;57        do {
000078  bf00                NOP
                |L1.122|
;;;58           x += 2;
00007a  1c89                ADDS      r1,r1,#2
;;;59           } while (x < 20);
00007c  2914                CMP       r1,#0x14
00007e  d3fc                BCC       |L1.122|
```

Listing 5.2   Assembly language listing file created by C compiler (filename suffix is .txt).

There are tools to disassemble object code into a listing file that shows additional information, such as encoded instructions. The compiler may also create an assembly language listing file to show the code it has generated for its source file. Listing 5.2 shows an example. The file is in a similar format to the assembly language file, but includes additional information:

- A numerical address (typically hexadecimal) is listed for each memory location. The address may be relative (an offset from the beginning of the module) or absolute (a fixed location in memory). In Listing 5.2 the addresses are relative since linking (described in the next section) hasn't been performed yet.

- The content of a memory location, shown as a hexadecimal value. For example, relative address 0x00007e holds a value of 0xd3fc, which is the encoding of the instruction BCC |L1.122|. Contents that depend on external references will have placeholders because they are currently undefined.

Note that tools may use different names to refer to the same register. For example, r1 and R1 both refer to register one.

Linker/Loader

A linker/loader creates an executable file from multiple object files. These object files may come from modules in the source program or from libraries. The data and code objects are arranged in appropriate sections of memory. The linker can then determine the numerical addresses for variables and functions. These addresses are then used to complete the machine instructions that refer to the symbolic names. The resulting memory image is described in an executable file with the ARM ELF format and a filename suffix of .axf. Keil µVision uses the armlink linker [4].

Programmer

When the CPU is powered up or reset, it does not have an operating system to load a program into memory. The memory must already contain the program. The program memory is nonvolatile (typically Flash ROM), so it will retain its contents even after power is removed.

The programmer is a tool that places the program into the MCU's memory according to the description in the executable file. The programmer has both hardware and software. The hardware is connected to the MCU's serial wire debug (SWD) interface, enabling the MCU's memory to be programmed. The software may be a stand-alone program or it may be built into the IDE.

Debugger

The debugger enables the developer to control program execution and examine the program state (e.g. current instruction, values of processor registers, and data memory) as it runs on the processor. Figure 5.2 shows an example of the debugger's interface. The source code is shown in the central window (delay.c), while the corresponding object code is in the Disassembly window above. The Registers window to the left shows the values of the processor's core registers. The Call Stack + Locals window on the lower right shows both the current subroutine call nesting and the values of those functions' local variables.

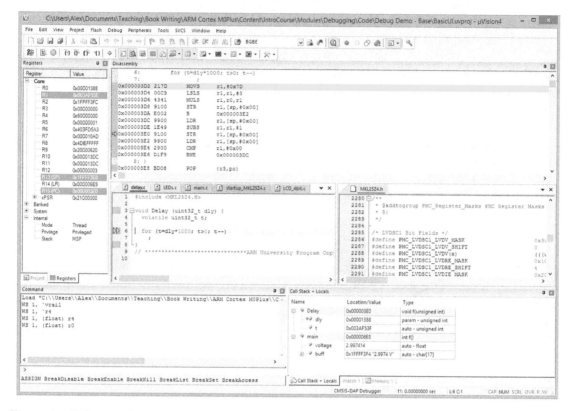

Figure 5.2 Debugger allows user to observe and control program execution, variables, and processor registers.

C Language Fundamentals

Program and Functions

A program is made of one or more functions, with each made of a series of statements. A function may take arguments (also called parameters) and may return a result value. A function may call other functions sequentially or in a nested (hierarchical) way. The function *call graph* is a diagram that shows possible function calls. In Figure 5.3 the main function calls functions J and K as *subroutines*, and J calls B as a subroutine.

call graph
Diagram showing subroutine calling relationships between functions in a program

subroutine
Program function which can be called by another function

Every C program must have a function called main. Running the program consists of running the main function. The main function for embedded systems software never completes, unlike a program you might run on your personal computer or smart phone.

```
void B(void) {          void main(void) {
   ...                     ...
}                          J();
                           ...
void J(void) {             K();
   ...                     ...
   B();                  }
   ...
}

void K(void) {
   ...
}
```

Figure 5.3 Source code and function call graph shows calling relationships between functions.

Functions use a *call stack* to hold temporary information. Calling a function creates a new *activation record* (stack frame) on top of the stack. Returning from a function destroys that activation record, freeing up the space for future function calls. For example, when main is executing, the call stack holds the activation record for main. When J is executing, the call stack holds the activation records for J and main. After J completes and control returns to main, the activation record for J is removed from the call stack.

call stack
Stack of activation records/stack frames of functions which have started executing but have not yet completed

activation record
Temporary storage in memory for function's preserved registers, arguments, local variables, return address, etc. Exists only from function's start to end.

Start-Up Code

When the CPU first starts running (e.g. after power-up or reset) it will execute the code for the reset exception handler. This is called Reset_Handler and is located in startup_MKL25Z4.s. The MCU is not ready for the user's main function yet and needs to be prepared.

First, some basic hardware settings may need to be configured. As with many other MCUs, the KL25Z MCU comes out of reset running in a low-speed mode. To run at full speed, a high-speed oscillator needs to be configured and selected after it has stabilized. The reset exception handler performs this clock configuration by calling the function SystemInit (defined in system_MKL25Z4.c).

Second, the runtime environment for the C program needs to be set up. For example, the stack pointer and variables need to be initialized. This is done in part by a runtime support function called __scatterload, which also sets certain variables to their correct initial values. We will discuss this further later in this chapter.

After performing these steps, the CPU can start executing the code in the main function.

Types of Memory

We saw in Chapter 4 that a microcontroller may use several types of memory. We can classify memory based on certain key characteristics:

- Can we write data to the memory? If so, how easy is it to do?
- Is the memory volatile or persistent? Volatile memory loses its contents when power is removed, whereas persistent memory does not.
- Does the memory need to be refreshed periodically?

Read-only memory (ROM) can only be read. It is nonvolatile (persistent) and retains its contents after power is removed. There are several types of ROM. The most basic ROM contains data that is specified when the IC is fabricated. Electrically erasable programmable ROM (EEPROM) can be erased and reprogrammed one location at a time. The erasing and programing operations take some time and may involve multiple steps. Flash EEPROM (typically called Flash or Flash ROM) allows an entire page of data to be erased or programmed at a time, saving time.

RAM is volatile and loses its contents when power is removed. There are two common types of RAM. Static RAM (SRAM) is built with digital latches, so it is fast and remembers data until power is removed. Dynamic RAM (DRAM) is built with a transistor acting like a capacitor, so it is slower and needs to be refreshed periodically. However, a DRAM cell is much smaller than an SRAM cell, so it is much less expensive.

MCUs typically have integrated Flash ROM and SRAM. Some may also have EEPROM to allow persistent storage of data that may need to change (e.g. configuration data). Some MCUs have (or can be configured to provide) address and data buses on their pins to allow external memory expansion. This allows external SRAM, DRAM, Flash ROM, and other devices to be added to the system. These MCUs typically also include DRAM memory refresh controllers.

A Program's Memory Requirements

What memory does a program need? Let's look at the several key characteristics of the information that will be stored in the memory.

- Does the information need to persist after power is removed? This information will need to be placed in ROM, EEPROM, or Flash ROM.
- Will the program only read the information? If so, this read-only (RO) information can be placed in ROM, Flash ROM, or EEPROM. If the program changes the information, this read/write (RW) information will probably need to be placed in RAM.
- How long does the information need to exist? What is its **lifetime**? Information that must exist for the entire duration of the program must be given a permanent location in memory. This is called **static data**. Temporary information can be stored in read/write memory that is reused by different parts of the program. The program can use two reusable memory sections. The call stack is used to automatically allocate space on function entry and deallocate (free) it on function exit. The heap is used for explicit dynamic memory allocation and deallocation; the programmer must manage these operations.

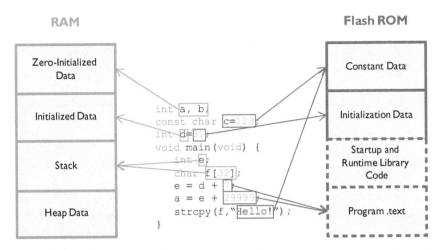

Figure 5.4 RAM and ROM are used to hold a program's data. Code is located in Flash ROM in the program.text or library regions.

Now we can look at the memory requirements of a C program. Figure 5.4 shows that data and instructions are allocated space in different memory areas.

Program instructions must be persistent and are generally read-only, so they are typically placed in Flash ROM. However, some MCUs also provide a small section of read/write memory to hold code that reprograms the Flash ROM when updating code.

Constant data values (c), data tables, text strings ("Hello!"), and similar read-only items can be placed in Flash ROM.

Data variables can be read and written, so they must be placed in RAM. If a data variable is used only by a small part of the program, the compiler may optimize it by not allocating a memory location for it. Instead the compiler will just use a CPU register temporarily for the variable until the value is needed no more.

Data variables are handled differently based on whether they are initialized and whether they are statically allocated. Later in this chapter we will see how variables in memory are accessed.

- Initialization is done in one of two ways. Static data (d) has a fixed memory address, so it is initialized at program start-up by copying the initial values from ROM. Automatically allocated data (e, f) is initialized by specific program instructions upon allocation, since the memory location may be used for different data before this use.
- Uninitialized variables are handled in two ways. Uninitialized static variables (a, b) have fixed memory addresses and they are initialized to zero. Uninitialized automatically or dynamically allocated variables (e, f) have undefined values, as their memory may have been used previously by other data.

Making Functions

A function's object code contains three sections. The *prolog* prepares the processor and memory, the **body** of the function performs the work specified by the source code's function body, and the *epilog* cleans up, prepares the return value (if any), and returns control to the calling function.

> **prolog**
> *Initial code in function which preserves registers and prepares activation record*

> **epilog**
> *Final code in function which restores preserved registers, prepares return value, frees activation record and returns control to caller function*

Register Use Conventions

The ARM architecture procedure calling standard (AAPCS) defines various behaviors, including how general-purpose registers are shared between a function and a subroutine. The calling function expects some registers to be overwritten by the subroutine, whereas others (called **preserved registers**) are expected to retain their values. If the subroutine needs to use a preserved register, it needs to save the value before overwriting it. Before completing, the subroutine needs to restore the preserved register to its original value.

Figure 5.5 shows that a subroutine must preserve the value of registers r5 through r11. Registers r0 through r3 can be modified without the need to be restored. Registers r0 through r3 may also be used for arguments, and r0 and r1 may be used for a return value.

Register Description	Symbol	On function exit, must be restored to original value?	Special use for subroutines?
Program Counter	PC (R15)	No	No
Link Register	LR (R14)	No	Holds return address after BL, BLX instructions
Stack Pointer	SP (R13)	Yes	Yes, points to top of stack
High general-purpose registers	R12	No	No
	R11	Yes	No
	R10	Yes	No
	R9	Yes	No
	R8	Yes	No
Low general-purpose registers	R7	Yes	No
	R6	Yes	No
	R5	Yes	No
	R4	Yes	No
	R3	No	Argument 4
	R2	No	Argument 3
	R1	No	Argument 2, result 2
	R0	No	Argument 1, result 1

Figure 5.5 Registers use conventions.

Function Arguments

The arguments (or parameters) for a subroutine are passed according to the AAPCS. Arguments may be passed by register or by memory. Using registers is much faster, so the compiler tries to pass arguments in registers when possible. However, there are only four 32-bit registers available for argument use.

Each argument is extended to be a multiple of four bytes long. Arguments are then assigned to registers starting with r0; 64-bit arguments are allocated to even-numbered registers. Remaining arguments are passed on the stack.

For example, consider a function with three arguments: char x, int y, and double z. Argument x is eight bits long because it is of type char, so is extended to 32 bits and uses r0. Argument y is 32 bits long, so it uses r1 and does not need extension. Argument z is 64 bits long because it is a double precision float, so it uses r2 and r3. Now consider changing the order of the arguments to be char x, double z, and int y. Argument x is passed in r0, argument z is passed in r2 and r3, and argument y is passed on the stack.

Function Return Value

A function returns a value using r0, r1, or the stack. Return value types up to 32 bits use r0; shorter types are extended to 32 bits as mentioned earlier. Return value types up to 64 bits use r0 and r1, with shorter types extended. Longer types are returned on the stack.

Prolog and Epilog

In this section we will examine the prolog and epilog for the C function shown in Listing 5.3.

```
int fun4(char a, int b, char c) {
    int x[8];
    x[0] = a * b;
    x[c] = b;
    return a+b+c;
}
```

Listing 5.3 Example source code.

Prolog

The prolog has several responsibilities, including saving preserved registers, setting up the activation record on the call stack, and initializing automatic variables when needed.

Registers r4 through r11 must be preserved across function calls, as specified in Figure 5.5. If the body of the function might use any of these registers, then the prolog will save these registers on the stack with a PUSH instruction. If the body of the function might make a subroutine call, then the return address in LR must also be saved. This is the address of the next instruction to execute in the calling function after the subroutine completes. In Listing 5.4, the PUSH instruction will save r4 and the link register on the stack.

```
            fun4  PROC
;;;101    int fun4(char a, int b, char c) {
0000ba  b510            PUSH      {r4,lr}
0000bc  b088            SUB       sp,sp,#0x20
;;;102      int x[8];
```

Listing 5.4 Prolog code for function fun4 saves register r4 and link register, then allocates 32 bytes of space on call stack for integer array x.

The prolog may allocate space on the stack for automatic variables. In Listing 5.4, the SUB instruction will grow the stack by subtracting 0x20 (32 decimal) from the stack pointer. This allocates the space needed for the automatic variable x, an array of eight integers. As each integer takes 4 bytes, 32 bytes are needed in total. Note that the compiler tries to promote variables from stack memory into registers, so some automatic variables will use only registers and no stack space.

Figure 5.6 shows how the PUSH and SUB instructions create the activation record on the stack.

	Memory Address	Contents	Description
3. SP after SUB sp,sp,#0x20 →	A – 0x28	x[0]	
	A – 0x24	x[1]	
	A – 0x20	x[2]	
	A – 0x1C	x[3]	
	A – 0x18	x[4]	Array x
	A – 0x14	x[5]	
	A – 0x10	x[6]	
	A – 0x0C	x[7]	
2. SP after PUSH {r4,lr} →	A – 0x08	LR	Return address
	A – 0x04	r4	Preserved register
1. SP on entry to function, before PUSH {r4,lr} →	A		Caller's stack frame

Figure 5.6 Activation record creation.

Epilog

The epilog needs to place the return value (if present) in the correct location, restore preserved registers to their original values, and return control to the calling function.

When a subroutine is called, the return address is placed in the link register (LR) by the branch and link (BL) or branch and link and exchange (BLX) instruction. Control can be returned to the calling function by executing the BX LR instruction, resulting in a branch to the address stored in LR. However, if this subroutine has called another subroutine, then the first return address (in LR) will be overwritten by the second call. To prevent this, a subroutine that may call another subroutine will save the return address on the stack with a PUSH {LR} instruction. In this case, the return instruction will be POP {PC}, which pops the return address from the stack into the program counter. Note that if other registers were pushed onto the stack in the prolog, the POP instruction may have a list of multiple registers.

```
;;;105        return a+b+c;
0000ca  1840            ADDS      r0,r0,r1
0000cc  1880            ADDS      r0,r0,r2
;;;106    }
0000ce  b008            ADD       sp,sp,#0x20
```

	Memory Address	Contents	Description
1. SP before ADD sp,sp,#0x20 →	A – 0x28	x[0]	
	A – 0x24	x[1]	
	A – 0x20	x[2]	
	A – 0x1C	x[3]	Array x
	A – 0x18	x[4]	
	A – 0x14	x[5]	
	A – 0x10	x[6]	
	A – 0x0C	x[7]	
2. SP after ADD sp,sp,#0x20 →	A – 0x08	LR	Return address
	A – 0x04	r4	Preserved register
3. SP after POP {r4,pc} →	A		Caller's stack frame

Figure 5.7 Activation record deletion.

```
0000d0  bd10              POP        {r4,pc}
                          ENDP
```

Listing 5.5 Epilog code for function fun4 computes return value, deallocates 32 bytes from stack, then restores original values of registers r4 and link register.

Listing 5.5 shows that the source code return statement is implemented with a two ADDS instructions that place the result (a+b+c) in r0. The next ADD instruction adds 0x20 (32 decimal) to the stack pointer to deallocate the space for the array x. The last instruction (POP) has two effects. First, it restores r4 to its original saved value, as required by the register use conventions. Second, it loads the PC with the saved value of the link register, which is the address of the instruction in the calling function that follows the subroutine call. After the POP instruction executes, the CPU will continue executing the calling function.

Figure 5.7 shows how the ADD and POP instructions delete the activation record from the stack.

Exception Handlers

The compiler generates code for exception handlers (including interrupt service routines) in a similar way to regular functions. The compiler identifies an exception handler with the __irq qualifier in its declaration. There are three main differences between exception handlers and regular functions.

First, a handler must have no arguments or return values. The compiler will signal an error if a function declared with __irq takes arguments or returns a value. Recall that the CMSIS support for an MCU declares standard names for the MCU's exception handlers; these declarations include the __irq qualifier.

Second, because the handler can execute anywhere in the program, **all registers** must be treated as preserved registers. When responding to an exception, the CPU automatically saves certain general-purpose registers on the stack: r0, r1, r2, r3, and r12. The handler does not need to save the value of these registers. If the handler uses any other general-purpose registers (r4 through r11), it will need to save their values upon entry and restore them before exiting. The C compiler generates prolog and epilog code for a handler that does this.

Third, the handler must return using an instruction that triggers exception return processing.

There is no "return from interrupt" instruction for ARMv6-M processors. Instead, we use an instruction to update the PC with a special exception return code (EXC_RETURN) to trigger the CPU's exception processing hardware and specify which stack pointer and processor mode to use. Recall that this code was loaded into the link register when first responding to an exception. If the exception return code is still in the link register, we use a branch indirect to the link register (BX LR). Otherwise the code was pushed onto the stack because the handler may have called a subroutine, so we need to pop the code from the stack into the PC.

```
                    PIT_IRQHandler PROC
;;;15
;;;16      void PIT_IRQHandler() {
000000  b430              PUSH        {r4,r5}

; (handler body code here)

000086  bc30              POP         {r4,r5}
000088  4770              BX          lr
;;;61
                    ENDP
```

Listing 5.6 Prolog and epilog of exception handler.

Listing 5.6 shows the prolog and epilog of a timer peripheral's ISR in assembly code. Note that registers r4 and r5 are preserved with a PUSH instruction. The body of the handler uses registers r0 through r5. The values of r4 and r5 are restored with the POP. The return from exception operation is performed by executing the BX lr instruction; this restores the values of r0 through r3 (as well as r12, LR, PC, and xPSR).

Controlling the Program's Flow

In this section we examine the assembly code that implements the C control flow structures for conditionals and loops and subroutine calls.

Conditionals

The C language offers if/else and switch code structures to select one of the multiple code blocks to execute.

If/Else

```
if (x){
    y++;
} else {
    y--;
}
```

Listing 5.7 C source code with if/else statement.

```
;;;39          if (x){
000056   2900                    CMP         r1,#0
000058   d001                    BEQ         |L1.94|
;;;40              y++;
00005a   1c52                    ADDS        r2,r2,#1
00005c   e000                    B           |L1.96|
                         |L1.94|
;;;41          } else {
;;;42              y--;
00005e   1e52                    SUBS        r2,r2,#1
                         |L1.96|
;;;43          }
```

Listing 5.8 Assembly code listing for if/else statement.

If/else statements are simple, requiring a test, code for the true (if) case and code for the false (else) case. In Listing 5.7 the if statement tests the value of variable x. If x is nonzero, then the y++ statement is executed. If x is zero, then the y--statement is executed. Listing 5.8 shows the assembly code generated by the compiler. Figure 5.8 shows the control flow of the assembly code. Register r1 holds the variable x.

- The CMP r1, #0 instruction (at address 000056) compares r1 with the immediate value zero and sets the processor's condition code flags according to the result. If the two values (r1 and zero) are equal, then the Z flag will be set to one. Otherwise it will be cleared to zero.
- The BEQ |L1.94| instruction (at address 000058) will branch to label |L1.94| if the values are equal (since the Z flag is set). Otherwise the BEQ instruction will allow program execution to continue to the next instruction (at address 00005a).

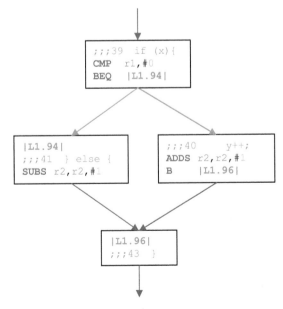

Figure 5.8 Control flow of if/else statement code.

- The code for the true case starts at address 00005a. The ADDS r2, r2, #1 instruction adds one to r2, which is used for the variable y. The B |L1.96| instruction (at address 00005c) forces the program to branch to label |L1.96| to skip over the false case code.
- The code for the false case starts at address 00005e, which is also the value of label |L1.94|. The instruction SUBS r2, r2, #1 subtracts one from register r2, which is used for the variable y.
- The label |L1.96| marks the merge point of the if and else cases, and is the address of the first instruction after the if/else statement.

Switch

```
switch (x) {
case 1:
   y += 3;
   break;
case 31:
   y -= 5;
   break;
default:
   y--;
   break;
}
```

Listing 5.9 C source code with switch statement.

Switch statements can be implemented in different ways. The approach shown in Listing 5.10 performs a test for each case, similar to the if/else structure. Other approaches are to use a jump table or a computed jump, which eliminate the need for multiple tests. Figure 5.9 shows the control flow of the assembly code.

```
;;;45            switch (x) {
000060  2901                    CMP       r1,#1
000062  d002                    BEQ       |L1.106|
000064  291f                    CMP       r1,#0x1f
000066  d104                    BNE       |L1.114|
000068  e001                    B         |L1.110|
                     |L1.106|
;;;46          case 1:
;;;47             y += 3;
00006a  1cd2                    ADDS      r2,r2,#3
;;;48          break;
00006c  e003                    B         |L1.118|
                     |L1.110|
;;;49          case 31:
;;;50             y -= 5;
00006e  1f52                    SUBS      r2,r2,#5
;;;51          break;
000070  e001                    B         |L1.118|
                     |L1.114|
;;;52          default:
;;;53             y--;
000072  1e52                    SUBS      r2,r2,#1
```

```
;;;54          break;
000074  bf00                    NOP
                |L1.118|
000076  bf00                    NOP                        ;48

;;;55          }
```

Listing 5.10 Assembly code listing of switch statement.

There are three different cases based on the value of x: a case for 1, a case for 31, and a default case. The code starts by comparing x to each of the values.

- The instruction CMP r1, #1 (at address 000060) compares x to 1.
- If they are equal, then the BEQ |L1.106| instruction (at address 000062) causes the program to branch to the corresponding case code at label |L1.106| (at address 00006a).
- If r1 is not equal to 1, then the code will continue with the next test instruction: CMP r1, #0x1f (at address 00006e), and #0x1f is the immediate value of 31 represented in hexadecimal.
- If they are not equal, then the BNE |L1.114| instruction (at address 000066) causes the program to branch to the default case code at label |L1.114| (at address 000072).

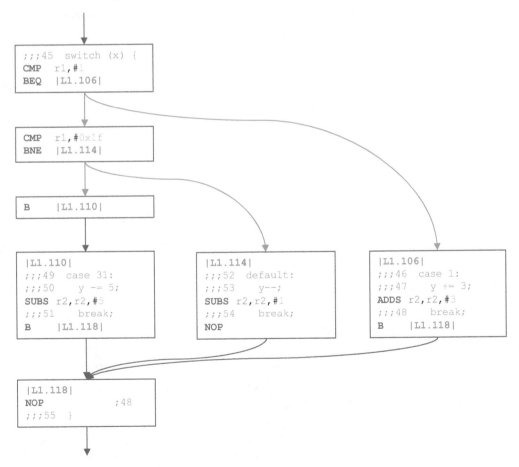

Figure 5.9 Control flow of switch statement code.

- If r1 is equal to 31, then the code will continue with the next instruction, which is B |L1.110| (at address 000068). This will cause the program to jump to label |L1.110| (at address 00006e) and execute the code starting there.
- The code for each of the cases is similar. First, register r2 (holding the variable y) is modified. Then the program unconditionally branches to the merge point of |L1.118| (at address 000076) because of the break statement. The last case does not need such a branch case because the execution will naturally proceed to the merge point. A NOP instruction is added as a placeholder for debugging at address 000074.

Loops

Code structures for loops include a loop body and a loop test. The test may be performed before the body is executed (top-test) or after (bottom-test).

Do While

The do/while loop is simple, executing the loop body first (adding 2 to x) and then testing whether to repeat the body (if x < 20). The assembly code is shown in Listing 5.12, whereas Figure 5.10 shows the control flow.

```
do {
   x += 2;
} while (x < 20);
```

Listing 5.11 C source code with do/while loop.

```
;;;57        do {
000078  bf00                    NOP
                |L1.122|
;;;58           x += 2;
00007a  1c89                    ADDS      r1,r1,#2
;;;59           } while (x < 20);
00007c  2914                    CMP       r1,#0x14

00007e  d3fc                    BCC       |L1.122|
```

Listing 5.12 Assembly code of do/while loop.

- A NOP instruction (address 000078) serves as a placeholder for debugging.
- The body of the loop adds 2 to x using the instruction ADDS r1, r1, #2 (address 00007a).
- The loop test starts by comparing x to 20 (hexadecimal 0x14) using CMP r1, #0x14 (address 00007c). This instruction checks for the result of subtracting r1 from 20, but doesn't update r1. Instead, it only updates the condition code flags.
- The loop test then can branch back to the loop body or else continue with the next instruction. If x is less than 20, then the comparison mentioned does not result in a borrow (indicated by the carry flag), so the C flag will be zero. Branch if carry cleared (BCC) performs a branch if the carry bit is cleared (zero). If x is not less than 20, then the C flag will be one, so the BCC will not execute, and the program will proceed to the next instruction after the loop.

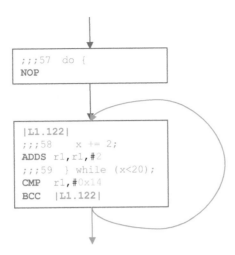

Figure 5.10 Control flow of do/while loop.

While

The while loop's assembly code appears in Listing 5.14, and Figure 5.11 shows the control flow. The while loop performs the test first, and then executes the loop body. However, the code is laid out in a different order. The start of the loop has a branch over the loop body to the test at the end. So the loop test is executed first, before the body has a chance to execute.

```
while (x > 10) {
   x = x + 1;
}
```

Listing 5.13 C source code with while loop.

```
;;;61          while (x/green>
000080   e000             B          |L1.132|
                 |L1.130|
;;;62         x = x + 1;
000082   1c49             ADDS       r1,r1,#1
                 |L1.132|
000084   290a             CMP        r1,#0xa                  ;61
000086   d3fc             BCC        |L1.130|

;;;63         }
```

Listing 5.14 Assembly code listing of while loop.

- B |L1.132| (at address 000080) branches to label |L1.132|, which is the start of the loop test.
- The loop test starts at |L1.132|. Instruction CMP r1, #0xa (address 000084) compares r1 to 10 (0xa in hexadecimal) and sets the condition code flags according to the result.
- If r1 is less than 10, then the Carry flag will be cleared, so BCC |L1.130| (address 000086) will cause the program to branch to that label.
- The loop body starts at label |L1.130| with the instruction ADDS r1,r1,#1 (address 000082) that adds 1 to register r1 (holding variable x).

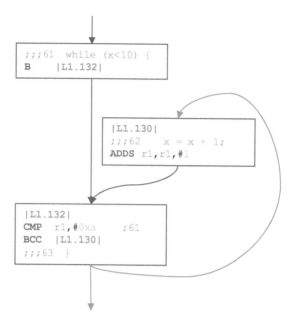

Figure 5.11 Control flow of while loop.

For

The for loop is the most complex loop. It contains initialization code (i = 0) that executes before the loop starts, a loop test (i < 10), the loop body (x + = i), and loop index update code (i++). The assembly code appears in Listing 5.16, while Figure 5.12 shows the control flow.

```
for (i = 0; i < 10; i++){
   x += i;
}
```

Listing 5.15 C source code with for loop.

```
;;;65          for (i = 0; i < 10; i++){
000088  2300            MOVS    r3,#0
00008a  e001            B       |L1.144|
                |L1.140|
;;;66           x += i;
00008c  18c9            ADDS    r1,r1,r3
00008e  1c5b            ADDS    r3,r3,#1              ;65
                |L1.144|
000090  2b0a            CMP     r3,#0xa              ;65
000092  d3fb            BCC     |L1.140|

;;;67        }
```

Listing 5.16 Assembly code listing of for loop.

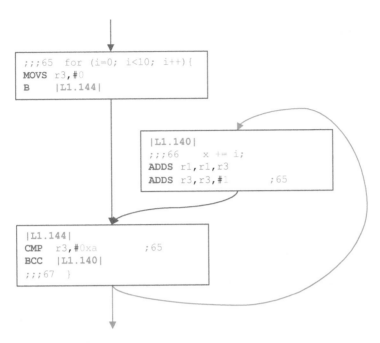

```
;;;65   for (i=0; i<10; i++){
MOVS  r3,#0
B     |L1.144|
```

```
|L1.140|
;;;66     x += i;
ADDS  r1,r1,r3
ADDS  r3,r3,#1          ;65
```

```
|L1.144|
CMP   r3,#0xa          ;65
BCC   |L1.140|
;;;67  }
```

Figure 5.12 Control flow of for loop.

- The loop initialization code (i = 0) is performed by MOVS r3,#0 (address 000088). Register r3 holds variable i, which serves as a loop counter. The code then branches to the loop test with the instruction B|L1.144| (address 00008a).
- The loop test code is marked with label |L1.144| and starts with instruction CMP r3,#0xa (address 000090). This compares the loop counter i (r3) with 10 (hexadecimal 0xa). The branch instruction BCC |L1.140| will branch to the loop body if r3 is less than 10.
- The loop body code is marked with label |L1.140|. It uses the instruction ADDS r1, r1, r3 (address 00008c) to add i to x.
- The loop index update code follows the loop body. It uses the instruction ADDS r3, r3, #1 (address 00008e) to add one to the variable i.

Note that the code is laid out in the sequence of initialization code, loop body, loop index update, and test. However, it is executed in a different order, with the test performed before the loop body.

Calling Subroutines

Calling a subroutine requires preparing the arguments (if any) and then calling the subroutine. After the return, the result value (if any) can be used. Let's consider the C source code shown in Listing 5.17, which shows main calling fun5 as a subroutine. The function fun5 has four arguments: one char (a), two ints (b, c), and another char (d). The assembly code is presented in Listing 5.18.

```
extern int fun5(char a, int b, int c, char d);
int main(void)
{
  int n;
  n = fun5(1,2,3,4);
}
```

Listing 5.17 C source code calling function fun5 as subroutine.

```
;;;16                    n = fun5(1,2,3,4);
00001a   2304                    MOVS     r3,#4
00001c   2203                    MOVS     r2,#3
00001e   2102                    MOVS     r1,#2
000020   2001                    MOVS     r0,#1
000022   f7fffffe                BL       fun5
000026   9000                    STR      r0,[sp,#0]
```

Listing 5.18 Assembly code calling function fun5 as subroutine.

First the arguments are loaded into the appropriate registers: r0 for argument a, r1 for b, r2 for c, and r3 for d. The arguments are loaded in reverse order, but any order would work.

Second, the subroutine is called either with BL or BLX instruction. The BL instruction contains the address of the subroutine. The BLX instruction needs the subroutine's address to be loaded into register r0. Both of these instructions will place the address of the following instruction in the LR to allow the subroutine to return control to the calling function. Listing 5.18 shows that the subroutine is called with the instruction BL fun5 (at address 000022).

Third, after fun5 completes its returns control to main, its result will be in r0. The instruction STR r0, [sp,#0] (at address 000026) stores that result to the memory for the main's automatic variable n.

Accessing Data in Memory

Let's see how to access data in memory. A data variable must be in a register in order for the program to operate on it. The access method depends on the variable's location (e.g. static memory vs. on the stack) and other factors (e.g. using pointers, whether in an array).

Statically Allocated Memory

A variable in a statically allocated memory can be anywhere in the CPU's 32-bit memory space, so we need 32 bits to specify its address. There is not enough space to hold both a 32-bit address and an operation specifier in a Thumb instruction, since most are 16 bits long (with a few being 32 bits long).

To solve this problem, we take advantage of the program-counter-relative addressing mode. The variable's address is stored in memory near the instructions that need it. The program uses an LDR instruction to load a register with the variable's address. The program then uses that register to specify the memory location.

```
                                              AREA  ||.text||, CODE, READONLY, ALIGN=2
;;;20          siA = 2;
00000e 2102              MOVS      r1,#2
000010 4a49              LDR       r2,|L1.312|
000012 6011              STR       r1,[r2,#0]    ; siA
;;;21          aiB = siC + siA;
000014 4949              LDR       r1,|L1.316|
000016 6809              LDR       r1,[r1,#0]    ; siC
000018 6812              LDR       r2,[r2,#0]    ; siA
00001a 1889              ADDS      r1,r1,r2
00001c 9103              STR       r1,[sp,#0xc]
; Pointers to static data
                 |L1.312|
                              DCD        ||siA||
                 |L1.316|
                              DCD        ||siC||
; Static data
                              AREA  ||.data||, DATA, ALIGN=2
                 ||siA||
                              DCD        0x00000000
                 ||siC||
                              DCD        0x00000003
```

Listing 5.19 Code to access variables in statically allocated memory.

For example, the code in Listing 5.19 first assigns a value of 2 to static integer siA, and then reads the values of siC and siA. The variables siA and siC are allocated space in the data memory section with the DCD assembler directives.

Automatically Allocated Memory

Automatically allocated variables are stored on the stack. Each such variable is located in memory at a specific offset from the stack pointer. This sp-relative addressing mode is specified in assembly code as [sp, #offset]. The offset ranges from 0 to 1020 and must be a multiple of four.

```
;;;14    void static_auto_local( void ) {
000000 b50f            PUSH          {r0-r3,lr}
;;;15          int aiB;
;;;16          static int siC=3;
;;;17          int * apD;
;;;18          int aiE=4, aiF=5, aiG=6;
000002 2104            MOVS          r1,#4
000004 9102            STR           r1,[sp,#8]
000006 2105            MOVS          r1,#5
000008 9101            STR           r1,[sp,#4]
00000a 2106            MOVS          r1,#
600000c 9100            STR           r1,[sp,#0]
```

Listing 5.20 Code to access variables in automatically allocated memory.

Address	Contents	Description
SP	aiG	Automatic variables
SP + 0x04	aiF	
SP + 0x08	aiE	
SP + 0x0c	aiB	
SP + 0x10	r0	Preserved registers
SP + 0x14	r1	
SP + 0x18	r2	
SP + 0x1c	r3	
SP + 0x20	LR	Return address
SP + 0x24		Caller's stack frame

Figure 5.13 Contents of activation record.

The three store instructions in Listing 5.20 initialize the variables aiE, aiF, and aiG in memory at specific offsets from the stack pointer. The activation record on the stack is shown in Figure 5.13.

Dynamically Allocated Memory and Other Pointers

A pointer variable holds the address of a data item, such as another data variable. Pointers are used to access memory that is dynamically allocated (using malloc, calloc, or realloc).

```
;;;22        apD = & aiB;
00001e  a803              ADD       r0,sp,#0xc
;;;23        (*apD)++;
000020  6801              LDR       r1,[r0,#0]
000022  1c49              ADDS      r1,r1,#1
000024  6001              STR       r1,[r0,#0]
```

Listing 5.21 Code to access a variable using a pointer.

The statement apD = & aiB loads the address of the variable aiB into the variable apD. Listing 5.21 shows how this is implemented in assembly code. The variable aiB is located at the location SP+0x0c, as shown in Figure 5.13. The instruction at address 00001e calculates this address by adding SP and 0x0c and then places the result in r0, which holds apD and serves as a pointer to aiB.

The statement (*apD)++ will increment the variable pointed to by apD. This is performed in three steps:

- The LDR instruction (address 000020) loads r1 with the memory value to which apD points (which is aiB),

- The ADDS instruction (address 000022) adds one to r1
- The STR instruction (address 000024) stores r1 back to memory via pointer apD.

Array Elements

In order to access an array element, its address must be determined, which is the sum of the array's starting address and an offset. For a one-dimensional array, the offset is the product of the element size (in bytes) and index of the particular element. For a two-dimensional array, the offset must also include the size of rows before the desired element's row.

Let's look at the one-dimensional array declared as unsigned char buff2[3]. This array of characters has three elements. Each element is a character, so each takes one byte. The entire array takes three bytes and is laid out in memory as shown in Figure 5.14.

Address	Contents
buff2	buff2[0]
buff2 + 1	buff2[1]
buff2 + 2	buff2[2]

Figure 5.14 Memory layout of array declared as unsigned char buff2[3].

```
;;;72   unsigned int arrays(unsigned char n, unsigned char j) {
00009c b508                   PUSH        {r3,lr}
00009e 4602                   MOV         r2,r0
;;;73  volatile unsigned int i;
;;;74
;;;75  i = buff2[0] + buff2[n];
0000a0 4827                   LDR         r0,|L1.320|
0000a2 7800                   LDRB        r0,[r0,#0]  ; buff2
0000a4 4b26                   LDR         r3,|L1.320|
0000a6 5c9b                   LDRB        r3,[r3,r2]
0000a8 18c0                   ADDS        r0,r0,r3
0000aa 9000                   STR         r0,[sp,#0]
; Static data
            |L1.320|
                   DCD         buff2
```

Listing 5.22 Code to access and add two elements in a one-dimensional array.

The code to add two elements in the array (buff2[0] and buff2[n]) is shown in Listing 5.22 and explained in Figure 5.15.

Now let's look at the two-dimensional array declared as short int buff3[5][7]. This array of short integers has five rows and seven columns, with seven elements per column. Each element is a short integer, so each takes two bytes. The entire array takes $2 \times 5 \times 7 = 70$ bytes and is laid out in memory as shown in Figure 5.16.

Instruction	Description
`00009c PUSH {r3,lr}`	This instruction saves r3 and the return address on the stack.
`00009e MOV   r2,r0`	The parameter n is passed into the function through register 0. This instruction copies that value into register r2, freeing up r0 for other use.
`0000a0 LDR   r0,|L1.320|`	The starting address of the array buff2 is loaded into register r0.
`0000a2 LDRB  r0,[r0,#0]`	The code needs to calculate the offset of each element from the array's starting address (buff2). Because the first element is a constant (zero), the offset will be a constant which the compiler can calculate. This simplifies the assembly code. Element 0 is located at an offset of 1 byte/element * 0 elements = 0 bytes. So the address of buff2[0] is buff2 + 0, or simply buff 2. This instruction reads a byte from memory at location r0 and places the result in r0.
`0000a4 LDR   r3,|L1.320|`	The starting address of the array buff2 is loaded into register r3 with this instruction.
`0000a6 LDRB  r3,[r3,r2]`	The offset of buff2[n] is 1 byte/element * n elements = n bytes. The address of buff2[n] is therefore buff2 + n. This instruction reads a byte from memory at location r3+r2 and places the result in register r3.
`0000a8 ADDS  r0,r0,r3`	This instruction adds r0 (element buff2[0]) and r3 (element buff2[n]) and places the result in r0.
`0000aa STR   r0,[sp,#0]`	This instruction stores the sum on the stack at offset 0.

Figure 5.15 Explanation of code implementing i = buff2[0] + buff2[n].

The code to add the element buff3[n][j] to variable i is shown in Listing 5.23. The element's address is calculated based on several parts: the array's starting address, the row offset (based on the row size and the row number), and the column offset (based on the column number and the element size). Each instruction in the code is explained in Figure 5.17.

```
;;;76  i += buff3[n][j];
0000ac 200e               MOVS      r0,#0xe
0000ae 4350               MULS      r0,r2,r0
0000b0 4b24               LDR       r3,|L1.324|
0000b2 18c0               ADDS      r0,r0,r3
0000b4 004b               LSLS      r3,r1,#1
0000b6 5ac0               LDRH      r0,[r0,r3]
0000b8 9b00               LDR       r3,[sp,#0]
0000ba 18c0               ADDS      r0,r0,r3
0000bc 9000               STR       r0,[sp,#0]
; Static data
                   |L1.324|
                     DCD       buff3
```

Listing 5.23 Code to access element in two-dimensional array.

Address	Contents	Comment
buff3	buff3[0][0]	Row 0
buff3 + 1		
buff3 + 2	buff3[0][1]	
buff3 + 3		
(etc.)		
buff3 + 10	buff3[0][5]	
buff3 + 11		
buff3 + 12	buff3[0][6]	
buff3 + 13		
buff3 + 14	buff3[1][0]	Row 1
buff3 + 15		
buff3 + 16	buff3[1][1]	
buff3 + 17		
buff3 + 18	buff3[1][2]	
buff3 + 19		
(etc.)		
buff3 + 68	buff3[4][6]	Row 4
buff3 + 69		

Figure 5.16 Memory layout of array declared as short int buff3[5][7].

Instruction	Description
0000ac MOVS r0,#0xe	The row size is two bytes/element * 7 elements per row = 14 bytes. This instruction loads the hexadecimal value 0xe (which is decimal 14) into r0.
0000ae MULS r0,r2,r0	The row offset is the row size multiplied by the row number (n, which is still in r2). This instruction calculates the row offset.
0000b0 LDR r3,|L1.324|	The starting address of the array buff3 is loaded into register r3 with this instruction.
0000b2 ADDS r0,r0,r3	The starting address (r3) and the row offset (r0) are added with this instruction and placed back in r0.
0000b4 LSLS r3,r1,#1	The column offset is element's column number multiplied by the number of bytes per element (two). The column number j is passed as an argument through r1. It is multiplied by two by shifting it left by one bit position with this instruction and stored in r3.
0000b6 LDRH r0,[r0,r3]	The array element's address is the sum of the base address and the row offset (in r0) and the column offset (in r3), and is formed with [r0,r3]. The halfword at that address is loaded into register r0.
0000b8 LDR r3,[sp,#0]	Register r3 is loaded with the value of variable i, which is located on the stack at offset 0.
0000ba ADDS r0,r0,r3	The array element and i are added together and placed in r0.
0000bc STR r0,[sp,#0]	The sum calculated above is stored to the memory location for variable i.

Figure 5.17 Explanation of code implementing i += buff3[n][j].

Summary

In this chapter, we have examined the assembly code that the compiler generates to implement the C language source program. We examined the program build tools, which translate program modules between languages and then link them together. We then saw how functions are built from a prolog, an epilog, and a body with control flow and data access operations. We also evaluated how exception handlers differ from regular functions.

Exercises

Consider the following assembly code that the compiler has generated for a C function. Explain what each assembly instruction does and describe what data is in any registers used.

	Assembly code listing				Explanation
1.	`;;;5`		`void fn(int8_t * a, int32_t *`		
	`b, float * c) {`				
	`000000`	`b5f0`	`PUSH`	`{r4-r7,lr}`	
2.	`000002`	`b085`	`SUB`	`sp,sp,#0x14`	
3.	`000004`	`4604`	`MOV`	`r4,r0`	
4.	`000006`	`460d`	`MOV`	`r5,r1`	
5.	`000008`	`4616`	`MOV`	`r6,r2`	
6.	`;;;6`		`volatile int8_t a1, a2;`		
	`;;;7`		`volatile int32_t b1, b2;`		
	`;;;8`		`volatile float c1, c2;`		
	`;;;9`				
	`;;;10`		`a1 = 15;`		
	`00000a`	`270f`	`MOVS`	`r7,#0xf`	
7.	`;;;11`		`a2 = -14;`		
	`00000c`	`200d`	`MOVS`	`r0,#0xd`	
8.	`00000e`	`43c0`	`MVNS`	`r0,r0`	
9.	`000010`	`9004`	`STR`	`r0,[sp,#0x10]`	
10.	`;;;12`		`*a = a1*a2;`		
	`000012`	`9804`	`LDR`	`r0,[sp,#0x10]`	
11.	`000014`	`4378`	`MULS`	`r0,r7,r0`	
12.	`000016`	`b240`	`SXTB`	`r0,r0`	
13.	`000018`	`7020`	`STRB`	`r0,[r4,#0]`	
14.	`;;;13`				
	`;;;14`		`b1 = 15;`		
	`00001a`	`200f`	`MOVS`	`r0,#0xf`	
15.	`00001c`	`9003`	`STR`	`r0,[sp,#0xc]`	

	Assembly code listing				Explanation

16. `;;;15        b2 = -14;`
    `00001e   200d      MOVS   r0,#0xd`

17. `000020   43c0      MVNS   r0,r0`

18. `000022   9002      STR    r0,[sp,#8]`

19. `;;;16        *b = b1*b2;`
    `000024   9902      LDR    r1,[sp,#8]`

20. `000026   9803      LDR    r0,[sp,#0xc]`

21. `000028   4348      MULS   r0,r1,r0`

22. `00002a   6028      STR    r0,[r5,#0]`

23. `;;;17`
    `;;;18        c1 = 15;`
    `00002c   4809      LDR    r0,|L1.84|`

24. `00002e   9001      STR    r0,[sp,#4]`

25. `;;;19        c2 = -14;`
    `000030   4809      LDR    r0,|L1.88|`

26. `000032   9000      STR    r0,[sp,#0]`

27. `;;;20        *c = c1*c2;`
    `000034   9900      LDR    r1,[sp,#0]`

28. `000036   9801      LDR    r0,[sp,#4]`

29. `000038   f7fffffe  BL     __aeabi_fmul`

30. `00003c   6030      STR    r0,[r6,#0]`

31. `;;;21`
    `;;;22     }`
    `00003e   b005      ADD    sp,sp,#0x14`

32. `000040   bdf0      POP    {r4-r7,pc}`

References

[1] *ARM Compiler v5.06 for µVision Version 5: armcc User Guide*, ARM Ltd., 2015
[2] *ARM Compiler v5.06 for µVision Version 5: armasm User Guide*, ARM Ltd., 2015.
[3] *ARMv6-M Architecture Reference Manual*, DDI 0419C, ARM Ltd., 2010.
[4] *ARM Compiler v5.06 for µVision Version 5: armlink User Guide*, ARM Ltd., 2015.

6

Analog Interfacing

Chapter Contents

Overview

This chapter presents the concepts and methods that enable the interfacing of a digital micro-controller with analog circuitry. It covers quantization and sampling concepts, and then presents digital-to-analog conversion and the reverse. We examine examples such as waveform generation, temperature measurement, and proximity sensing using infrared energy.

Introduction

Motivation

Embedded computers often need to monitor the characteristics of the surrounding environment, such as sound, temperature, pressure, acceleration, strain, and light intensity. These character-istics are analog because they can take on an infinite number of possible values (even within a limited range). For example, a temperature sensor might indicate its reading by setting its output signal's voltage to 0.05 V per degree C. A reading of 0.5 V would indicate a temperature of 10°C, whereas a reading of 0.50005 V would indicate 10.001°C. This analog signal must be converted to a digital (numerical) value for the program to process it; this is done with an analog-to-digital converter (ADC). Whether the ADC will be able to differentiate between these two temperatures depends on its resolution and other factors.

In order to generate sounds accurately (with little distortion), the MCU must generate analog voltage signals to drive headphones or speakers. The digital values representing the sound signal can be converted to an analog voltage using a digital-to-analog converter (DAC).

Concepts

Interfacing with analog devices involves *quantization* and *sampling*. To understand these con-cepts, let us consider how to generate a sound using an MCU and a speaker. We would like to drive the speaker with the signal shown in Figure 6.1. This signal varies continuously in both voltage and time, but an MCU cannot generate such a signal accurately for two reasons. First, there are **quantization** issues: the MCU is digital so it can generate only a limited (discrete) number of volt-ages on an output. Second, there are **sampling** issues: the MCU can update an output only at a limited rate, with some minimum time between updates. Our MCU's approximation of the desired output is limited by both quantization and sampling characteristics. These limits affect both digi-tal signal processing [1] and digital control systems [2].

quantization
Process of selecting a discrete digital value to represent an analog value

sampling
Process of converting a continuous-time signal to a series of discrete-time samples

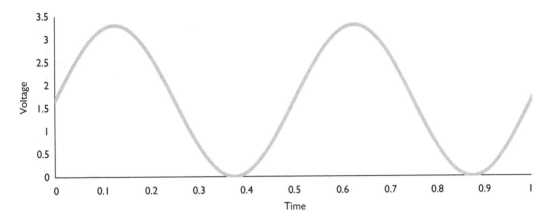

Figure 6.1 Sine wave signal has analog (continuous) voltage that varies continuously over time.

Quantization

In Chapter 2 we learned about the digital general-purpose outputs of the MCU. If we use such an output in order to generate the sine wave, we will get the signal labeled "two-level quantization" shown in Figure 6.2. This is a rather inaccurate reconstruction of our desired sine wave.

The problem is that our output can generate only two possible voltage levels. If our MCU could generate more than two different voltage levels, then our output sine wave would be more accurate. The number of discrete values available for use defines the resolution of the quantization. In Figure 6.2, the signal labeled "eight-level quantization" shows the sine wave when generated with eight quantization levels.

An analog value can take on an infinite number of possible values along a continuous range. Quantization is the process of selecting one of multiple possible quantized (discrete) values to represent the analog value. Each quantized output value represents a range of possible analog input values. Figure 6.3 shows an example of quantization, identifying which output value represents each range of input values. For example, any voltage between 0.5 V and 0.75 V will be quantized to 2. The same code will be returned for 0.51 V and 0.74 V, making them indistinguishable to the MCU.

Two voltage references (V_{+ref} and V_{-ref}) are needed to define the boundaries of the conversion range. Often the positive supply rail (e.g. 3.3V) is used as the positive reference and ground is used as the negative reference.

Digital electronics work with binary values, so the number of discrete output values is typically a power of 2. The resolution describes the number of bits (B) used to hold the output value. For example, a code with eight-bit resolution has $2^8 = 256$ possible output values. The example in Figure 6.3 shows a two-bit quantization.

Note that an output value n does not represent an exact voltage, but instead a range of voltages:

$$V_{range} = \frac{n}{2^B}\left(V_{+ref} - V_{-ref}\right)$$

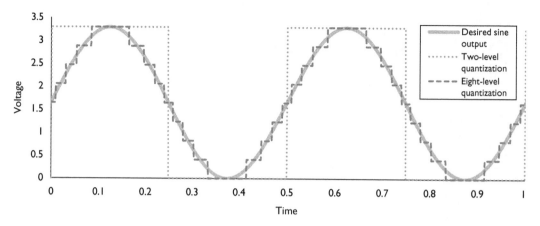

Figure 6.2 More quantization levels improves accuracy of generated sine wave.

Input Voltage	Quantized Value		
	Decimal	Binary	
$V_{+ref} = 1$ V	3	11	Out of range
	3	11	
0.75 V			
	2	10	
0.5 V			
	1	01	
0.25 V			
	0	00	
$V_{-ref} = 0$ V			
	0	00	Out of range

Figure 6.3 Example of two-bit quantization of analog input voltage.

As the resolution B increases, the quantization becomes more accurate. The maximum quantization error is typically half of this voltage range.

A *transfer function* defines the quantization mathematically. The following is an example of a common transfer function:

$$n = \text{round}\left(\frac{V_{in} - V_{-ref}}{V_{+ref} - V_{-ref}} 2^B \right)$$

transfer function
Mathematical equation describing relationship between input and output values

Sampling

We have just seen that better resolution for quantization improves our MCU's output signal accuracy. The other factor we need to consider is time: how often do we need to update an output or sample an input to get an adequate signal?

A sampled signal is a discrete-time representation (a series of individual samples) of a continuous-time signal. The sampling rate determines how often an input is measured, or how often an output is updated. Note that each sample may be an analog value (one of an infinite number of possible values) until it is quantized.

Any information between the samples is lost. Figure 6.4 shows that sampling the sine wave at a low frequency (slow sampling) results in a poor approximation. Raising the sampling rate (fast sampling) improves the approximation.

If the continuous-time signal changes more often than it is sampled, we will lose that high-frequency information. To understand this, let us consider the signal's frequency spectrum. Figure 6.5 shows the spectrum of a signal, with the horizontal axis representing frequency and the vertical axis showing power. The spectrum is symmetric across the 0 Hz frequency.

Sampling a signal in effect makes copies of the signal's spectrum centered at multiples of the sampling frequency f_s, as shown in Figure 6.6. The Nyquist criterion states that if the signal has

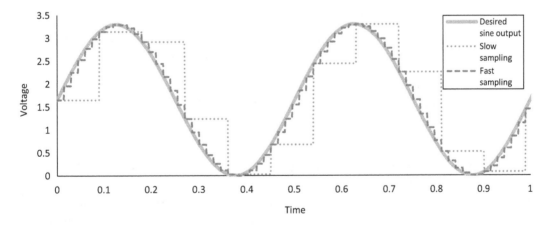

Figure 6.4 Faster sample rate improves accuracy of generated sine wave.

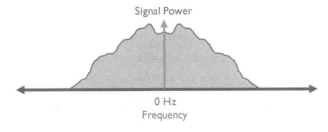

Figure 6.5 Signal spectrum shows distribution of power across frequencies.

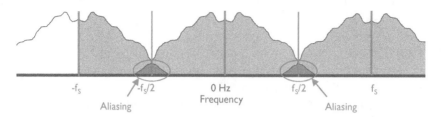

Figure 6.6 Sampling too slowly causes aliasing.

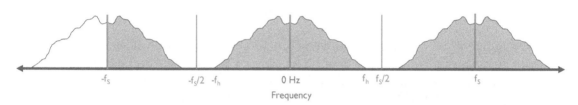

Figure 6.7 Raising sampling frequency f_s above signal's highest frequency component f_h eliminates aliasing.

any energy at a frequency of $f_s/2$ or higher, those signal components will appear in the sampled signal at different (lower) frequencies, distorting the sampled signal with *aliasing*.

> aliasing
> *Distortion of signal resulting from sampling at too low a frequency*

Two complementary methods are used to prevent aliasing. First, the sampling frequency f_s is chosen to be more than twice the frequency of the highest signal frequency of interest f_h as shown in Figure 6.7. Second, a low-pass anti-aliasing filter is used to remove or greatly weaken the signal components above f_h. In order to simplify the design of the anti-aliasing filter, the sampling frequency f_s is often double f_h or more.

Digital-to-Analog Conversion

Concepts

A digital-to-analog converter (DAC) generates an analog output signal based on the digital input value. The output signal may be a voltage or a current depending on the type of DAC. Here we will only consider voltage output DACs.

The minimum and maximum output voltages are defined by the DAC's lower and upper reference voltages. The lower reference voltage is often simply grounded at 0 V.

A transfer function defines the relationship between the digital input value n and the output voltage V_{out}. For a DAC with a lower reference voltage of 0 V, an upper reference voltage of V_{+ref}, and B bits of resolution, the general transfer function is:

$$V_{out} = n \frac{V_{+ref}}{2^B}$$

Converter Architectures

Two common DAC architectures are the resistor ladder and the R-2R ladder. An **N-bit resistor ladder** uses 2^N resistors of equal value connected in series between the upper and lower reference voltages. These resistors form a voltage divider with equally spaced voltages at the taps. An **R-2R resistor ladder** uses N resistors of one value (R) and N resistors of twice that value (2R).

Regardless of the type of DAC, an amplifier is typically used to buffer the output signal, enabling it to drive larger loads. This buffer amplifier is often located on-chip with the DAC to simplify application hardware design.

It is also possible to use a timer peripheral in pulse-width modulation (PWM) mode and a low-pass filter to create an analog output. We will discuss this in Chapter 7.

Kinetis KL25Z DAC

The Kinetis KL25Z has a 12-bit DAC, shown in Figure 6.8. There are two upper reference voltages available, and the lower reference voltage is connected to ground. An amplifier buffers the voltage output signal.

The control register DACx_C0 is shown in Figure 6.9 and controls various aspects of the DAC. There are other control registers (DACx_C1 and DACx_C2) that enable other operation modes using direct memory access (DMA), but we do not discuss them further.

- The DAC is enabled by writing a one to DACEN in DACx_C0.
- The output buffer's power consumption can be reduced by writing a one to LPEN in DACx_C0, at the cost of increasing the output's response time.
- The upper reference voltage can be connected to one of the two sources (V_{REFH}, V_{DDA}) using a multiplexer controlled by the DACRFS field in DACx_C0.

Output data for the DAC is 12 bits long and is stored in the DACDAT register. The output data's upper four bits (nibble) are written to DACx_DAT0H, while the lower byte is written to DACx_DAT0L.

The transfer function is similar to the general DAC transfer function, with an offset of one added to n. This offset allows the output voltage to range from $V_{+ref}/4096$ to V_{+ref}.

$$V_{out} = (n+1)\frac{V_{+ref}}{2^{12}}$$

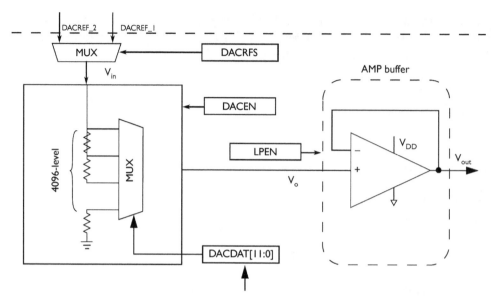

Figure 6.8 KL25Z 12-bit DAC [3].

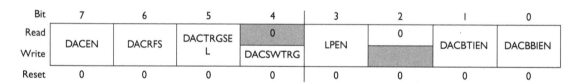

Bit	7	6	5	4	3	2	1	0
Read	DACEN	DACRFS	DACTRGSEL	0	LPEN	0	DACBTIEN	DACBBIEN
Write				DACSWTRG				
Reset	0	0	0	0	0	0	0	0

Figure 6.9 DAC control register 0, DACx_C0.

The DAC also offers a buffered output mode. In this mode, new data can be written to DACx_DAT0H and DACx_DAT0L. However, the DAC continues to generate the old output voltage until it receives a trigger signal from a hardware timer or a software write to the DACSWTRG field in DACx_C0. This makes it possible to preload the DAC data register but still have the output change at fixed times. This simplifies the design of systems that require output updates to be precisely timed.

Example Application: Waveform Generator

Let's use the DAC to create a simple waveform generator. The output for DAC0 is connected to pin PTE30. Listing 6.1 shows the function Init_DAC, which initializes the DAC and related peripherals.

```
#define DAC_POS (30)

void Init_DAC(void) {
   // Enable clock to DAC and Port E
   SIM->SCGC6 |= SIM_SCGC6_DAC0_MASK;
   SIM->SCGC5 |= SIM_SCGC5_PORTE_MASK;

   // Select analog for pin
   PORTE->PCR[DAC_POS] &= ~PORT_PCR_MUX_MASK;
   PORTE->PCR[DAC_POS] |= PORT_PCR_MUX(0);

   // Disable buffer mode
   DAC0->C1 = 0;
   DAC0->C2 = 0;

   // Enable DAC, select VDDA as reference voltage
   DAC0->C0 = DAC_C0_DACEN_MASK | DAC_C0_DACRFS_MASK;
}
```

Listing 6.1 Function to initialize DAC.

The second function Triangle_Output (in Listing 6.2) sweeps the DAC output voltage up and down repeatedly. Note that two macros (DAC_DATL_DATA0 and DAC_DATH_DATA1, defined in MKL25Z4.H) are used to format the output data for the upper and lower output data registers. However, we still need to shift the data to the right by eight positions to position the upper four bits correctly for the macro.

```
void Triangle_Output(void) {
    int i=0, change=1;

    while (1) {
        DAC0->DAT[0].DATL = DAC_DATL_DATA0(i);
        DAC0->DAT[0].DATH = DAC_DATH_DATA1(i >> 8);

        i += change;
        if (i ==0) {
          change = 1;
        } else if (i == DAC_RESOLUTION-1) {
          change = -1;
        }
    }
}
```

Listing 6.2 Function to generate triangle wave output.

When the function Triangle_Output is called, the system creates the waveform shown in Figure 6.10.

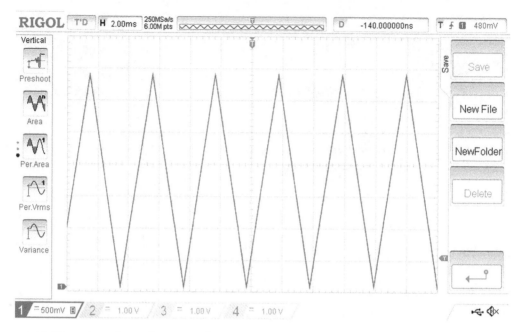

Figure 6.10 Triangle analog voltage waveform created by DAC and function Triangle_Output.

Analog Comparator

Concepts

Figure 6.11 shows an analog *comparator*, which is a circuit that compares two analog voltages and indicates which is greater. This can be used to determine if a voltage is above or below a given level. The comparator has two inputs that are labeled plus and minus. We apply a voltage to each input: V_{inP} to plus, V_{inM} to minus. If $V_{inP} > V_{inM}$, then the comparator output will be a logic one. Otherwise the output will be a logic zero. The program can read the comparator output directly with software. Most comparators are able to generate an interrupt request when their output changes.

> comparator
> *Circuit which compares two analog inputs to identify larger value*

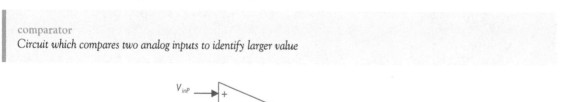

Figure 6.11 Analog comparator indicates which input voltage is greater.

Connecting one of the inputs to a known reference voltage enables us to determine if the other input is above or below that voltage. Using the comparator this way quantizes an input voltage into one of two possible values, zero or one, providing one bit of data. Some MCUs supplement their comparators with multiple fixed reference voltages, or even a DAC for greater flexibility.

Kinetis KL25Z Comparator

The comparator peripheral of the KL25Z MCU is shown in Figure 6.12. In this section we examine the key features of the peripheral; other features (filtering, hysteresis, low-power, DMA) are described in the reference manual, FRDM-KL2 5Z user's manual [4].

In order to enable the comparator, the clock gating must be enabled by writing a one to the CMP bit in the SIM_SCGC4, and then writing one to the comparator enable bit (EN) in CMPx_CR1, shown in Figure 6.13.

Each comparator input can be connected to one of eight possible signals (Table 6.1). The comparator's CMPx_MUXCR register shown in Figure 6.14 contains the fields PSEL and MSEL to control with which signals the plus and minus inputs are connected. The possible settings are shown below: six external input signals, a programmable voltage generated by the comparator's

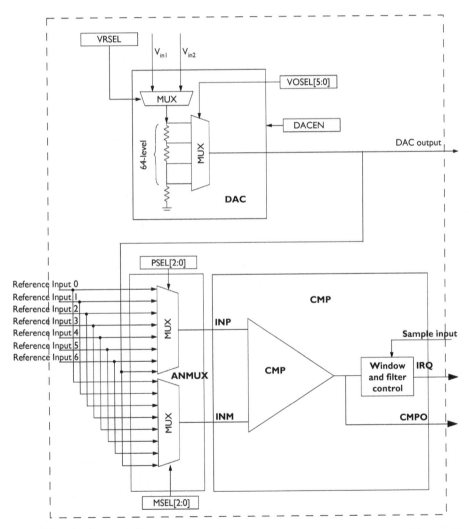

Figure 6.12 Overview of comparator peripheral in Kinetis KL25Z MCU [3]. The comparator (lower center) is supplemented with input multiplexers, a DAC for generating a reference voltage, and output processing logic.

Bit	7	6	5	4	3	2	I	0
Read Write	SE	WE	TRIGM	PMODE	INV	COS	OPE	EN
Reset	0	0	0	0	0	0	0	0

Figure 6.13 CMPx_CR1 controls general comparator settings.

Table 6.1 Comparator Input Multiplexer Settings and Freedom KL25Z Connections

PSEL or MSEL	Input selected for comparator	MCU signal (with ALT0 multiplexer setting)	Freedom KL25Z connector and pin number
000	CMP0_IN0	PTC6	J1 11
001	CMP0_IN1	PTC7	J1 1
010	CMP0_IN2	PTC8	J1 14
011	CMP0_IN3	PTC9	J1 16
100	12b DAC0 Reference / CMP0_IN4	PTE30	J10 11
101	CMP0_IN5	PTE29	J10 9
110	Bandgap	–	–
111	6b DAC0 Reference	–	–

Bit	7	6	5	4	3	2	I	0
Read Write	0	PSTM	PSEL		PSEL	MSEL	MSEL	
Reset	0	0	0	0	0	0	0	0

Figure 6.14 Plus and minus input multiplexers are controlled by CMPx_MUXCR register.

Bit	7	6	5	4	3	2	I	0
Read Write	DACEN	VRSEL	VOSEL					
Reset	0	0	0	0	0	0	0	0

Figure 6.15 Comparator DAC is controlled by CMPx_DACCR register.

6-bit DAC, a programmable voltage generated by the 12-bit DAC peripheral described previously, and a fixed 1 V bandgap voltage reference.

In order to use the comparator's 6-bit DAC, the DAC must be enabled by writing a one to DACEN in CMPx_DACCR, shown in Figure 6.15. Writing a value of n to the VOSEL field of CMPx_DACCR results in a DAC output voltage of $(n+1) \times V_{Ref}/64$. VRSEL controls whether the DAC's upper reference voltage is connected to V_{REFH} (zero) or V_{DD} (one).

The comparator's output signal CMP0_OUT can drive a digital output pin. To do this, set the OPE bit in CMPx_CR1 to one and configure the appropriate pin control register multiplexer as shown in Table 6.2.

Table 6.2 Possible Comparator Output Locations on Freedom KL25Z Board

MCU signal	Multiplexer setting	Freedom KL25Z connector and pin number
PTC0	5	J1 3
PTC5	6	J1 9
PTE0	5	J2 18

The output of the comparator can be read using the COUT field of the CMPx_SCR register shown in Figure 6.16. The comparator can generate an interrupt or DMA request on either a rising edge, a falling edge, or both. Setting the IER or IEF fields to one will enable the comparator to generate an interrupt on a rising edge (IER) or a falling edge (IEF). The CFR and CFF fields are set to one by the comparator hardware automatically whenever COUT rises from zero to one (CFR) or falls from one to zero (CFF). The ISR must clear these fields by writing one to them.

Bit	7	6	5	4	3	2	1	0
Read	0	DMAEN	0	IER	IEF	CFR	CFF	COUT
Write						w1c	w1c	
Reset	0	0	0	0	0	0	0	0

Figure 6.16 CMPx_SCR register shows comparator output, control interrupts, and DMA activity.

Example Application: Voltage Transition Monitor

Let's see how to use the comparator to generate an interrupt whenever an analog voltage crosses an arbitrary voltage (1.85 V in this case). We initialize the comparator as shown in Listing 6.3. Note that the comparator's minus input is connected to the comparator DAC. To generate an output voltage of approximately 1.85 V given a reference voltage of 3.3 V, we load the VOSEL field with a rounded value of $64 \times (1.85/3.3) = 35.879$, which is 36. We configure the comparator to generate interrupts on both rising and falling edges of the comparator output, and then enable the comparator interrupt in the NVIC.

```
void Init_Comparator(void) {
    // Enable clock to comparator
    SIM->SCGC4 |= SIM_SCGC4_CMP_MASK;

    // Enable Comparator
    CMP0->CR1 = CMP_CR1_EN_MASK;

    // Select input channels
    // Plus: channel 5 on Port E bit 29
    // Minus: CMP DAC is channel 7
    CMP0->MUXCR = CMP_MUXCR_PSEL(5) | CMP_MUXCR_MSEL(7);

    // Enable DAC, set reference voltage at 1.85 V. 64*1.85/3.3 = 36.
    CMP0->DACCR = CMP_DACCR_DACEN_MASK | CMP_DACCR_VOSEL(36);
```

```
    // Enable interrupt for Comparator on both edges
    CMP0->SCR = CMP_SCR_IEF_MASK | CMP_SCR_IER_MASK;

    NVIC_SetPriority(CMP0_IRQn, 128);
    NVIC_ClearPendingIRQ(CMP0_IRQn);
    NVIC_EnableIRQ(CMP0_IRQn);
}
```

Listing 6.3 Code to configure comparator to detect input voltage crossing 1.85 V level.

```
void CMP0_IRQHandler(void) {
    // set break point here to observe operation
    if (CMP0->SCR & CMP_SCR_CFR_MASK) { // rising
            // light green LED
            Control_RGB_LEDs(0, 1, 0);
    } else if (CMP0->SCR & CMP_SCR_CFF_MASK) { // falling
            // light red LED
            Control_RGB_LEDs(1, 0, 0);
    }
    // clear flags, keep interrupt on both edges enabled
    CMP0->SCR = CMP_SCR_IEF_MASK | CMP_SCR_IER_MASK |
                    CMP_SCR_CFR_MASK | CMP_SCR_CFF_MASK;
}
```

Listing 6.4 Interrupt handler to light green LED on rising edges, red LED on falling edges.

The interrupt handler shown in Listing 6.4 checks to determine if the interrupt was caused by a rising or falling comparator output edge, and lights the LEDs accordingly. It then clears the rising and falling flags to prepare for the next transition.

Analog-to-Digital Conversion

Concepts

An ADC is similar to an analog comparator in that it quantizes an analog input voltage to create a binary output code. One major difference is that it provides more quantization levels and therefore more bits of resolution, allowing higher-quality measurements of analog values.

Converter Architectures

There are various approaches to building an ADC. We will discuss the flash and successive approximation architectures. There are others as well (e.g. sigma-delta, dual-slope integrating) but we will not discuss them here.

The comparator we saw earlier is essentially a 1-bit ADC. A B-bit ADC can be built out of 2^B analog comparators operating in parallel, each with a different reference voltage. The resulting B-bit code is created with digital logic that encodes the output bits of the 2^B comparators. This is called a flash architecture because it is extremely fast. The conversion time consists of

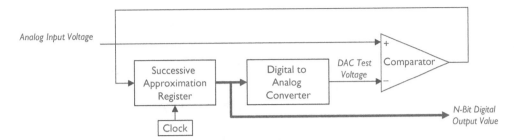

Figure 6.17 Architecture of successive approximation ADC.

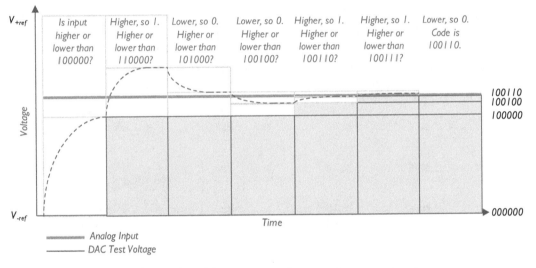

Figure 6.18 Performing analog-to-digital conversion with successive approximation.

the comparator delay and the digital encoder delay. However, this approach requires many comparators: increasing the resolution by one bit doubles the number of comparators needed. This increases power use and circuit area and therefore cost.

We can use a single comparator to make a series of comparisons, changing its reference voltage for each. The successive approximation architecture uses this approach and performs a binary search to quantize the input. Figure 6.17 shows the hardware for this converter, including a successive approximation register (SAR), a DAC, an analog comparator, and control logic.

Figure 6.18 shows how the converter works. The converter first clears all bits in the SAR to zero. It then sets the most significant bit in the SAR to one. The comparator determines if the input voltage is greater than the DAC output voltage. If so, the first bit is left as one, or else it is cleared to zero. This process advances to the next bit and repeats until all bits have been determined.

A successive approximation ADC is not as fast as a flash ADC, as it requires one comparison for each bit of the result. However, the circuitry is much smaller and does not grow quickly as resolution is increased. Adding one bit of resolution slows down the conversion slightly, as it requires one more comparison. However, the circuit area increase is marginal. Because of these positive characteristics, most MCUs with built-in ADCs use a successive approximation ADC.

Inputs

ADCs often include an input multiplexer to allow a single ADC to select one of the multiple input channels to measure. We store a channel select code in a control register to specify the input channel.

An ADC requires two voltage references to define the conversion range. These voltage references are used in the transfer function. Often the positive supply rail (e.g. 3.3V) is used as the positive reference, and ground is used as the negative reference.

Many types of ADC (including those using successive approximation) will produce incorrect results if the input changes much during the conversion process. A sample and hold circuit can be used to sample the input signal and then hold it fixed during the conversion time, eliminating this source of error. Conceptually, this circuit consists of a capacitor and a switch. Figure 6.19 shows the operation of the circuit. When the switch is closed, the circuit will **sample** the input by charging the capacitor to the input voltage. Opening the switch disconnects the capacitor from the input, so the circuit will **hold** the saved value of the input voltage for the ADC to perform its conversion. The capacitor does not charge instantaneously when in sample mode, but is limited by the resistance of the input voltage source and switch and the capacitance. As a result, the switch must be closed for a minimum sample time.

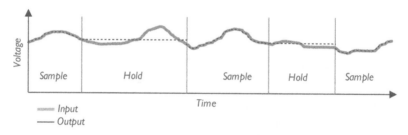

Figure 6.19 Sample and hold circuit tracks input voltage or holds last value depending on mode.

A single-ended signal represents information with the voltage difference between the signal and ground. Differential signals represent information with the voltage difference between two signals, neither of which is ground. This reduces the effects of noise. Some ADCs support differential signal inputs. These ADCs contain hardware that allows direct measurement of the voltage difference, making conversion a single-step process. An ADC without differential input signal support needs to convert each of the two signals separately, and then use software to find the difference.

Triggering

The trigger is a signal that tells the ADC to start sampling and converting an input. An ADC will typically include two types of triggers: software and hardware. A software trigger requires the software (or DMA, discussed in Chapter 9) to write a value to a specific ADC control register to start the conversion. A hardware trigger requires a hardware signal to be asserted by a circuit, whether outside the MCU or within it. For example, a hardware timer could generate a signal every millisecond to trigger the ADC operation.

The ADC performs sampling and conversion and then indicates that the conversion has completed. This is done by setting a flag in an ADC status register, and possibly also signaling an interrupt request. At this point the result of the conversion is available in digital form in an ADC result register.

Kinetis KL25Z ADC

The Kinetis KL25Z MCU contains an ADC with many features; an overview appears in Figure 6.20. In this section we will examine the basic features. Full details can be found in the ADC chapter of the MCU reference manual [3] and in the MCU data sheet [5].

Analog input data is routed through an input multiplexer to the SAR converter. A trigger signal starts the conversion process; the control sequencer steps through a series of activities at a rate determined by the clock signal. The output of the SAR converter may be processed before being placed into a result register. The ADC may generate an interrupt when the conversion completes. Compare logic can be used to discard the results in (or outside of) a specified range. We will now examine the ADC in more detail.

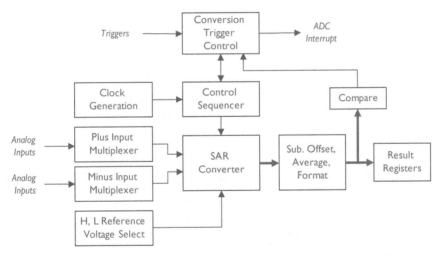

Figure 6.20 Overview of KL25Z ADC.

Analog Inputs

The input multiplexer can select one of 24 single-ended inputs or one of four pairs of differential inputs. The input channel is selected by the ADCH field of the SC1n register. Differential input mode is selected by setting the DIFF bit in SC1n register to one; otherwise single-ended inputs are used.

There are several special multiplexer inputs.

- Channel 26 is connected to an on-chip temperature sensor.
- Channel 27 is connected to an on-chip fixed 1.0 V voltage reference (called a band gap reference).

- Channel 29 is connected to the high-reference voltage V_{REFSH}.
- Channel 30 is connected to the low-reference voltage V_{REFSL}.

Voltage References

The ADC uses two reference voltages, V_{REFSH} and V_{REFSL}. These can be selected from two pairs of reference voltages: V_{REFH} and V_{REFL}, or V_{ALTH} and V_{ALTL} using the REFSEL bit of the ADCx_SC2 register. On the KL25Z, V_{ALTH} is connected to the analog supply voltage V_{DDA}, which is nominally 3.3 V.

SAR Converter

The ADC in the KL25Z MCU uses successive approximation for quantization, supporting various resolutions from 8 to 16 bits in signed or unsigned formats. Resolution is specified by the MODE field of ADCx_CFG1, as shown in Table 6.3.

There are other conversion options available as well:

- Low-power conversions save power by reducing the maximum ADC clock speed. Set bit ADLPC1 in ADCx_CFG1 to enable this option.
- Input noise can be reduced by using a longer sample time. Set bit ADLSMP in ADCx_CFG1 to one to enable long samples, and then use the ADLSTS field in ADCx_CFG2 to add from 6 to 20 ADCK cycles to each conversion's sample time.
- Continuous (back-to-back) conversions are enabled by setting ADCO in ADCx_SC3 to one. Without this, only one conversion will be performed per conversion start request.

Table 6.3 Codes for ADC Conversion Modes

MODE	Conversion mode
00	Single-ended 8-bit, differential 9-bit
01	Single-ended 12-bit, differential 13-bit
10	Single-ended 10-bit, differential 11-bit
11	Single-ended 16-bit, differential 16-bit

Conversion Trigger

A trigger is needed to start the conversion process. The ADTRG bit in SC2 selects either software triggering (zero) or hardware triggering (one).

- Software triggering consists of writing to SC1A to start the conversion. This is typically done by software, but could also be performed by the direct memory access peripheral (discussed further in Chapter 9).
- Hardware triggering consists of starting the conversion with a specific hardware signal that indicates when an event has occurred. These events include timer signals, comparator output,

and an external trigger signal. The trigger source is selected using the ADC0TRGSEL field of the register SIM_SOPT7, as shown in Table 6.4.

Table 6.4 Codes for Selecting Hardware Trigger Signal for ADC0

ADC0TRGSEL	Trigger selected for ADC0
0000	External trigger pin input
0001	HSCMP0 (comparator) output
0100	PIT (timer) trigger 0
0101	PIT (timer) trigger 1
1000	TPM0 (timer) overflow
1001	TPM1 (timer) overflow
1010	TPM2 (timer) overflow
1100	RTC (real-time clock) alarm
1101	RTC (real-time clock) seconds
1110	LPTMR0 (timer) trigger
other	Reserved

Conversion Clock

The conversion clock signal ADCK determines how quickly the ADC samples and then converts input data. Depending on the ADC's configuration, a sample can take from 4 to 26 ADCK cycles, and a conversion can take from 20 to 71 ADCK clock cycles. The complete timing details can be found in the user manual and data sheet.

The ADCK signal has frequency restrictions: it must be between 1 and 18 MHz when the ADC is operating with the resolution of up to 13 bits, or between 2 and 12 MHz for higher resolutions.

There are four possible inputs to the conversion clock: the bus clock (e.g. 24 MHz), the bus clock divided by two, ADACK (a local clock that can keep running when the rest of the CPU is stopped), and ALTCLK (an alternate clock source). The input is selected with the ADICLK field of the ADCx_CFG1 register.

The input clock is divided by a factor specified by a code in the ADIV field of register ADCx_CFG1. Table 6.5 shows there are four possible division factors: 1, 2, 4, and 8.

Table 6.5 Codes for ADC Clock Division Factors

ADIV	Clock division factor
00	1
01	2
10	4
11	8

Conversion Completion and ISR

A completed conversion can be indicated in two ways. First, the control hardware sets COCO bit in SC1x to one. Second, the ADC can generate an interrupt (if AIEN in SC1 is set to one). The name for the ADC ISR is ADC0_IRQHandler.

After the conversion has been completed, the ADC will begin the next conversion automatically if in continuous conversion mode (flag ADCO in ADCx_SC3 is one).

Special Output Processing

The ADC has dedicated hardware that can process the results from the SAR and greatly reduce the software processing needed in many cases. This hardware is shown in Figure 6.21.

The first component is a subtractor that can remove offsets determined during ADC calibration. This is useful for applications requiring extremely high accuracy.

The next component will average multiple conversion results automatically if bit AVGE in ADCx_SC3 is set to one. This can eliminate the software processing required to average input signals. The number of samples to be averaged is selected from 1, 4, 8, 16, or 32 using the AVGS field of ADCx_SC3. Note that conversion completion will be indicated with the COCO bit and ADC interrupt only after all of the samples have been taken.

The next component converts the data to the correct format, performing justification and extension to create a 16-bit result. The data is right-justified, so the LSB of the conversion data is always in bit 0. For conversion formats shorter than 16 bits, the upper unused bits need to be filled. Single-ended conversions produce positive results in an unsigned format, so the upper bits are filled with zeros. Differential conversions produce positive or negative results in a two's-complement signed format, so the upper bits are filled by sign, extending the result. The formatted conversion result can be read from the ADC data result register ADCx_Rn.

A compare function can detect conversion results that exceed a certain threshold or range and then generate an interrupt. Various comparisons are possible: less than threshold, greater than or equal to threshold, inside range, and outside range. Threshold comparisons will compare the ADC result with the comparison value located in ADCx_CV1. Range comparisons will compare it with both ADCx_CV1 and ADCx_CV2. The comparison performed is selected with the ACFGT and ACREN fields of the ADCx_SC2 register. The inside/outside range selection depends on whether ADCx_CV1 is greater than ADCx_CV2 or not.

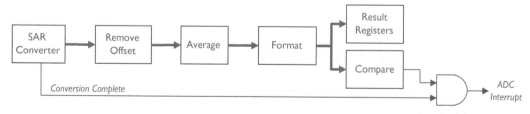

Figure 6.21 SAR output data processing hardware.

Using the KL25Z ADC on the Freedom Board

The MCU family data sheet provides information on connections between ADC channels and MCU pins, whereas the FREEDOM-KL25Z manual explains how MCU pins are connected to the board's header connectors. The relevant information for analog inputs is summarized in Table 6.6.

Table 6.6 ADC Inputs and Multiplexer Settings on KL25Z Freedom Board

ADC channel (single-ended)	MCU signal (with ALT0 multiplexer setting)	Freedom KL25Z connector and pin number
0	PTE20	J10 1
3	PTE22	J10 5
4	PTE21 (a), PTB29 (b)	J10 3 (a), J10 9 (b)
5	PTD1 (b)	J2 12 (b)
6	PTD5 (b)	J2 4 (b)
7	PTE23 (a), PTD6 (b)	J10 7 (a), J2 17(b)
8	PTB0	J10 2
9	PTB1	J10 4
11	PTC2	J10 10
12	PTB2	J10 6
13	PTB3	J10 8
14	PTC0	J1 3
15	PTC1	J10 12
23	PTE30	J10 11

Example Applications

Next we will examine two applications of the ADC. Both use polling to determine when the conversion is complete, but in the next chapter we will use the ADC's interrupt to reduce processor overhead and simplify multitasking.

Hotplate Temperature Sensor

We can measure the temperature of the hotplate using a device called a thermistor, which is a sensor whose resistance varies with temperature. One type of thermistor (called negative temperature coefficient, or NTC) has a resistance that falls with increasing temperature. Figure 6.22 shows an example of an NTC thermistor whose resistance at 25°C is 33 kΩ. The manufacturer provides this information in the device's data sheet.

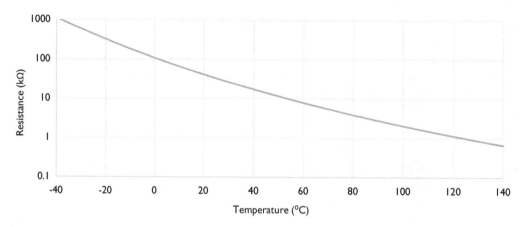

Figure 6.22 Resistance of NTC resistor falls with rising temperature. Note that the vertical axis is logarithmic.

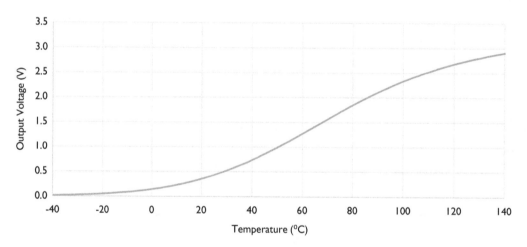

Figure 6.23 Output voltage of 3.3 V divider created with 33 kΩ NTC resistor (upper) and a 5 kΩ fixed resistor (lower).

We can create a voltage divider with an NTC thermistor and a fixed resistor. The output voltage V_{Temp} will depend on the temperature as shown in Figure 6.23.

How can we convert this voltage reading to a temperature? Rather than use a look-up table, let's use a spreadsheet program to create an equation through a process called curve-fitting. The equation that follows will calculate the approximate temperature in Celsius given the ADC conversion result n, assuming a 16-bit conversion and $V_{Ref} = 3.3$ V.

$$\text{Temperature} = \left(-1.13090 \times 10^{-25} \times n^6\right) + \left(2.32656 \times 10^{-20} \times n^5\right) - \left(1.84630 \times 10^{-15} \times n^4\right)$$
$$+ \left(7.18641 \times 10^{-11} \times n^3\right) - \left(1.43216 \times 10^{-6} \times n^2\right) + \left(0.0155762 \times n\right) - 36.9861$$

We will connect V_{Temp} to pin one of connector J10, which will send the signal through PTE20 to ADC channel 0.

The code to initialize the ADC appears in Listing 6.5.

```
#define ADC_POS (20)

void Init_ADC(void) {

    SIM->SCGC6 |= SIM_SCGC6_ADC0_MASK;
    SIM->SCGC5 |= SIM_SCGC5_PORTE_MASK;

    // Select analog for pin
    PORTE->PCR[ADC_POS] &= ~PORT_PCR_MUX_MASK;
    PORTE->PCR[ADC_POS] |= PORT_PCR_MUX(0);

    // Low power configuration, long sample time, 16 bit single-ended conversion
    // Bus clock input
    ADC0->CFG1 = ADC_CFG1_ADLPC_MASK | ADC_CFG1_ADLSMP_MASK | ADC_CFG1_MODE(3) |
            ADC_CFG1_ADICLK(0);
    // Software trigger, compare function disabled, DMA disabled
    // Voltage references VREFH and VREFL
    ADC0->SC2 = ADC_SC2_REFSEL(0);
}
```

Listing 6.5 Code to initialize ADC to read temperature sensor circuit.

The code to read the ADC and calculate the temperature appears in Listing 6.6. The code starts a conversion on channel 0 and uses polling to determine when the conversion is complete. It then reads the ADC result and calculates the temperature using a polynomial approximation. The equation given is reorganized to reduce the complexity and improve execution speed.

```
float Measure_Temperature(void){
    float n, temp;

    ADC0->SC1[0] = 0x00; // start conversion on channel 0

    // Wait for conversion to finish
    while (!(ADC0->SC1[0] & ADC_SC1_COCO_MASK))
        ;
    // Read result, convert to floating-point
    n = (float) ADC0->R[0];

    // Calculate temperature (Celsius) using polynomial equation
    // Assumes ADC is in 16-bit mode, has VRef = 3.3 V
    temp = -36.9861 + n*(0.0155762 + n*(-1.43216E-06 + n*(7.18641E-11
            + n*(-1.84630E-15 + n*(2.32656E-20 + n*(-1.13090E-25))))));
    return temp;
}
```

Listing 6.6 Code to read ADC and convert result to Celsius temperature value.

Infrared Proximity Sensor

We can use the ADC to create a sensor that uses reflected *infrared (IR)* light to detect if an object is nearby. The sensor uses an IR emitter (LED) and an IR detector (phototransistor) pointing in the same direction, as shown in Figure 6.24. If there is no object in front of the sensor, then no IR energy will be reflected back to the detector. If an object is present, then there will be a reflection and the detector will see it. The strength of the reflection depends on the object's distance, size, reflectivity, and orientation.

> infrared (IR)
> *Electromagnetic energy immediately past the visible portion of the spectrum; also called invisible light*

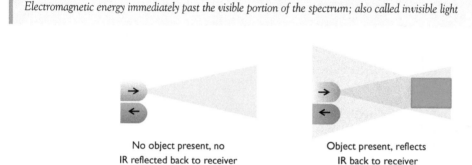

No object present, no   Object present, reflects
IR reflected back to receiver   IR back to receiver

Figure 6.24 Proximity sensor method of operation.

The proximity sensor works with a combination of hardware and software. Simply keeping the emitter on and measuring the detector's signal will not work well because the system will be very vulnerable to changes in ambient light levels. We will use a more sophisticated approach that compares the IR levels with the emitter off and on in order to subtract out the effects of ambient light.

Sensing occurs in two steps: First, the software measures the IR light level (using IR-sensitive phototransistor Q1 and the ADC) when the IR-emitting LED is turned **off**. Second, the software measures the IR light level when the IR LED is turned **on**. An object that reflects the IR back will increase this IR brightness level. The difference between the two readings indicates the reflected signal's strength.

Circuit Description

The circuit is shown in Figure 6.25. The IR energy is emitted by IR LED D1, which the MCU controls with a GPIO pin output called IR_LED_DRIVE. The IR energy is detected by an IR-sensitive phototransistor Q1. Q1 forms a voltage divider with R2. A higher level of IR energy lowers the phototransistor's resistance and therefore lowers the voltage on signal IR_SENSE.

The traces in Figure 6.26 show the operation of the circuit. The IR LED is on when the upper trace is low and off when it is high. There is no reflecting object present, but the IR LED emits a small amount of energy laterally. This IR energy strikes the phototransistor, resulting in a minor signal.

Figure 6.27 shows the circuit's behavior with an object about 5 cm away, whereas Figure 6.28 shows the results from an object about 1 cm away. Note that the phototransistor takes time to respond to the change in IR energy, as shown by the curves in the lower traces. Our software must

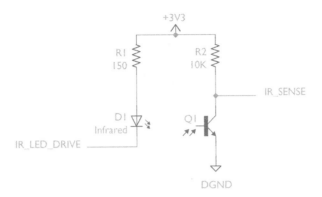

Figure 6.25 Schematic diagram of infrared proximity sensor circuit.

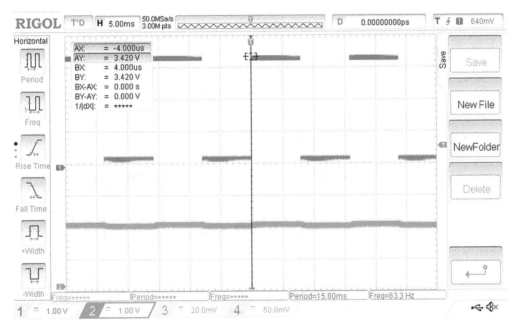

Figure 6.26 No reflecting object nearby. Upper trace is LED (transmitter) drive signal, lower trace is receiver (phototransistor) signal.

wait after switching IR_LED_DRIVE before it measures IR_SENSE. The longer it waits, the more sensitive the system will be.

Figure 6.29 shows the result of sweeping four separated fingers over the proximity sensors. The oscilloscope has been adjusted to show a longer time period.

Control Software
The control software uses several functions to do its work. These functions use the definitions in the header file shown in Listing 6.7.

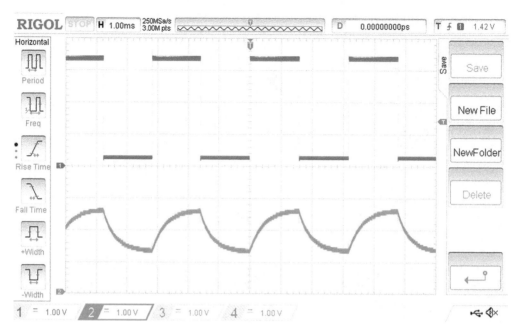

Figure 6.27 Transmitter and receiver signals with reflecting object 5 cm away.

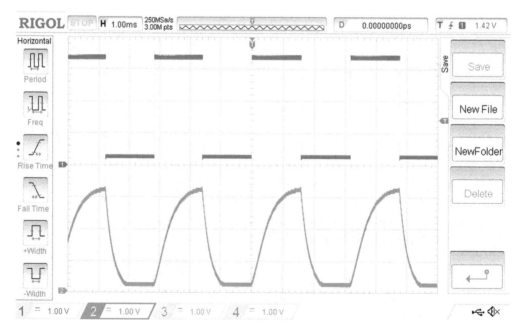

Figure 6.28 Transmitter and receiver signals with reflecting object 1 cm away.

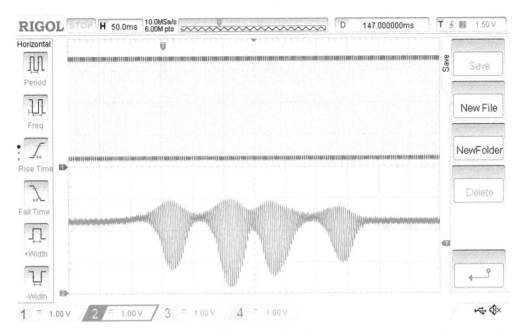

Figure 6.29 Transmitter and receiver signals detecting four fingers passing over proximity sensor in sequence.

```
#define IR_LED_POS (1) // on port B bit 1
#define IR_PHOTOTRANSISTOR_CHANNEL (8) // on port B bit 0

#define T_DELAY_ON (1000)
#define T_DELAY_OFF (1000)

#define NUM_SAMPLES_TO_AVG (10)
```

Listing 6.7 Symbol definitions from header file.

```
void Init_ADC(void) {

    SIM->SCGC6 |= (1UL << SIM_SCGC6_ADC0_SHIFT);
    ADC0->CFG1 = ADC_CFG1_ADLPC_MASK | ADC_CFG1_ADIV(0) | ADC_CFG1_ADLSMP_MASK |
    ADC_CFG1_MODE(3) | ADC_CFG1_ADICLK(0); // 16 bit conversion mode
    ADC0->SC2 = ADC_SC2_REFSEL(0); // Select default voltage reference pins
}

void Init_IR_LED(void) {
    PORTB->PCR[IR_LED_POS] &= ~PORT_PCR_MUX_MASK;
    PORTB->PCR[IR_LED_POS] |= PORT_PCR_MUX(1);
    PTB->PDDR |= MASK(IR_LED_POS);

    // Start off with IR LED turned off
    Control_IR_LED(0);
}
```

Listing 6.8 Functions to initialize ADC and IR LED.

The Init_ADC function (in Listing 6.8) configures the GPIO pins and ADC input as needed. The Init_IR_LED function configures a GPIO pin and a bit in Port B to drive the LED.

```c
void Control_IR_LED(unsigned int led_on) {
    if (led_on) {
                PTB->PCOR = MASK(IR_LED_POS);
    } else {
                PTB->PSOR = MASK(IR_LED_POS);
    }
}

unsigned Measure_IR(void) {
    volatile unsigned res=0;

    ADC0->SC1[0] = IR_PHOTOTRANSISTOR_CHANNEL; // start conversion on channel 0

    while (!(ADC0->SC1[0] & ADC_SC1_COCO_MASK))
        ; // Wait until conversion is complete

    res = ADC0->R[0];
    // Complement result since voltage falls with increasing IR level
    // but we want result to rise with increasing IR level
    return 0xffff-res;
}
```

Listing 6.9 Functions to control IR LED and measure IR level from phototransistor through ADC.

The Control_IR_LED function (in Listing 6.9) turns on or off the IR LED based on the function argument. The Measure_IR function starts an ADC conversion, blocks (waits) until the conversion is complete, reads the result, and then inverts the result so that larger values indicate brighter levels.

```c
void Delay(unsigned int time_del) {
    // This is a very imprecise and fragile implementation!
    time_del = 10*time_del;
    while (time_del--) {
            ;
    }
}
```

Listing 6.10 Simple busy-waiting time delay function.

The Delay function (in Listing 6.10) waits for an amount of time proportional to the input parameter. Note that the actual time delay is not specified, and will vary based on processor speed, compiler settings, and other factors.

```c
int Threshold[NUM_RANGE_STEPS] = {34000, 27000, 20000, 14000, 8000, 0};

const int Colors[NUM_RANGE_STEPS][3] = {{ 1, 1, 1},   // white
                                        { 1, 0, 1},   // magenta
                                        { 1, 0, 0},   // red
                                        { 1, 1, 0},   // yellow
                                        { 0, 0, 1},   // blue
                                        { 0, 1, 0}    // green
```

```
};
void Display_Range(int b) {
      unsigned i;

      for (i=0; i<NUM_RANGE_STEPS-1; i++) {
            if (b > Threshold[i])
                  break;
      }

      Control_RGB_LEDs(Colors[i][RED], Colors[i][GREEN], Colors[i][BLUE]);
}
```

Listing 6.11 Function and data to light LED based on IR reflectance.

The Display_Range function (in Listing 6.11) lights the RGB LED according to the input argument (IR brightness difference), and uses a table to define thresholds and colors.

```
int main (void) {
      static int on_brightness=0, off_brightness=0;
      static int avg_diff;
      static int diff;
      unsigned n;

      Init_ADC();
      Init_RGB_LEDs();
      Init_IR_LED();
      Control_RGB_LEDs(0, 0, 0);

      while (1) {
            diff = 0;
            for (n=0; n<NUM_SAMPLES_TO_AVG; n++) {
                  // Measure IR level with IRLED off
                  Control_IR_LED(0);
                  Delay (T_DELAY_OFF);
                  off_brightness = Measure_IR();

                  // Measure IR level with IRLED on
                  Control_IR_LED(1);
                  Delay(T_DELAY_ON);
                  on_brightness = Measure_IR();

                  // Calculate difference
                  diff += on_brightness - off_brightness;
            }
            // Calculate average difference
            avg_diff = diff/NUM_SAMPLES_TO_AVG;
            // light RGB LED according to range
            Display_Range(avg_diff);
      }
}
```

Listing 6.12 Main function that controls IR LED, measures IR phototransistor voltage, and calculates reflectance.

The main function (in Listing 6.12) initializes the system and then measures IR reflectance. To do this, it repeatedly measures the difference in brightness caused by lighting the IR LED and then calls a function to indicate the range with color coding on the RGB LED. In order to reduce noise, it averages at least ten measurements before each update of the LED color.

Summary

In this chapter we have seen how a digital microcontroller can measure and generate analog signals. We began by examining quantization and sampling. We then examined various peripherals. A digital-to-analog converter allows the MCU to generate an analog signal. A comparator allows the MCU to determine which of the two analog voltages is greater. Using a known reference voltage as one of the inputs allows us to determine whether the other input is above or below that voltage. An analog-to-digital converter measures an analog voltage and provides a proportional digital representation.

Exercises

For all of these questions, assume the KL25Z peripherals are used unless specified otherwise.

1. Consider a 12-bit ADC with a reference voltage of 3.3 V operating in single-ended mode. Given an input voltage of 0.92 V, what will the output code be?
2. Consider an 8-bit ADC with a reference voltage of 2.7 V operating in single-ended mode. What input voltage range will lead to an output code of 0x34?
3. Consider a 12-bit ADC with an unknown reference voltage operating in single-ended mode. What is the reference voltage if sampling the 1.0 V band gap reference results in a code of 0x513?
4. Consider a 12-bit ADC with a reference voltage of 3.3 V operating in single-ended mode. If it samples the internal temperature sensor and reads a voltage of 0.621 V, what is the temperature? Assume $V_{Temp}25=719$ mV and m = 1.175 mV/°C.
5. Consider a 12-bit DAC with a reference voltage of 3.3 V. What input code will result in an output of 1.43 V?
6. Consider a 10-bit DAC with a reference voltage of 2.7 V. Given that the input code is 0x104, what is the output voltage?
7. What is the output voltage resolution of an 8-bit DAC with a reference voltage of 3.0 V?
8. How would you configure the comparator in the KL25Z to trigger whenever the input voltage rises above 2.0 V? Assume the reference voltage is 3.3 V.

References

[1] L. Tan and J. Jian, *Digital signal processing: Fundamentals and applications*, 2nd ed., Elsevier Inc., 2013.

[2] C. L. Philips, T. Nagle, and A. Chakrabortty, *Digial control system analysis and design*, 4th ed., Pearson, 2014.

[3] *KL25 Sub-Family Reference Manual*, KL25P80M48SF0RM, Rev. 3rd ed., NXP Semiconductor, B.V., 2016.

[4] FRDM-KL25Z User's Manual, rev. 2.0, NXP Semiconductor, B.V., 2016.

[5] *Kinetis KL25 Sub-Family Data Sheet*, KL25P80M48SF0, Rev. 5th ed., NXP Semiconductor, B.V., 2016.

7

Timers

Chapter Contents

Overview

In this chapter, we show how timer peripherals work to measure elapsed time, count events, generate events at specified times, help the processor recover from an out-of-control program, and perform other more advanced features. Using timers, it is also possible to output a square wave with a controllable frequency and duty cycle. We will cover the concepts behind these features and how to use them.

Concepts

The core of a *timer* or *timer/counter* peripheral is a digital *counter* whose value changes by one each time the counter is clocked. The faster the clocking rate, the faster the device counts. If the timer's input clock frequency is 10 MHz, then its period is the inverse of 10 MHz: 1/10 MHz or 0.1 μs. Hence one count (increment or decrement) of the register represents 0.1 μs. We can measure how much time has passed since the counter was reset by reading the counter value and multiplying it by 0.1 μs. For example, if the counter value is 15821, and the count direction is up (incrementing), then we know that 1582.1 μs have passed since the counter was reset.

timer/counter
Peripheral which measures time or counts events

counter
Digital circuit which counts number of input pulses

Timer Circuit Hardware

Figure 7.1 shows the block diagram of a basic timer peripheral's hardware. A transition on the input signal may represent either an event or a fixed time interval. Regardless, the transition causes the counter to change (e.g. increment by one). The timer peripheral can therefore count events or measure time. Other hardware is often added to make it even more flexible. Timer peripherals are typically able to measure elapsed time, count events, generate events at fixed times, generate waveforms, or measure pulse widths and frequencies. This circuitry controls factors such as:

- Which signal source it counts. If it counts a signal with a known frequency, then we can use it to measure elapsed time
- When it starts and stops running
- Whether it counts rising or falling edges
- Which direction it counts
- What happens when it overflows
- If and how it is reloaded
- Whether its value is captured by another register
- Whether it generates a signal or an interrupt

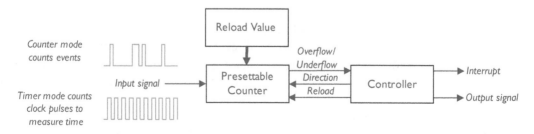

Figure 7.1 Timer peripheral hardware is built around a counter.

Example Timer Uses

Periodic Timer Tick

One of the most basic uses of a timer peripheral is to generate a periodic interrupt event. The time between interrupts is steady because it is controlled by hardware and not affected by software delays. We may want to monitor elapsed time, for example, to generate a time-stamp for logged events. The timer's counter register measures the current time with a high resolution. If needed, we can extend the timer's range by using its overflow interrupt to trigger an interrupt service routine that increments an overflow counter.

Many software tasks in embedded systems require time delays. A task could use a busy-waiting time delay loop to wait, but this does not share the processor with other tasks. A periodic timer interrupt can be used instead to track the time delay and start the task after it has elapsed.

Watchdog Timer

It is difficult to make a program for an embedded system completely perfect. One reason is that developers sometimes translate their ideas into code (and peripheral configurations) incorrectly, introducing bugs. This may be from misunderstanding what a C code statement really means, how a peripheral really operates, or how different parts of a system might interact (e.g. preemption). Another reason is that the developer has translated an imperfect idea to code. It is difficult for humans to imagine all possible sequences of combinations of inputs to an embedded system, so we often leave some of these out of our specification of how the system should behave, and don't consider them when designing the system to meet that specification.

We can reduce the number of both types of bug with various methods (e.g. testing, rigorous design process, design reviews), but eliminating all bugs will be expensive and probably infeasible. So bugs are present essentially in all embedded system software. We still want the system to operate correctly most of the time. One way to do this is to restart the program automatically if an error is detected.

A *watchdog timer (WDT)* is a peripheral that tries to detect if the program goes out of control, in which case the WDT resets the processor to restart the program. The WDT uses a counter to keep track of the elapsed time and expects to be signaled (serviced) by the program periodically, such as once per second. If the WDT is not serviced within the expected time, then it will reset the processor. If the WDT is serviced, then it will reset its counter to begin a new time measurement.

> watchdog timer (WDT)
> *Hardware peripheral used to reset out-of-control program*

The program is responsible for servicing the WDT at correct times. There are many types of bugs in the program that can keep it from timely WDT servicing, making this a useful error detection method. Nearly all MCUs provide a WDT, and good embedded systems use them. However, bugs that do not affect the timing of the WDT servicing will not be detected.

Figure 7.2 Cup anemometer used to measure wind speed. Photo by author.

Time and Frequency Measurement

We can measure a signal's frequency or period with a timer peripheral. For example, an anemometer generates a pulse signal with a wind-dependent frequency. The anemometer in Figure 7.2 has a rotating section with three arms and cups and one or more magnets mounted near the axle. A magnetic sensor (such as a reed switch) is mounted on the fixed mast. The magnetic sensor generates a pulse each time a magnet passes by, so the frequency of the signal f_{anem} will be proportional to the wind speed, neglecting the errors caused by inertia and friction. We can then calculate the wind speed v_{wind} based on the f_{anem} and the distance $\mathbf{r}$ of the anemometer cups from the axis.

$$v_{wind} = 2\pi r f_{anem}$$

How do we find the signal's frequency or period (the inverse of the period)?

- We can measure the signal's **frequency** by counting how many pulses have occurred during a fixed time period. We configure the peripheral in **event counter** mode. To make a measurement, we clear the timer, start it running, wait for the fixed measurement time, and then read the counter value. Dividing the count value by the measurement time gives the signal frequency, which we then scale to provide wind speed.
- We can measure the signal's **period** by measuring the time between successive rising edges. We configure the peripheral in **timer** mode, so it counts at a fixed rate. We then start the timer running. When the input signal has a rising edge on the input signal, we capture the value of the timer's counter with an interrupt service routine. We then wait for the next rising edge and capture the new value of the timer's counter. The period of the signal is equal to the difference in the count values divided by the count frequency. We invert the period and then scale it to determine wind speed.

Timer peripherals typically have additional support circuitry to simplify these measurement procedures to improve accuracy and reduce software processing and complexity, as we will see shortly.

PWM Signal Generation

Pulse-width modulation (PWM) is a method to send more than one bit of information on a single digital signal line. Rather than encode the information serially as a series of bits (as we will see in the next chapter), the information is encoded as the fraction of time that the signal is a logic one (called the *duty cycle*). Because the signal is sent in a digital format, it is much less vulnerable to electrical noise.

> Pulse-width modulation (PWM)
> *Method for encoding information onto a single digital signal based on duty cycle*

> Duty cycle
> *Fraction of time that a digital signal is asserted*

Some devices can be driven by a PWM signal or a buffered version that can provide more power, voltage, and current. For example, a PWM signal may drive a motor at a reduced speed or partially dim a light. The high-frequency components of the signal are averaged by the inertia of the motor or the persistence of human vision. A PWM signal can be averaged with a low-pass filter to create an analog voltage if we do not have a DAC.

Remember the hot-plate example from the first chapter? We can use PWM to control the heating element. Rather than being only fully on or fully off, the heating element can take on intermediate heating values, proportional to the duty cycle. This will enable more precise control with less error and overshoot.

Figure 7.3 shows an example of a PWM signal with a duty cycle of about 70%. There are several terms that describe PWM signal characteristics:

- The on-time T_{On} is the amount of time the signal is true.
- The off-time T_{Off} is the amount of time the signal is false.
- The signal frequency f indicates how many pulses are sent per second.
- The period T is the inverse of the frequency: $T = 1/f$. It is also the sum of the on and off times: $T = T_{On} + T_{Off}$
- The duty cycle D is the on-time divided by the period: $D = T_{On}/T$
- The polarity of the signal may be active-high or active-low. For active-high signals, the signal is on (true) when it is a logic one. For active-low signals, the signal is on (true) when it is a logic zero.

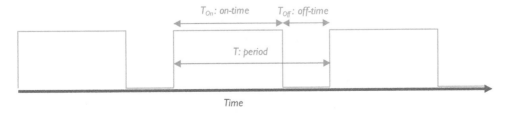

Figure 7.3 Example of pulse-width modulated signal.

Timer Peripherals

SysTick Timer

The Cortex-M0+ core contains a simple timer peripheral called the SysTick timer, shown in Figure 7.4. It is designed to provide a periodic tick for system operation, such as in a scheduler or operating system kernel. Regardless of MCU device manufacturer, all Cortex-M processors (M0, M0+, M3, M4, and M7) have one. This helps make the system software more portable across different devices.

The counter in the *SysTick timer* is 24 bits long and decrements when clocked. Its current value can be read from the VAL register field, shown in Figure 7.5. When first enabled, the counter is loaded from the 24-bit LOAD[1] field in Figure 7.6. It then counts down with each input clock pulse. After the counter reaches zero it reloads itself with the RELOAD value and can generate a SysTick exception (if enabled). Writing anything to the SYST_CVR clears that register to zero.

> SysTick timer
> *Timer peripheral available in Cortex-M CPU cores, typically used to generate periodic time tick*

The counter divides the input frequency by a factor of LOAD+1. In order to divide an input frequency f_{in} by a factor of N, we store N-1 in the LOAD register.

The CTRL register controls and indicates the status for the SysTick timer.

- The CLKSOURCE field selects the clock source, which can be either the processor clock (one) or an external reference clock (zero). On the KL25Z MCU, the processor clock runs at up to 48 MHz, and the external reference clock is the processor clock divided by 16.
- The TICKINT field controls whether counting down to zero will enable SysTick Exception request (one) or not (zero).
- The ENABLE field enables the counter when set to one.
- The COUNTFLAG field returns a one if the timer has counted down to zero since the last time this register was read. Reading SYST_CSR clears COUNTFLAG to zero, as does writing any value to SYST_CVR.

The SYST_CALIB register provides support for calibrating the timer and is not discussed further here. Further information on the SysTick timer can be found in the ARM documentation and other texts [1], [2].

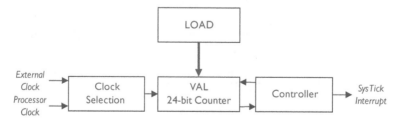

Figure 7.4 Overview of SysTick timer circuitry.

---

[1] This text uses the CMSIS names for these registers. The ARM documentation uses different names: SYST_RVR for LOAD, SYST_CVR for VAL, SYST_CSR for CTRL [1].

31	24	23	22	21	20	19	18	17	16	15	14	13	12	11	10	9	8	7	6	5	4	3	2	1	0
												VAL													

Figure 7.5 SysTick Timer current value register (VAL or SYST_CVR).

31	24	23	22	21	20	19	18	17	16	15	14	13	12	11	10	9	8	7	6	5	4	3	2	1	0
												LOAD													

Figure 7.6 SysTick Timer reload value register (LOAD or SYST_RVR).

31	17	16	15	14	13	12	11	10	9	8	7	6	5	4	3	2	1	0
		COUNTFLAG														CLKSOURCE	TICKINT	ENABLE

Figure 7.7 SysTick Timer control and status register (CTRL or SYST_CSR).

CMSIS definitions for the SysTick timer peripheral are located in the core_cm0plus.h include file. That file also defines a function SysTick_Config that can be used to configure the timer. The exception handler is called SysTick_Handler, and the exception number is SysTick_IRQn.

Example: Periodic 1 Hz Interrupt

Let's configure the SysTick timer to generate an interrupt every second, assuming the processor clock is 48 MHz. We need to divide the processor clock down by a factor of 48 MHz/1 Hz = 48,000,000. The value of 47,999,999 is too large to fit into the 24-bit LOAD field, so we will need to use the alternate clock source, which runs at 48 MHz/16 = 3 MHz. The new division factor is 3 MHz/1 = 3,000,000, and the LOAD value of 2,999,999 does fit into 24 bits.

```
void Init_SysTick(void) {
  SysTick->LOAD = (48000000L/16);         // Set reload to get 1 s interrupts
  NVIC_SetPriority (SysTick_IRQn, 3);     // Set interrupt priority
  SysTick->VAL  = 0;                      // Force load of reload value
  SysTick->CTRL = SysTick_CTRL_TICKINT_Msk | // Enable interrupt, alt. clock source
            SysTick_CTRL_ENABLE_Msk;      // Enable SysTick timer
}
```

Listing 7.1 Function to initialize SysTick Timer to generate 1 Hz interrupts.

The Init_SysTick function in Listing 7.1 configures the timer. It first writes the LOAD value, enables the SysTick IRQ in the NVIC, initializes the current count value, and finally configures CTRL to use the alternate clock source, enable interrupts, and enable the timer.

```
void SysTick_Handler() {
  static int n=0;
  Control_RGB_LEDs(n&1,n&1,n&1);
  n++;
}
```

Handler for SysTick exception runs every second, turns LEDs on or off.

The exception handler for the SysTick Timer in Listing 7.2 runs each time the timer reaches zero, which is 1 Hz in this example.

Kinetis KL25Z COP Watchdog Timer

The KL25Z MCUs feature a watchdog timer called the computer operating properly (COP) [3]. The COP will reset the MCU if it is not serviced when required.

Figure 7.8 shows the basic operation of the COP. When the MCU comes out of reset, the program starts running and can configure the COP operation. The COP counts up as the application program runs. Eventually the program services the COP, resetting its counter to zero. The COP resumes counting from zero, expecting to be serviced again by the program before reaching its time-out value. The diagram shows a case in which the program starts running out of control (e.g. due to a bug or electrical noise) and the COP is not serviced. Eventually, the COP times out, resetting the MCU and causing the program to restart.

With the window mode, the COP must be serviced within a specific portion of the time period, as shown in Figure 7.9 in green. This provides more robust protection against faults, because if the watchdog is serviced too early or too late (outside of the green window area) it will reset the CPU. The KL25Z COP can be configured so the valid window is the last 25% of the watchdog period.

Hardware Configuration

The COP is controlled by two registers in the system integration module (SIM). Shown in Figure 7.10, the SIM_COPCTRL register configures the COP.

- The COPCLKS field selects the clock source for the COP. A zero selects the internal low-power oscillator (LPO) that runs at about 1000 Hz, whereas one selects the bus clock (e.g. 24 MHz).

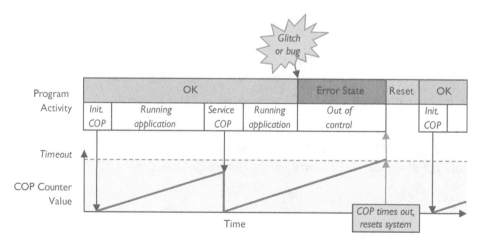

Figure 7.8 COP Watchdog timer detects program that is out of control, resets system to restart program.

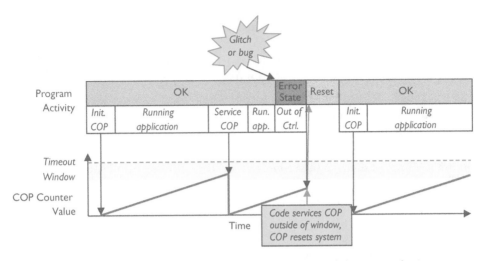

Figure 7.9 Windowed watchdog resets system if serviced outside of valid time window.

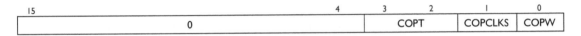

Figure 7.10 SIM_COPCTRL control register.

The exact frequency of the LPO may vary between 909 Hz and 1111 Hz as described in the MCU datasheet [4].

• Setting the COPT field to a nonzero value enables the COP and sets the time-out period. A value of one selects a time-out period of 2^5 LPO cycles or 2^{13} bus clock cycles, a value of two selects a time-out period of 2^8 LPO cycles or 2^{16} bus clock cycles, and a value of three selects a time-out period of 2^{10} LPO cycles or 2^{18} bus clock cycles.

• The COPW field enables windowed mode when set to one and the bus clock is used (i.e. COPCLKS is one).

The initial value of SIM_COPCTRL after reset is 0x0C, so the COP is enabled with a time-out period of 1024 LPO cycles in nonwindowed mode. The COPCTRL register accepts only the first data written to it after the processor has been reset. Subsequent writes are ignored to improve system reliability.

The SIM_SRVCOP control register is used to service the COP, which resets its counter. To service the COP, the code must write 0x55 and then 0xAA to SIM_SRVCOP in order.

The processor can read the reset control module's status register zero to determine the cause of the reset. As shown in Figure 7.11, the WDOG bit is set to one if a reset has been caused by the watchdog timer and cleared otherwise. Other causes which can be distinguished include power-on reset, external reset pin, loss of PLL lock, loss of external clock, low voltage detection, and wakeup from a low-leakage stop mode.

7	6	5	4	3	2	1	0
POR	PIN	WDOG	0	LOL	LOC	LVD	WAKEUP

Figure 7.11 Reset control module status register RCM_SRS0 indicates cause of reset.

How to Use a WDT

Now we know how to configure and service the COP WDT. How should we use it? Here are some common best practices; these and others are discussed in greater depth elsewhere [5] [6].

How Long Should the WDT Period Be?

The WDT period sets the maximum detection delay, so choose one that is appropriate for the system. An MCU controlling a cordless power tool (e.g. a drill) needs a short WDT because the tool can injure the user, or damage the environment, the drill itself, and the battery.

If we shorten its period, the WDT must be serviced more frequently. This requires a better understanding of the program's timing behavior, which may be more complex than expected.

Where Should the WDT Be Serviced, and How Often?

Do not service the watchdog in an interrupt service routine, because ISRs are likely to run even if the rest of the software has crashed. Instead service the watchdog in mainline non-ISR code, preferably low-priority code that is vulnerable to system crashes.

Do not scatter WDT service commands throughout the code. First, this lack of design leads to sloppy use of the WDT, making it much less effective. Second, having multiple WDT service locations will complicate finding the cause of WDT resets.

Embedded systems have code for two phases: the start-up code configures and prepares the system, whereas the operational code handles everything else. The WDT may need to be serviced multiple times during system start-up if there are operations that take a long time to complete. Once the system is in its operational mode, the WDT should be serviced in few places, preferably only one.

How Do We Debug a System with a WDT?

A WDT complicates debugging, as it will reset the system shortly after the program hits a break-point. To prevent this problem, the KL25Z's COP will not run while the MCU is in debug or stop mode. Other WDTs typically have an equivalent feature.

Example: Tilt Sensor

Let us use the COP WDT and trigger it when the FRDM-KL25Z board is not horizontal. We will use the MMA8451Q inertial sensor, which is described in Chapter 8 and the device's datasheet [7]. After starting up, the code will initialize the COP WDT and LEDs. It will then flash the RGB LED three times to indicate if this is a start-up after a regular reset (green) or after a WDT reset (red). The code will next initialize the I²C communications bus and inertial sensor. Finally the code will enter its main loop, in which it reads the inertial sensor and computes the board's roll and pitch angles. If the board is sufficiently horizontal, the LED will be lit green and the COP WDT will be serviced. If the board is tilted enough, the LED will be lit yellow and the COP WDT will not be serviced. If the COP WDT is not serviced within about 1.024 seconds, it will reset the system. The code will restart, flashing the LED red to indicate the WDT reset cause.

```
void Init_COP_WDT(void) {
    // Select 1 kHz clock and 1024 cycle time-out
    SIM->COPC = SIM_COPC_COPT(3) & ~SIM_COPC_COPCLKS_MASK & ~SIM_COPC_COPW_MASK;
}

void Service_COP_WDT(void) {
    SIM->SRVCOP = 0x55;
    SIM->SRVCOP = 0xaa;
}
```

Listing 7.3 Functions to initialize and service COP WDT.

The two functions to initialize and service the COP WDT are shown in Listing 7.3 and are quite simple.

```
#define NUM_STARTUP_FLASHES (5)
#define STARTUP_FLASH_DURATION (20)

void Flash_Reset_Cause(void) {
    unsigned n;

    for (n=0; n<NUM_STARTUP_FLASHES; n++) {
        if (RCM->SRS0 & RCM_SRS0_WDOG_MASK)
            Control_RGB_LEDs(1, 0, 0); // Red: WDOG caused reset
        else
            Control_RGB_LEDs(0, 1, 0); // Green: WDOG did not cause reset

        Delay(STARTUP_FLASH_DURATION);
        Control_RGB_LEDs(0, 0, 0);
        Delay(2*STARTUP_FLASH_DURATION);
    }
}
```

Listing 7.4 Function to flash LEDs with color determined by the reset cause.

The code to determine the cause of the reset and flash the LEDs accordingly is shown in Listing 7.4. The code reads the reset control module status register and lights the correct LEDs. After a delay, all the LEDs are turned off. After another delay the loop repeats or exits.

```
#define MAX_ANGLE (30)

int main (void) {

    Init_COP_WDT();
    Init_RGB_LEDs();
    Flash_Reset_Cause();            // Show system is starting up by flashing LEDs
    Service_COP_WDT();

    i2c_init();                     // Init i2c
    if (!init_mma()) {              // Init mma peripheral
        Control_RGB_LEDs(1, 0, 1);  // Light purple error LED
        while (1)                   // Not able to initialize MMA
            ;
    }
```

```
    Service_COP_WDT();
    Delay(300);                          // Delay before starting rest of program
    while (1) {
        read_full_xyz();
        convert_xyz_to_roll_pitch();
        if ((fabs(roll) > MAX_ANGLE) | (fabs(pitch) > MAX_ANGLE)) {
            Control_RGB_LEDs(1, 1, 0); // Light yellow LED as warning
        } else {
            Control_RGB_LEDs(0, 1, 0); // Light green LED - OK!
            Service_COP_WDT();
        }
    }
}
```

Listing 7.5 Main function for using COP WDT to reset system when board is tilted excessively.

The main function is shown in Listing 7.5. After initializing the COP WDT, the program services the WDT before continuing to initialize other hardware peripherals. Note that the COP is serviced twice during this initialization sequence. This depends on the timing of the initialization code, with service operations inserted within 1.024 s of each other. Here the Flash_Reset_Cause function and I²C and MMA code may take a long time to execute, so we service the COP between them.

The while loop holds the regular operation portion of the code. The code first reads the x, y, and z axis accelerations from the MMA8451Q sensor using the I²C communications bus. It then calculates the roll and pitch from these accelerations. On the basis of the absolute values of the angles, it determines which LEDs to light and whether to service the COP WDT.

Kinetis KL25Z Timer/PWM Module

The *timer/PWM module (TPM)* consists of a core with a 16-bit counter and multiple channels that use the core counter's value to measure the timing of input signals or generate output signals. Figure 7.12 shows a block diagram of the TPM circuitry. The KL25Z family of MCUs has three TPMs: TPM0 has six channels, whereas TPM1 and TPM2 each have two channels. Full information is available in the documentation [3] [4].

timer/PWM module (TPM)
Timer peripheral in Kinetis KL25Z MCU which can also generate PWM signals

TPM Core and Basic Timer Mode

The heart of the TPM is a 16-bit preloadable up/down counter called TPMx_CNT. The CPWMS field in TPMx_SC sets the count direction to up only (zero) or alternating between up and down (one).

The TPM status and control register (TPMx_SC) controls the basic operation of the TPM's core and is shown in Figure 7.13. The CMOD field of TPMx_SC determines the clock source for the TPM. It can be an external clock signal (LPTPM_EXTCLK), the module's LPTPM clock, or it can be disconnected to disable the TPM.

The prescaler is a hardware circuit that divides down the input signal's frequency by a factor of 1, 2, 4, 8, 16, 32, 64, or 128, as controlled by the PS field of the TPMx_SC register.

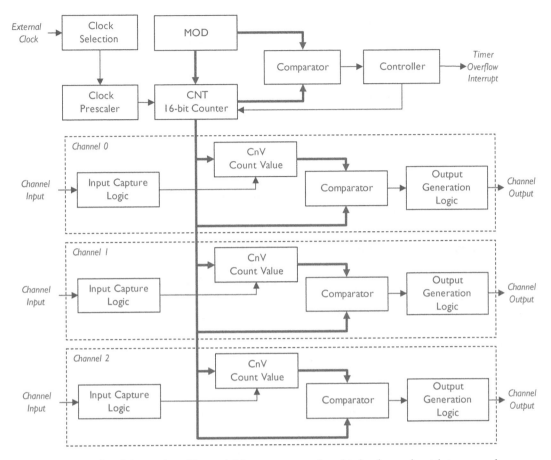

Figure 7.12 Timer/PWM peripheral has a 16-bit counter and multiple channels with input and output
          processing support.

The TPMx_STATUS register, shown in Figure 7.14, indicates the status of the TPM core and
its channels.

The MOD register defines how high the CNT register counts. A comparator detects the overflow condition that occurs when CNT tries to count past MOD. The controller logic responds to
the overflow by performing the following actions:

- The overflow flag TOF is set to one.
- If the TOIE field of TPMx_SC is set to one, the TPM will generate a TPMx interrupt.
- If the DMA field of TPMx_SC is set to one, the TPM will generate TPMx DMA request.
- The counter is modified according to the value of the CPWMS bit:
    - If the counter is configured for up-counting (CPWMS is zero), then CNT is cleared to zero.
    - If the counter is configured for up/down-counting (CPWMS is one), then the direction is set
      to down-counting and CNT is decremented (to MOD-1).

When in up/down counting mode, counting down to zero results an underflow condition, so the
count direction changes to up. The next clock input will increment CNT to one.

15	14	13	12	11	10	9	8	7	6	5	4	3	2	1	0
			0				DMA	TOF	TOIE	CPWMS	CMOD		PS		

Figure 7.13 TPMx_SC status and control register.

15	14	13	12	11	10	9	8	7	6	5	4	3	2	1	0
								TOF		CH5F	CH4F	CH3F	CH2F	CH1F	CH0F

Figure 7.14 TPMx_STATUS register indicates if counter has overflowed and if any channel events have occurred.

The TPM will overflow at a frequency of $f_{clock/ (prescaler*(MOD+1))}$ when in up-counting mode, and $f_{clock/ (prescaler*2*MOD)}$ when in up/down-counting mode.

Example: Analog Waveform Generation

We can use the timer to generate a regular interrupt in order to generate a waveform with precise timing. Listing 7.6 shows the DAC-based triangle waveform generator function from the previous chapter. There are two major limitations to this approach.

```
void Triangle_Output(void) {
    int i=0, change=1;

    while (1) {
        DAC0->DAT[0].DATL = DAC_DATL_DATA0(i);
        DAC0->DAT[0].DATH = DAC_DATH_DATA1(i >> 8);

        i += change;
        if (i ==0) {
          change = 1;
        } else if (i == DAC_RESOLUTION-1) {
          change = -1;
        }
    }
}
```

Listing 7.6 Simple triangle waveform generator function from previous chapter has timing and processor sharing limitations.

First, the program's structure makes it difficult to share the processor's time with other processing activities. The function Triangle_Output uses an infinite loop and never completes. Second, the program's timing behavior is very fragile. On some loop iterations the conditional code in an **if** statement will be executed (e.g. change =1, if (i == DAC_RESOLUTION-1), change = –1), taking an additional amount of time. The DAC playback of a sample following such an iteration will be delayed, distorting the signal. Adding any other processing will slow down the waveform generator, delaying its sample generation and distorting the output signal. Changing compiler settings will probably change the timing of the sample playback. These changes will force the developer to adjust the time delay in the loop.

We can eliminate this timing variability and also simplify processor time sharing by using a periodic interrupt to update the DAC at regular intervals. The ISR operates asynchronously from the main program, improving the timing stability. Our waveform generation code is short and simple enough to embed within the ISR, as shown in Listing 7.7.

```c
void TPM0_IRQHandler() {
    static int change=STEP_SIZE;
    static uint16_t out_data=0;

    FPTD->PSOR = MASK(BLUE_LED_POS); // Debug signal: Entering ISR
    TPM0->SC |= TPM_SC_TOIE_MASK;    // reset overflow flag

    // Do ISR work
    out_data += change;
    if (out_data < STEP_SIZE) {
                change = STEP_SIZE;
    } else if (out_data >= DAC_RESOLUTION-STEP_SIZE) {
                change = -STEP_SIZE;
    }
    DAC0->DAT[0].DATH = DAC_DATH_DATA1(out_data >> 8);
    DAC0->DAT[0].DATL = DAC_DATL_DATA0(out_data);
    FPTD->PCOR = MASK(BLUE_LED_POS); // Debug signal: Exiting ISR
}
```

Listing 7.7 Interrupt service routine generates waveform using DAC.

We have modified the code to change the output data by STEP_SIZE rather than just one, making the code more configurable. In this example STEP_SIZE is 16 and DAC_RESOLUTION is 4096.

We have also added two lines of code to set Port D bit 1 upon entering the ISR and to clear it upon exiting. We can monitor this signal with an oscilloscope to determine when the processor is executing the ISR. Remember that there is additional minor time overhead for the CPU to respond to the interrupt before the ISR begins executing.

```c
void Init_TPM(void)
{
    // Turn on clock to TPM
    SIM->SCGC6 |= SIM_SCGC6_TPM0_MASK;
    // Set clock source for tpm
    SIM->SOPT2 |= (SIM_SOPT2_TPMSRC(1) | SIM_SOPT2_PLLFLLSEL_MASK);
    // Load the counter and mod, given prescaler of 32
    TPM0->MOD = (F_TPM_CLOCK/(F_TPM_OVFLW*32))-1;
    // Set TPM to divide by 32 prescaler, enable counting (CMOD) and interrupts
    TPM0->SC = TPM_SC_CMOD(1) | TPM_SC_PS(5) | TPM_SC_TOIE_MASK;
    // Enable interrupts in NVIC
    NVIC_SetPriority(TPM0_IRQn, 3);
    NVIC_ClearPendingIRQ(TPM0_IRQn);
    NVIC_EnableIRQ(TPM0_IRQn);
}
```

Listing 7.8 Function to initialize TPM to generate periodic interrupt.

Listing 7.8 shows the code that initializes the TPM0 to generate an interrupt at a frequency of F_TPM_OVERFLOW (100 kHz here), given an input clock rate of F_TPM_CLOCK (48 MHz). We use the prescaler to divide the input frequency by a factor of 32.

Figure 7.15 shows the output of the DAC (upper trace) and the debug signal, which is one when the ISR is executing. The period of the DAC signal is about 5.1 ms, so the frequency is about 196 Hz. These show the system is working correctly.

Let's take a closer look at the timing of the signals. Figure 7.16 shows the DAC is updated within the ISR, as expected. The ISR takes about 1 μs to execute, so at least 10% of the CPU's

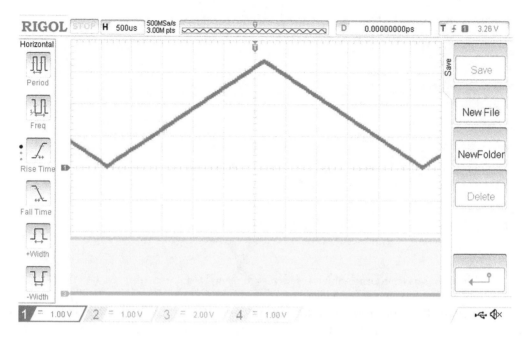

Figure 7.15 Output of ISR-based triangle waveform generator program. Upper trace is DAC output, lower trace is ISR activity (Port D bit 1).

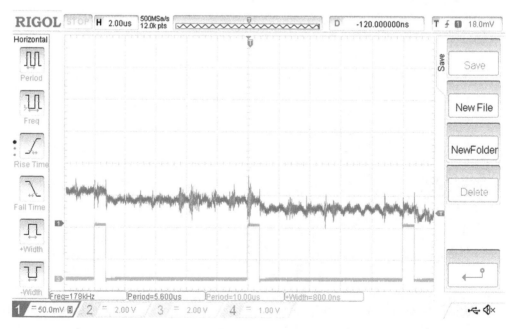

Figure 7.16 DAC output is updated every 10 μs, when ISR is active (lower trace is high). ISR is active for 1 μs.

time is used for the waveform generation. This leaves nearly 90% of the CPU time for other processing, unlike the code of Listing 7.6.

The ISR does not always take the same amount of time to execute because of the conditional code within it. We can see the variability of the execution time in Figure 7.17, in which the oscilloscope's infinite persistence feature is used to display all traces, erasing none. The ISR normally takes 1.0 μs to execute, but occasionally it takes 0.94 μs or 1.04 μs. With the CPU's 48 MHz clock rate, these times represent 48, 45, and 50 clock cycles respectively. Examining the ISR code shows the DAC is updated after this conditional code, so the DAC output waveform will be early or late in these cases. We could eliminate this timing variability by updating out_data after updating the DAC, rather than before.

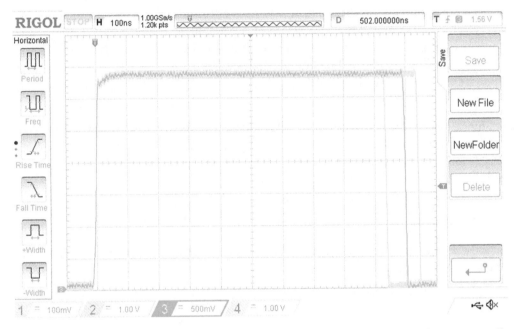

Figure 7.17 Detailed view of ISR execution time signal. ISR usually takes 1.000 μs, but occasionally takes slightly more or less time.

TPM Channels

Each TPM channel has a status and control register (TPMx_CnSC), shown in Figure 7.18. Each channel can be configured to operate in input capture or output generation mode, as controlled by the mode select (MSB and MSA) and edge select fields (ELSB and ELSA) in TPMx_CnSC.

Each TPM channel also has an I/O signal called TPMx_CHn[2] that can be used to provide a single-bit digital input or output signal. When using this signal, the appropriate pin's PCR must be configured to select that signal.

15	14	13	12	11	10	9	8	7	6	5	4	3	2	1	0
								CHF	CHIE	MSB	MSA	ELSB	ELSA		DMA

Figure 7.18 TPMx_CnSC channel status and control register.

---

[2] This is called FTMx_CHn in the FRDM-KL25Z documentation.

All channel flags are also accessible through the TPMx_STATUS register. This simplifies the code needed to identify which channel flags are set.

Input Capture Mode

Using input capture mode makes time measurement of input signals much less vulnerable to delays in processing interrupts because the channel hardware automatically captures the timer value without the need for any software intervention.

When the channel is in input capture mode, the input signal is monitored for a specific transition (rising edge, falling edge, or either). When that transition occurs, the value of the TPMx_CNT register is captured in the VAL field of the channel's CnV register, and the channel flag CHF in TPMx_CnSC is set to one. If the channel interrupt enable field (CHIE) is one, then TPMx will generate an interrupt. The ISR must copy the captured value out of the channel's TPMx_CnV register and use it. The ISR must also clear the channel flag by writing one to it. If the DMA field is set, then a DMA transfer will be requested.

We configure TPMx_CnSC as follows:

- Select input capture mode by setting the MSB and MSA bits to 0:0. CPWMS must also be zero.
- Select which edges trigger a capture using ELSnB:ELSnA: 0:1 for rising edges, 1:0 for falling edges, 1:1 for both rising and falling edges.
- If used, enable interrupts by setting CHIE to one.
- If used, enable DMA by setting DMA to one.

Example: Anemometer Using Period Measurement

Let's see how to use the input capture mode to measure the period of the input signal from the anemometer. This initialization code for the TPM is shown in Listing 7.9.

```
extern volatile int32_t g_anem_period, g_new_data;

void Init_TPM_IC(void) {
  // Clock gating for TPM1, Port E
  SIM->SCGC6 |= SIM_SCGC6_TPM1_MASK;
  SIM->SCGC5 |= SIM_SCGC5_PORTE_MASK;

  //set clock source for tpm
  SIM->SOPT2 |= (SIM_SOPT2_TPMSRC(1) | SIM_SOPT2_PLLFLLSEL_MASK);

  //load the counter and mod.
  TPM1->MOD = 0xffff;

  //set channel to input capture (rising edge) with interrupt
  TPM1->CONTROLS[0].CnSC = TPM_CnSC_ELSA_MASK | TPM_CnSC_CHIE_MASK;

  // Select pin mux to connect to timer
  PORTE->PCR[20] &= ~PORT_PCR_MUX(7);
  PORTE->PCR[20] |= PORT_PCR_MUX(3);

  // Enable interrupts, use /128 prescaler
  TPM1->SC = TPM_SC_CMOD(1) | TPM_SC_PS(7) | TPM_SC_TOIE_MASK;
  NVIC_SetPriority(TPM1_IRQn, 3);
  NVIC_ClearPendingIRQ(TPM1_IRQn);
  NVIC_EnableIRQ(TPM1_IRQn);
}
```

Listing 7.9 Function to initialize TPM1 with channel 0 in input capture mode.

First, we need to set up the TPM core to count. We will set the prescaler to divide by 128, so the counting frequency is 48 MHz/128 = 375 kHz. Setting MOD to 0xFFFF will set the overflow frequency to 375 kHz/65536 = 5.722 Hz.

Second, we will use channel 0 in input capture mode, so rising input edges will trigger the capture and also generate an interrupt request. The ISR will read the captured value from CnV and compute the difference from the previous captured value. The difference is saved in a global variable g_anem_period for later conversion to wind speed by other (noninterrupt) code. The ISR will also set a flag indicating that there is new data available. Finally, if the time delay between two edges is too long, then the period will be set to zero to indicate invalid data.

We use a low-count frequency because our anemometer pulse frequency is very slow compared with the MCU's counting frequency of up to 48 MHz. If the anemometer is rotating too slowly, then the timer will overflow before being able to measure one anemometer period. For example, with a wind speed of 100 km/h, an anemometer with a 70 mm arm length will rotate at about 63 Hz, so the period will be 15.87 ms.

The lowest wind speed the timer can measure is 5.722 Hz$\times 2 \times \pi \times r$ = 2.516 m/s, or 9 km/h. In order to allow measurement of lower wind speeds, we will extend the time range in the software beyond the counter's 16 bits. We configure the TPM to generate an interrupt on timer overflow. The ISR will increment an overflow counter for each overflow that occurs. Because MOD is set to 0xFFFF, each overflow count represents 0x10000 timer counts. As a result, we can create a 32-bit timestamp using the overflow count as the upper 16 bits and the counter value as the lower 16 bits. Finding the time difference simply involves taking the difference between two successive 32-bit timestamps. The final ISR is shown in Listing 7.10.

```c
void TPM1_IRQHandler() {
    static uint32_t overflows=0;
    static uint32_t prev_count=0;
    uint32_t timer_val;

    PTD->PTOR = MASK(BLUE_LED_POS); // Debug signal
    if (TPM1->STATUS & TPM_STATUS_TOF_MASK) { // Overflow detected
        overflows++;
    }
    if (TPM1->STATUS & TPM_STATUS_CH0F_MASK) {
        timer_val = TPM1->CONTROLS[0].CnV; // Unsigned extension to 32_bits
        timer_val |= overflows << 16;  // Each overflow is 2^16 counts
        g_anem_period = timer_val - prev_count;
        prev_count = timer_val;
        g_new_data = 1;
    }
    if (overflows > (prev_count >> 16) + 20) { // Almost no wind, so zero period
        g_anem_period = 0;
    }
    TPM1->STATUS |= TPM_STATUS_TOF_MASK | TPM_STATUS_CH0F_MASK |
                    TPM_STATUS_CH1F_MASK; // reset all flags
    PTD->PTOR = MASK(BLUE_LED_POS); // Debug signal
}
```

Listing 7.10 ISR to capture rising input edge and compute period since previous rising edge.

We will calculate the wind speed in the main thread rather than the ISR. The ISR passes the period information through the global variable g_anem_period, and also sets the g_new_data flag to indicate new data is available. Shown in Listing 7.11, the main function checks to see if g_new_data is true. If so, it will call a function to calculate the wind speed. In this case, we want the wind speed in knots (1 kt = 1.852 km/h = 0.514 m/s).

```c
#define ANEM_R_MM (70)
#define ANEM_CLK_FREQ (375000) // 48 MHz clock, /128 prescaler
#define KTS_PER_MM_S (0.00194384)

volatile uint32_t g_anem_period=0;
volatile uint32_t g_new_data=0;

float Calculate_Windspeed_kt(void) {
    // calculate windspeed in knots
    float v;

    if (g_anem_period > 0)
        v = KTS_PER_MM_S*2*M_PI*ANEM_R_MM*ANEM_CLK_FREQ/g_anem_period;
    else
        v = 0;
    return(v);
}

int main (void) {
    float v_w=0;

    Init_TPM_IC();
    while (1) {
        if (g_new_data) {
            g_new_data = 0;
            v_w = Calculate_Windspeed_kt();
            // Use the wind speed information now
        }
    }
}
```

Listing 7.11 Code to calculate and display wind speed.

Output Modes

Each TPM channel has logic circuits that can detect when the TPM's counter CNT reaches a certain value. In response, the channel can change its output signal, trigger an interrupt, or trigger a DMA transfer (discussed in Chapter 9). The signal can change value when TPMx_CNT overflows, underflows, or matches TPMx_CnV. Various output signals are possible, including a single pulse with a specified width or delay, or a continuous stream of pulses with a specified duty cycle. The channel's flag CHF will be set to one when TPMx_CNT matches TPMx_CnV. If CHIE is set, then TPMx will generate an interrupt.

Output Compare Mode

The most basic output mode is output compare mode. In this case, the channel will respond each time that CNT reaches CnV (at the beginning of the cycle). The output can be configured to be set to one or cleared to zero on each match. This can be used to create a pulse with a fixed duration. After the first match, the output stays in its new state until the software explicitly changes it. The output can also be configured to toggle on each match, in which case the output signal is a square wave with a time offset (phase delay) determined by CnV.

PWM Signal Generation

Each channel of the TPM can generate a PWM signal with a duty cycle of CnV/MOD. The output signal's polarity can be selected to be high-true or low-true. Finally, the channel's pulses can be aligned by starting edges or centers.

Figure 7.19 shows an example of edge-aligned PWM mode, with MOD = 7 and CnV = 2. The TPM counter CNT counts up from zero to MOD, so its count period is $(MOD+1)/f_{count}$.

Each channel's output is initialized (e.g. to one) each time counter CNT overflows (e.g. from 7 to zero). CNT counts and eventually matches CnV, at which point the channel's output signal TPM_CHn is changed (e.g. to zero). CNT continues counting up and eventually matches MOD and overflows. At this point the cycle repeats. The resulting signal's pulse width is proportional to CnV, and the duty cycle is CnV/MOD. Note that the channel's output's starting edge is aligned with the overflow of CNT. If additional channels are enabled, they will all have starting edges at the same time.

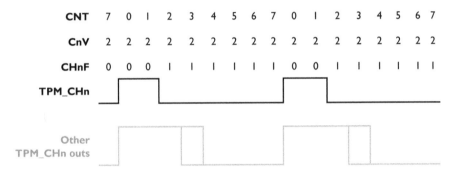

Figure 7.19 TPM operation with edge-aligned PWM.

Figure 7.20 shows an example of center-aligned PWM mode. The TPM counter CNT alternates between counting down and up, so its count period is $2*MOD/f_{count}$.

CNT is initialized to MOD, which also initialized the channel output (e.g. to zero). CNT then counts down and eventually matches CnV, at which time the channel output is toggled (e.g. zero

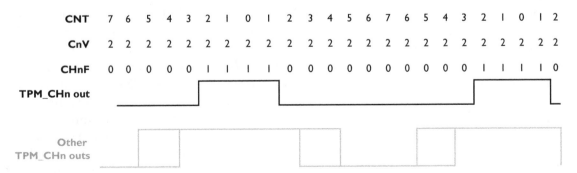

Figure 7.20 TPM operation with center-aligned PWM.

to one). CNT keeps counting and eventually reaches zero, at which point it changes count direction and starts counting up. CNT eventually matches CnV, at which time the channel output is toggled (e.g. one to zero). CNT continues until it reaches MOD, at which point it changes count direction and starts counting down. At this point the cycle repeats. The resulting signal's pulse width is proportional to CnV, and the duty cycle is (2*CnV)/(2*MOD) = CnV/MOD.

Note that each channel's output's signal is centered on the transition of CNT from one to zero. This center alignment is useful for switching circuits that require a time delay (dead time) between deactivating some components and enabling others (e.g. a synchronous buck power converter).

Example: LED Dimming

Let's drive an LED with a PWM output so we can dim it to partial brightness.

Figure 7.21 shows how the Freedom KL25Z board's RGB LED D3 has its cathodes connected to the MCU, with the blue LED connected to pin PTD1. We examine the MCU datasheet to find the signal multiplexing and pin assignments for PTD1 [4]. Pin PTD1 can be connected to TPM0 channel 1 (TPM0_CH1) by setting the MUX to 4. So we will need to use TPM 0 channel 1 to drive the LED.

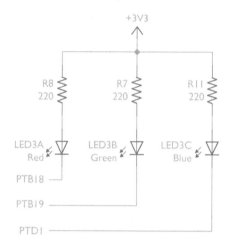

Figure 7.21 Freedom-KL25Z RGB LED connections.

Listing 7.12 shows the code to initialize the TPM to drive the blue LED with a PWM signal. We will use edge-aligned up-counting mode for simplicity. Because the LED will be lit when the output is low, we will configure the channel to generate a low-true output so that setting CnV to zero will turn off the LED. To turn the LED fully on we set CnV to MOD.

The frequency of the generated PWM signal should be at least 50 Hz to prevent visible flickering. Let's pick 500 Hz as the PWM frequency. The TPM input clock frequency of 48 MHz will need to be divided down to 500 Hz, so we need a division factor of 96000. We will use the prescaler to get this value down to no more than 65536, which is the maximum division factor for our 16-bit MOD register. We will need a prescaler factor of at least 96000/65536 = 1.46, so any factor of 2 or more is sufficient. Using the prescaler factor of 2 means the MOD value should be 96000/2 −1 = 48000 − 1 = 47999. We will be able to set the LED to one of 48000 brightness levels.

Note that the larger the prescaler factor, the fewer different PWM values will be available. Using the prescaler factor of 128 means the MOD value should be 96000/128 − 1 = 750 − 1 = 749. We would then be able to set the LED to one of only 750 brightness levels. For some applications this reduced resolution might be a problem.

For this example we do not enable interrupts. However, if we did, they would occur at 500 Hz, which could serve as a useful timing reference for other parts of the program.

```
void Init_Blue_LED_PWM(uint16_t period){
    // Enable clock to PORTD, TPM0
    SIM->SCGC5 |= SIM_SCGC5_PORTD_MASK;;
    SIM->SCGC6 |= SIM_SCGC6_TPM0_MASK;

    // Set pin to FTM
    // Blue FTM0_CH1, Mux Alt 4
    PORTD->PCR[BLUE_LED_POS] &= ~PORT_PCR_MUX_MASK;
    PORTD->PCR[BLUE_LED_POS] |= PORT_PCR_MUX(4);

    // Configure TPM
    // Set clock source for tpm: 48 MHz
    SIM->SOPT2 |= (SIM_SOPT2_TPMSRC(1) | SIM_SOPT2_PLLFLLSEL_MASK);
    // Load the counter and mod
    TPM0->MOD = period-1;
    // Set TPM count direction to up with a divide by 2 prescaler
    TPM0->SC = TPM_SC_PS(1);
    // Continue operation in debug mode
    TPM0->CONF |= TPM_CONF_DBGMODE(3);
    // Set channel 1 to edge-aligned low-true PWM
    TPM0->CONTROLS[1].CnSC = TPM_CnSC_MSB_MASK | TPM_CnSC_ELSA_MASK;
    // Set initial duty cycle
    TPM0->CONTROLS[1].CnV = 0;
    // Start TPM
    TPM0->SC |= TPM_SC_CMOD(1);
}
```

Listing 7.12 Function to initialize TPM0 Channel 1 to drive blue LED.

```
#define PWM_PERIOD (48000)

int main (void) {
    uint16_t i=0;
    volatile int32_t delay;
    Init_Blue_LED_PWM(PWM_PERIOD);
    // Flash forever
    while (1) {
        // Brighten LED
        for (i=0; i<PWM_PERIOD; i++) {
            TPM0->CONTROLS[1].CnV = i;
            for (delay=0; delay<100; delay++)
                ;
        }
        // Dim LED
        for (i=PWM_PERIOD-1; i>0; i--) {
            TPM0->CONTROLS[1].CnV = i;
            for (delay=0; delay<100; delay++)
                ;
        }
    }
}
```

Listing 7.13 Code to gradually brighten and dim the blue LED.

Listing 7.13 shows the main function that first initializes the timer and then adjusts the LED brightness. An infinite loop has two loops embedded within it. The first gradually brightens the LED by increasing the duty cycle, whereas the second gradually dims it by reducing the duty cycle. Note that for this simple example we use a software delay loop that increments a variable. It would be simple to modify this program to use the timer's ISR to adjust the signal's duty cycle, freeing up most of the processor's time for other processing.

Summary

This chapter has introduced three types of timer peripherals, the Cortex-M SysTick timer, the KL25Z COP watchdog timer, and the KL25Z TPM. The SysTick timer has a 24-bit counter and can be used to serve as a time reference, or generate periodic interrupts or a time delay. The COP watchdog timer enables a system to automatically detect and recover from faults or bugs that keep the watchdog from being serviced. The TPM has a 16-bit counter and channels. The TPM core has similar capabilities to the SysTick timer, but is enhanced by multiple channels that can be used in input capture or output generation mode. Input capture mode performs precise timing measurements on digital input signals. Output generation mode generates digital output signals (e.g. with pulse-width modulation) with precise timing.

Exercises

1. Specify how the SysTick control registers must be configured so that the timer generates interrupts with a frequency of 315 Hz, assuming a clock of 48 MHz. What is the actual frequency generated?
2. If the SysTick timer generates interrupts at 19199 Hz and the bus clock frequency is 48 MHz, what value is in the LOAD and CLOCKSOURCE fields?
3. If the SysTick Load register contains 0x00394391 and the CLOCKSOURCE is one, what is the interrupt period?
4. What is the lowest interrupt frequency that the SysTick timer on a KL25Z MCU can generate? Assume the CPU clock is 48 MHz.
5. What is the shortest time-out period available with the COP? Show the register settings needed.
6. What is the longest time-out period available with the COP? Show the register settings needed.
7. Specify how the control registers must be configured so that TPM2 generates interrupts at an approximate frequency of 2017.0101 Hz. What is the actual frequency of interrupts?
8. Specify how the control registers must be configured so that TPM0 channel 3 generates pulses that are high for 150 µs and low for 27 µs, assuming an input clock of 24 MHz. No interrupts are to be generated, but the pulses are to be generated on MCU Port D bit 3. What are the actual high and low times?

9. Specify how the control registers must be configured so that one of the channels in TPM0 measures the delay until the pulse applied to Port A bit 0 changes from one to zero. TPM also must generate an interrupt at that time. Each count in CnV must represent one-third of a microsecond.

10. What is the lowest interrupt frequency that a Timer/PWM module on a KL25Z MCU can generate? Assume the CPU clock is 48 MHz.

References

[1]   *Cortex-M0+ Devices Generic User Guide*, DUI 0662B, r0p1 ed., ARM Ltd., 2012.

[2]   J. Yiu, *The definitive guide to the ARM Cortex-M0 and Cortex-M0+ processors*, 2nd ed., Oxford: Newnes, 2015.

[3]   *KL25 Sub-Family Reference Manual*, KL25P80M48SF0RM, Rev. 3rd ed., NXP Semiconductor, B.V., 2016.

[4]   *Kinetis KL25 Sub-Family Data Sheet*, KL25P80M48SF0, Rev. 5th ed., NXP Semiconductor, B.V., 2016.

[5]   P. Koopman, *Better embedded system software*, Pittsburgh: Drumnadrochit Education LLC, 2010.

[6]   J. Ganssle, *The art of designing embedded systems*, 2nd ed., Elsevier Inc., 2008.

[7]   "MMA8451Q 3-axis, 14-bit/8-bit Digital Accelerometer Data Sheet," NXP Semiconductors, 2016.

8

Serial Communications

Chapter Contents

Overview

Serial communication simplifies the creation of complex embedded systems from separate hardware components. In this chapter we examine the basic ideas of wired serial communication and three common types of protocols: synchronous serial, asynchronous serial, and Inter-Integrated Circuit Bus (I^2C). For each protocol we examine the peripherals and supporting code. We discuss methods to structure the software to handle the lack of timing synchronization between program and communication activity. We also examine tools that simplify the development of systems using such protocols.

> serial
> *Organization in which parts of an item are sequentially available or active, but not simultaneously*

Concepts
Why?

Embedded systems are made of multiple hardware components that must communicate with each other. Why communicate **serially**?

Some of these components are integrated into the MCU. Because they are on a single chip, these components can communicate directly over the system's data bus using their native data type (e.g. bytes, 16-bit half-words, or 32-bit words). These internal buses are called *parallel* because they have a separate wire or signal for each bit of the data type. As a result they can send a data item in a single transaction, resulting in fast transfers.

> parallel
> *Organization in which all parts of item are simultaneously available or active*

Off-chip components are needed for many embedded systems. Using parallel communication to reach these off-chip parts may be fast but has disadvantages that grow as the communication distance or speed increase. First, the packages for the MCU and off-chip components must have a pin (or pad) for each bus signal. For example, a 32-bit bus requires 32 pins for data, multiple pins for addressing, and control lines to signal read or write operations. These large pin counts increase the package size and cost. Second, the printed circuit board (PCB) becomes more complex. A parallel bus has many signals that must be routed in a limited area. High-speed buses require more careful design to ensure signal timing integrity. Third, if the bus must be situated off the PCB, then the connectors and cables must be large enough to provide one connection or wire per signal.

One way to address these challenges is to transmit the data serially rather than in parallel; we send a *symbol* representing one or several bits (rather than all the bits) at a time. For example, sending a 32-bit word eight bits at a time would take four transmissions. Sending an 8-bit byte one bit at a time would take eight transmissions.

> symbol
> *A waveform or state transmitted on a communication channel to represent one or more bits of information*

Serialization reduces the number of pins needed on a chip package, the number of contacts in a connector, and the number of wires in cables. This enables smaller chip packages and connectors, which are less expensive and often significantly lighter. The circuit board design is simplified because there are fewer signals to route. Because of these benefits, most MCUs support serial communication, and there are many compatible components available.

How?

There are many different decisions to make when deciding how to communicate serially between computing systems. The Open System Interconnection (OSI) model from the International Organization for Standardization (ISO) defines seven layers of a communication system [1]. The three lowest layers are relevant for this chapter:[1]

- The **physical** layer (layer 1) specifies how symbols are represented on the communication medium (e.g. wire) as voltages or currents.
- The **data link** layer (layer 2) has two parts. The **media access control** determines when a node can transmit, defining how time on the bus is shared. The **logical link control** determines how the receiver identifies the start and end of a message from a stream of symbols on the physical layer. It also defines how errors are detected.
- The **network** layer (layer 3) defines how to address nodes, split up long data to fit into multiple messages, and handle errors, and other characteristics.

With this context, we can now examine the fundamental concepts of serial communication.

Serialization

Serialization is the conversion of data from a parallel to a serial format, whereas *deserialization* is the reverse. Each MCU and serial peripheral has internal shift registers to perform this. The serialized information is a stream of symbols that represent the data and control information. The communication protocols examined here can store one bit of data per symbol, but other examples improve speed by encoding multiple data or control bits in a single symbol. The rate at which the symbols are transmitted is called the *baud rate*.

> Serialization
> *The process of converting information from parallel to serial form*

> deserialization
> *Conversion of information from serial to parallel form*

> baud rate
> *Rate at which communication symbols are transmitted. Also called symbol rate.*

---

[1] The upper layers of the OSI model (**transport, session, presentation, application**) deal with higher level issues such as reliable communication and security.

A transmitting device uses a parallel-in-serial-out shift register that is first loaded with data from a multibit parallel input bus. To serialize the parallel data, a clock circuit applies a series of pulses to shift the data one bit position at a time and stream out the serial output.

A receiving device uses a serial-in-parallel-out shift register. To deserialize the serial data, a clock circuit applies a series of pulses to load the shift register one bit at a time from the serial input. After all bits of the shift register are loaded, the data can be read from the parallel output bus.

Symbol Timing

In order for the deserialization to work reliably, the receiver's clock pulses need to be applied at the right times. The serial data line must be sampled once per symbol (at the baud rate). This sampling should be at the middle of the symbol time in order to avoid signal transitions, where the signal may be corrupted due to noise or slow circuits.

With a *synchronous* approach the transmitter's clock signal is connected directly to the receiver's clock input. This approach is reliable but requires three signal connections: clock, data, and ground.

> synchronous
> *Activities which are synchronized with each other, or a protocol which sends clocking information*

With an *asynchronous* approach, the transmitter provides no clock signal. Instead, the receiver has a clock running at the same frequency as the transmitter that determines **when** to sample the signal line to capture each symbol.

> asynchronous
> *Activities that are not synchronized with each other, or a protocol that does not send clocking information*

Message Framing

How does the asynchronous receiver synchronize its clock with the transmitter's clock if there is no connection? This is done by adding a *framing symbol* to indicate the start of the message. The receiver clock starts running when it detects the framing symbol (such as a **start bit**) and then samples the input in the middle of each following symbol time. A framing symbol may also be used to indicate the end of a message (e.g. a **stop bit** or a **stop symbol**).

> framing symbol
> *Symbol used to indicate start or end of message*

Error Detection

Communication links are vulnerable to noise if they are long or poorly shielded. Some communication protocols add information to each message to detect transmission errors. Common error detection methods are **parity bits**, **checksums**, and **cyclic redundancy checks** [2]. With some protocols, there is a dedicated receive error notification bit in each message, allowing a receiver to notify the transmitter (and all other receivers) that the message was received incorrectly.

Acknowledgments

Some protocols include an *acknowledgment* field within each message, allowing a receiver to signal successful message reception. Other protocols may use a separate acknowledgment message, or nothing at all.

> acknowledgment
> *Device response indicating successful reception of message*

Media Access Control

If there are multiple possible transmitters on a single communication bus, then the transmitters need to follow a set of rules to share the time on the bus. These rules are called a *media access control (MAC)* method, and determine when a device can transmit. A master/slave MAC designates one device as the master. A slave can transmit only if it has been given permission by the transmitter. Other MACs use arbitration, token-passing, or other methods.

> media access control (MAC)
> *Rules controlling when a node can transmit a message on shared media*

Addressing

If there are multiple possible receivers on a single communication bus, then the transmitter may need to specify which receiver is the target of the communication. This information can be sent on separate select signals, or it may be included in the message itself.

Development Tools

There are several tools that will make it easier to develop embedded systems that use serial communication protocols. The most basic tool is an **oscilloscope**, which shows a signal's voltage over time. The developer needs to interpret the signals to determine the communication activity. The encoded data and precise timing relationships of serial communication can make it difficult to debug embedded systems. For example, what do the signals in Figure 8.1 mean?

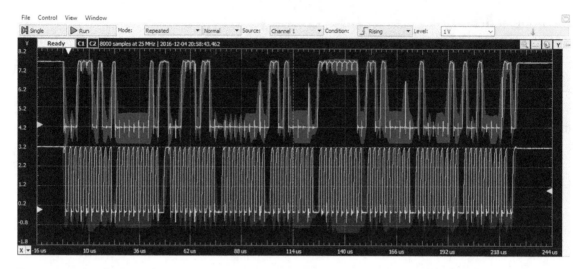

Figure 8.1 Oscilloscope shows voltage levels of signals over time.

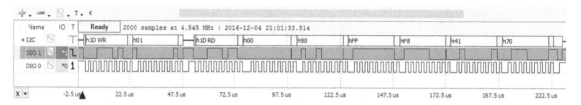

Figure 8.2 Logic analyzer interprets bus signals and displays message information.

Manual interpretation is often slow, tedious, and error-prone, so a much better tool is a **logic analyzer** with a **protocol decoder**. This tool interprets the signals automatically and displays them in an easily understood readable format.

Figure 8.2 shows the previous waveforms and their meaning when decoded according to the I²C communication protocol. First there is a write to device 1D of the value 01. Second there is a read from device 1D of 6 data bytes (00, 90, FF, F8, 41, and 70). Note that this program shows hexadecimal values with a prefix of **h**, whereas the C language uses a prefix of **0x**. The values are the same regardless of the prefix.

A logic analyzer may also save the received data for further analysis or processing. The developer typically needs to configure the protocol decoder to match the protocol in use, for example, setting the data rate or identifying a clock signal. Some oscilloscopes may also include logic analyzers and protocol decoders.

There are PC-based oscilloscopes and logic analyzers available, which are often less expensive than stand-alone devices. The Analog Discovery 2 from Digilent, Inc. is shown in Figure 8.3 and can serve as a logic analyzer, oscilloscope, waveform generator, and many other types of test equipment [3]. It offers a 16-input logic analyzer with support for various serial communication protocols. The PC-based software provides the graphical interface seen in Figure 8.1 and Figure 8.2.

Another useful tool is a PC-based bus interface, which allows a developer's PC to send and receive messages on the bus. One example is the Bus Pirate, which connects to the PC

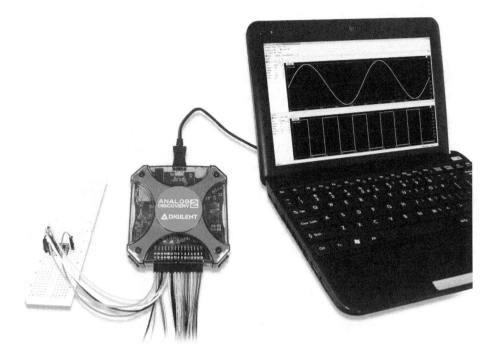

Figure 8.3 Multifunction device serves as 2-channel oscilloscope, 16-channel logic analyzer, and other tools. User interface program runs on a PC with USB connection. Image courtesy Digilent, Inc.

with a virtual serial port over USB [4]. The developer uses a terminal emulator program on the PC to control the Bus Pirate through a serial console interface. The Bus Pirate has many features: support for various serial communication protocols, scripting, and the ability to program flash memory and MCUs. It also offers switchable power supplies, ADC input, and PWM output.

Software Structures for Communication

Communications make it harder to share the CPU for two reasons. First, we don't know **which** program instruction will be executing when data is received. The program and the data reception are asynchronous. This means there is no timing relationship between the program's progress and data reception. Second, it takes a significant amount of time to send one data item. In this time, the program can execute many instructions, so it is not clear at **which** program instruction the transmitter will be ready to send another data item.[2] So we consider transmission to be asynchronous as well.

---

[2] Technically they are synchronous, but in a system with even minor complexity identifying the specific instruction(s) requires extensive (and impractical) program timing analysis each time the program is built. And there will be multiple instructions if there are multiple control flow paths.

Supporting Asynchronous Communication

We would like to create a timing relationship between the program and communication events. One approach is to use polling. For example, the program could spin in a loop until data has been received. Although simple, polling makes the CPU harder to share, as discussed in Chapter 3.

Another approach is to use interrupts, providing event-triggered processing. Every time the peripheral receives a data item, the peripheral will signal an interrupt and the CPU will run an ISR to get it. Every time the peripheral is ready to send an item, it will signal an interrupt and the CPU will run an ISR to start transmitting the next data item. The ISR may also execute a **callback** function (e.g. when all requested data items have been received).

We will split the work between the ISRs and the program's tasks to provide good responsiveness and to simplify scaling up the program later as we add other features. Recall that the longer an ISR takes to run, the longer all other ISRs can be delayed. To reduce these delays, the ISR will perform the most time-critical operations with the data and leave other processing for lower-priority code (e.g. task code). To do this we must somehow store data between the ISRs and the rest of the program.

This stored data will flow from the producer, which generates the data, to the consumer, which uses the data. For transmission, the producer is the task that creates the data to send, whereas the consumer is the transmit ISR that loads the peripheral's transmit data buffer. For reception, the producer is the receive ISR that reads the peripheral's received data buffer, whereas the consumer is the task that uses that data.

We will use a data buffer to hold the producer's output data until it is read by the consumer. In most cases we want the data to be delivered to the consumer in the order it was produced, using a first-in, first-out (FIFO) ordering. A **queue** is another name for a buffer with FIFO ordering. To **enqueue** an item is to add it to the queue. To **dequeue** an item is to remove it from the queue.

As communication systems typically provide both transmission and reception, we will need a queue for each direction. Figure 8.4 shows typical hardware and software components used for queued, interrupt-driven communication. At the left, the serial communication peripheral interfaces with the communication bus signals. It generates an interrupt after receiving a data item or when it is ready to transmit another.

Figure 8.5 shows the case where the peripheral is ready to transmit. The transmit ISR will dequeue the next data item from the transmit data queue and place it in the peripheral for transmission. A task enqueues data the transmit data.

Figure 8.6 shows the case where the peripheral has received data. The receiver ISR will read the data from the peripheral and enqueue it into the received data queue. A task will later dequeue the received data and use it.

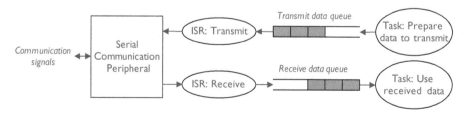

Figure 8.4   Software structure for interrupt-driven queued communication.

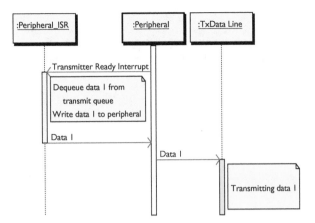

Figure 8.5 Sequence of activities for data transmission.

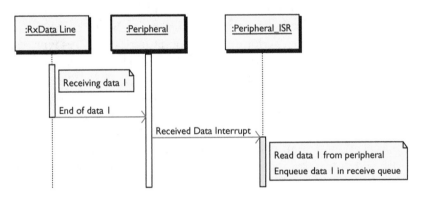

Figure 8.6 Sequence of activities for data reception.

Queue Implementation

We will create a queue data structure to hold data before the receiving code can process it. There are various ways to implement a queue, but the approach we use here is efficient and simple.

The data is stored in an array, as shown in Figure 8.7. Rather than move all of the data each time an item is added or removed, we will use indexes to keep track of the head and tail. The head indicates the oldest data element, which will be read in the next dequeue operation. The tail indicates the free space to use when enqueueing the next element.

```
#define Q_MAX_SIZE (256)
typedef struct {
    uint8_t Data[Q_MAX_SIZE];
    unsigned int Head;    // Index of oldest data element
    unsigned int Tail;    // Index of next free space
    unsigned int Size;    // Number of elements in use
} volatile Q_T;
```

Listing 8.1 Data structure definition for queue.

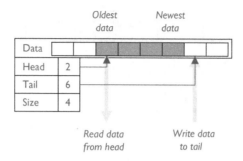

Figure 8.7 Queue data structure contains array to hold data, indexes for head and tail, and used size information.

The data structure definition for the queue is shown in Listing 8.1. Note that the entire data structure is defined as being volatile because it will be shared between ISRs and regular code. This will prevent the compiler from performing risky optimizations on this type of data structure. Instead, the compiler will generate code that forces the CPU to load the data values from memory each time the source code references the data.

How many elements should the queue be able to hold? In this example, up to 256 elements can be held, as defined by Q_MAX_SIZE. The correct value depends on how often an item may be enqueued, how long a delay can occur before the first item is dequeued, and how often subsequent items can be dequeued. We use a size field variable to track the number of elements currently in use. Note that we could instead calculate this value from the difference between the head and tail indices.

```c
int Q_Enqueue(Q_T * q, uint8_t d) {
    uint32_t masking_state;
    // If queue is full, don't overwrite data, but do return an error code
    if (!Q_Full(q)) {
        q->Data[q->Tail++] = d;
        q->Tail %= Q_MAX_SIZE;

        // protect q->Size++ operation from preemption
        // save current masking state
        masking_state = __get_PRIMASK();
        // disable interrupts
        __disable_irq();
        // update variable
        q->Size++;
        // restore interrupt masking state
        __set_PRIMASK(masking_state);
        return 1; // success
    } else
        return 0; // failure
}
uint8_t Q_Dequeue(Q_T * q) {
    uint32_t masking_state;
```

```
    uint8_t t=0;
    // Check to see if queue is empty before dequeueing
    if (!Q_Empty(q)) {
            t = q->Data[q->Head];
            q->Data[q->Head++] = '_'; // empty unused entries for debugging
            q->Head %= Q_MAX_SIZE;

            // protect q->Size-- operation from preemption
            // save current masking state
            masking_state = __get_PRIMASK();
            // disable interrupts
            __disable_irq();
            // update variable
            q->Size--;
            // restore interrupt masking state
            __set_PRIMASK(masking_state);
    }
    return t;
}
```

Listing 8.2 Functions for enqueueing and dequeueing data.

The enqueue and dequeue operations are shown in Listing 8.2. Adding an element to the queue will update the tail, whereas removing an element will update the head. The update operations are simply increments that are wrapped around to zero when the end of the array is reached. This type of implementation is called a ring buffer. Making the number of array elements a power of two will simplify the wrapping operation to simply masking off bits (e.g. with a bitwise and operation). Otherwise the modulus (remainder) operation will need to be performed, which is likely to be computationally expensive.

This queue is expected to share data between multiple threads with preemption due to interrupts. This introduces the risk of data corruption due to non-atomic access to the queue fields. As discussed in Chapter 3, for an ARM Cortex-M (or any other load/store architecture) processor to modify a variable stored in memory, that variable must be loaded from memory into a register first. The register can then be modified and stored back to memory. This sequence of code is a critical section that is vulnerable to corruption based on timing. Consider the case where a function has called Q_Dequeue. The Size field has a value of N, and is loaded from memory into a register to be decremented to $N-1$. Before the new value is stored to memory, another character arrives, causing the CPU to preempt Q_Dequeue and execute the ISR. The ISR calls Q_Enqueue, which loads N (the old value of Size) from memory into a register, increments it to $N+1$, and stores it to memory. Q_Enqueue completes, the ISR completes, and Q_Dequeue resumes executing, storing the value $N-1$ to memory. Size is now wrong: it should be N, but is $N-1$.

We protect the critical section of the code by disabling interrupts during its execution. To do this, our code first saves the current interrupt masking state using __get_PRIMASK, and then disables interrupts using __disable_irq. After executing the critical section, the code restores the previous interrupt masking state using __set_PRIMASK. These functions are defined in CMSIS-CORE.

Further examination would show that none of the other fields in the Q_T structure is vulnerable to Q_Enqueue preempting Q_Dequeue, or Q_Dequeue preempting Q_Enqueue. However, if we allow Q_Enqueue to preempt Q_Enqueue, the operations on Tail and Data become critical sections and must be protected. Similarly, allowing Q_Dequeue to preempt Q_Dequeue makes the operations on Head and Data critical sections that must be protected.

```
void Q_Init(Q_T * q) {
    unsigned int i;
    for (i=0; i<Q_MAX_SIZE; i++)
        q->Data[i] = 0; // To simplify our lives when debugging
    q->Head = 0;
    q->Tail = 0;
    q->Size = 0;
}
int Q_Empty(Q_T * q) {
    return q->Size == 0;
}
int Q_Full(Q_T * q) {
    return q->Size == Q_MAX_SIZE;
}
int Q_Size(Q_T * q) {
    return q->Size;
}
```

Listing 8.3 Functions for queue initialization and status checks.

Finally, the code for initialization and status checks is shown in Listing 8.3.

Queue Use

In order to use the queue, we need to decide whether we want our code to block and wait for data to be available (for dequeueing) or space to be available (for enqueueing). If our code should not block, then we will simply test the condition to determine whether to perform the queue operation. If the condition is true, then the code continues with the queue operation. If the condition is not true, then the code needs to defer this work for later. The actual approach will depend on the specifics of the application.

If our code should block, then we use a loop to wait for the appropriate condition to become true before performing the queue operation. Note that this blocking operation does not share the processor. When using a finite state machine to allow other code to run, this test code should be a separate state. If the condition is not true yet, the state should end and be repeated on the next call. If the condition is true, the code can continue with the queue operation and then advance to the next state. When using a task scheduler, if the condition is not true, the code should yield the processor briefly to other tasks.

Operations that might block should not be performed in interrupt handlers because they can introduce sporadic timing delays that are difficult to repeat and therefore debug. Instead, the handler should be prepared to discard the data (or handle it in some other way) and signal an error to the rest of the application.

Serial Communication Protocols and Peripherals

We can now examine three types of serial communication protocols and the corresponding peripherals. We start with a basic approach (synchronous serial), then advance to asynchronous serial and finish with I²C, which offers addressing and other higher-level features.

Synchronous Serial Communication

Protocol Concepts

Serial peripheral interface (SPI) is a type of synchronous serial communication with a master and one or more slaves (Figure 8.8). Typically the MCU is the master and peripheral devices are slaves. Some common slave SPI devices are ADCs, accelerometers, LCD controllers, and magnetometers. An MCU might instead be configured to operate as a slave, for example, to create a smart MCU-based peripheral subsystem in a larger system with a different MCU serving as the master.

SPI communication between a master and slaves uses three signals (clock and two data signals), a select signal for each slave and ground.

- The clock signal (SPSCK or SCK) indicates when data is to be sampled.
- The MOSI data signal is the master output and slave input.
- The MISO data signal is the master input and slave output.
- The master asserts the select line of the slave targeted for communication. This signal is typically active-low.

If bidirectional communication between the master and slaves is not needed, only one data line is needed (MOSI or MISO), depending on data transfer direction.

Communication

Figure 8.9 shows an example of communication between a master and a slave. The master selects a particular slave by asserting its slave select line. The master asserts the clock signal to indicate when its data output signal (MOSI) is valid and should be sampled by the slave. At the same time, the master can receive data from the slave on the MISO signal (not shown in the figure). Each clock pulse exchanges one bit between the shift registers of the master and the slave. For byte SPI transmissions, one byte is exchanged with every eight clock pulses. After the last new bit is shifted in, the receiver sets a status flag indicating completed reception. It may also generate an interrupt request. Finally, the slave select line can be released, though in some cases it is not, as described in further sections.

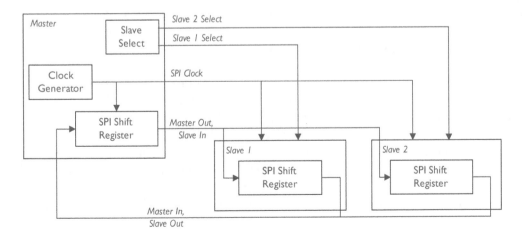

Figure 8.8 Overview of SPI system with master and two slave devices.

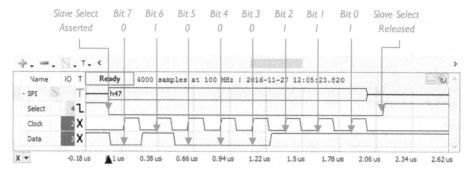

Figure 8.9 Master sending data 0x47 (01000111) to slave. Data is valid on the rising edge of the clock signal.

Clock Phase and Polarity

There are four different versions of SPI, based on the relationship between the clock and the data. Different peripherals may use different versions of SPI, so it is important to select the correct version. The clock polarity determines whether the clock signal is active-high or active-low.

The clock phase determines when the slave starts transmitting valid data on the MISO signal. In one case, the slave and master both transmit valid data when slave select is asserted. The first clock edge from inactive to active indicates the middle of the bit time, causing the master to sample MISO and the slave to sample MOSI. The next clock edge (from active to inactive) advances the shift registers. The slave select signal can remain active between transfers.

In the other case, data is not transmitted on MOSI or MISO until the inactive-to-active clock edge. It is sampled on the active-to-inactive clock edge. In addition, the slave select signal needs to go inactive between transfers.

KL25Z SPI Peripherals

The KL25Z128 microcontroller has two identical SPI peripherals, called SPI0 and SPI1. Each has the structure shown in Figure 8.10, with the SPI shift register at the core. Data to transmit is placed in the transmit buffer, and received data is read from the receive buffer. When the peripheral operates in the master mode, the shift register is clocked by the clock generator module.

The SPIx_C1 control register, shown in Figure 8.11, configures various aspects of the peripheral.

- MSTR selects whether the SPI module acts as a master (one) or slave (zero).
- LSBFE controls which data bit is transmitted first: the LSB (one) or the MSB (zero).
- CPOL and CPHA define clock polarity and phase. A CPOL value of zero selects an active-high clock, whereas one selects an active-low clock. A CPHA value of zero indicates valid data is transmitted starting with the slave select signal, so data can be sampled on the first clock edge (inactive to active). A value of one causes data to be sampled on the second clock edge (active to inactive).
- If the SSOE bit is one, then the SS pin will be asserted automatically during transmission.

The SPIx_C2 register controls other features such as DMA and operation in low-power, bidirectional, and stop modes. Please refer to Chapter 37 in the reference manual for further details [5].

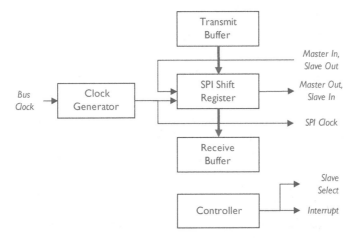

Figure 8.10 The KL25Z SPI peripheral structure is built around the SPI shift register.

7	6	5	4	3	2	1	0
SPIE	SPE	SPTIE	MSTR	CPOL	CPHA	SSOE	LSBFE

Figure 8.11 SPIx_C1 control register configures peripheral.

7	6	5	4	3	2	1	0
0	SPRR[2:0]			SPR[3:0]			

Figure 8.12 SPIx_BR register controls the baud rate of communication for master.

The SPIx_D register is used to access both the transmit buffer and the receive buffer. A write-to SPIx_D writes to the transmit buffer whereas a read of SPIx_D reads from the receive buffer.

To use an SPI peripheral, first enable its clock in the system integration module (SIM) register SIM_SCGC4 and then set the SPI system enable (SPE) bit in SPIx_C1.

Transmitter Baud Rate Generator

The master sets the rate at which data bits are shifted across the MOSI and MISO signals (Figure 8.12). The master's baud rate is derived by prescaling the bus clock by a factor of 1–8 and then dividing it by a factor of 2^1–2^9 (i.e. 2, 4, 8, 16, ... , 256, 512). The prescaler factor is determined by the SPPR field of SPIx_BR and is SPPR+1. The division factor is set by SPR in SPIx_BR, and is 2^{SPR+1}. The resulting baud rate is:

$$\text{Baud Rate} = \frac{f_{\text{BusClock}}}{(SPPR+1) \times 2^{SPR+1}}$$

Status and Interrupts

The SPI peripheral indicates events using status flags and interrupts (Figure 8.13). The SPIx_S register holds four status flags.

7	6	5	4	3	2	1	0
SPRF	SPMF	SPTEF	MODF		0		

Figure 8.13 SPIx_S status register indicates which SPI events have occurred.

- The SPTEF bit will be set if the SPIx transmit buffer is empty, indicating the transmit buffer can be loaded with new data. It is cleared by hardware automatically by the sequence of the code reading SPIx_S (when SPTEF is one) and then writing to SPIx_D.
- The SPRF bit will be set at the end of an SPI transfer when the SPIx receive buffer is full. It is cleared by hardware automatically by the sequence of the code reading SPIx_S (when SPRF is one) and then reading SPIx_D.
- The SPMF bit indicates that received data matches the contents of the SPIx_M register.
- The MODF bit indicates a mode fault, in which multiple masters attempt to drive the SPI clock and MOSI signals.

The SPI module can generate an interrupt request under certain conditions. Two important conditions are:

- If SPI transmit interrupt enable (SPTIE) is one, then an interrupt will generated when SPTEF is set.
- If SPIE is one, then an interrupt will be generated when SPRF is set.

Transmission/Reception Activity

Listing 8.4 shows the basic software to transmit and receive SPI data using polling. Before it can transmit, the MCU must first wait until the transmitter buffer is empty, which is indicated by the SPTEF flag. The MCU can then write the byte to the SPI data register. This write triggers the simultaneous transmission and reception of bytes to MOSI and from MISO and also clears the SPTEF flag. When the entire byte has been received, the receiver buffer is marked full, indicated by the SPRF flag. The MCU can then read the received data from the SPI data register, which also clears the SPRF flag.

```
while(!(SPI1->S & SPI_S_SPTEF_MASK))
    ; //Wait for transmit buffer empty
SPI1->D = d_out;

while (!(SPI1->S & SPI_S_SPRF_MASK))
    ; // wait for receive buffer full
d_in = SPI1->D;
```

Listing 8.4 Code to transmit and receive one byte with SPI using polling.

Interrupts can be used to improve system responsiveness. Recall that data is loaded into the transmit buffer by writing to SPIx_D, which in turn starts simultaneous data transmission and reception. When the byte exchange is complete, the receive buffer is full, setting the SPRF flag and triggering an interrupt. The SPI ISR reads the received data from SPIx_D and can load a new byte to transmit.

If even faster transmission is needed, the communication can be accelerated by using the transmit buffer empty flag (SPTEF) to trigger an interrupt. SPTEF is set when the transmit buffer is empty and ready to accept new data. This happens as soon as the transmit buffer is copied into the SPI shift register. The ISR needs to check the flags to determine which flag is set. If SPTEF is set, the ISR can load the new data into the transmit buffer immediately. The shift register is starting to receive the new data on the MISO signal, so that data is not available yet. However, if SPRF is set, then the data received from the previous transmission can be read from SPIx_D.

Other Features

There are several other features available that we do not cover here. For example, the peripheral can generate an interrupt if the received data matches the value in the SPIx_M (match) register. This is useful for creating a slave device that recognizes a specific address. There is a low-power mode that can operate even if the rest of the MCU is in sleep mode.

Example: SPI Loopback Test

We can examine the basic SPI communication with a loopback test. We will connect the output data signal MOSI to the input data signal MISO. The program will then transfer a data byte. If the received data matches the transmitted data, the program will light the green LED. Otherwise the red LED will be lit.

```c
void Init_SPI1(void) {
    // enable clock to SPI1
    SIM->SCGC4 |= SIM_SCGC4_SPI1_MASK;
    SIM->SCGC5 |= SIM_SCGC5_PORTE_MASK;

    // disable SPI1 to allow configuration
    SPI1->C1 &= ~SPI_C1_SPE_MASK;

    // set PTE2 as SPI1_SCK -- ALT2
    PORTE->PCR[2] &= ~PORT_PCR_MUX_MASK;
    PORTE->PCR[2] |= PORT_PCR_MUX(2);
    // set PTE3 as SPI1_MOSI -- ALT5
    PORTE->PCR[3] &= ~PORT_PCR_MUX_MASK;
    PORTE->PCR[3] |= PORT_PCR_MUX(5);
    // set PTE1 as SPI1_MISO -- ALT5
    PORTE->PCR[1] &= ~PORT_PCR_MUX_MASK;
    PORTE->PCR[1] |= PORT_PCR_MUX(5);
    // set PTE4 as SPI1_PCS0 -- ALT2
    PORTE->PCR[4] &= ~PORT_PCR_MUX_MASK;
    PORTE->PCR[4] |= PORT_PCR_MUX(2);

    // Select master mode, enable SS output
    SPI1->C1 = SPI_C1_MSTR_MASK | SPI_C1_SSOE_MASK;
    SPI1->C2 = SPI_C2_MODFEN_MASK;
    // Select active high clock, first edge sample
    SPI1->C1 &= ~SPI_C1_CPHA_MASK;
    SPI1->C1 &= ~SPI_C1_CPOL_MASK;
```

```
    // BaudRate = BusClock / ((SPPR+1)*2^(SPR+1))
    SPI1->BR = SPI_BR_SPPR(2) | SPI_BR_SPR(1);

    // enable SPI1
    SPI1->C1 |= SPI_C1_SPE_MASK;
}
```

Listing 8.5 Code to initialize SPI1 peripheral.

The initialization code in Listing 8.5 configures the SPI1 peripheral and connects its signals to MCU pins (SCK: PTE2, MISO: PTE1, MOSI: PTE3, CS0: PTE5). The baud rate is set to 48 MHz/(3×2^2) = 48 MHz/12 = 4 MHz, or 250 ns per bit. Interrupts are not used. Be sure to connect MOSI (PTE3) and MISO (PTE1) for this test.

```
uint8_t Test_SPIsend(uint8_t d_out)
{
    while(!(SPI1->S & SPI_S_SPTEF_MASK))
      ; //Wait for transmit buffer empty
    SPI1->D = d_out;

    while (!(SPI1->S & SPI_S_SPRF_MASK))
      ; // wait for receive buffer full
    return SPI1->D;
}
```

Listing 8.6 Code to send and receive one byte with SPI1 with polling.

The function test_SPI_Loopback performs SPI communication with polling, as shown in Listing 8.6. The function first waits until the transmitter buffer is empty (indicated by the SPTEF flag). At that point the output data d_out is written to the SPI data register. The code then waits until the receiver buffer is full (indicated by the SPRF flag). The code reads the received data from the SPI data register and returns it to the calling function.

```
void Test_SPI_Loopback(void) {
    uint8_t out='A', in;
    while (1) {
        in = Test_SPIsend(out);
        if (in != out) {
            // Red: error, data doesn't match
            Control_RGB_LEDs(1, 0, 0);
        } else {
            // Green: data matches
            Control_RGB_LEDs(0, 1, 0);
        }
    }
    out++;
    if (out > 'z')
        out = 'A';
    }
}
```

Listing 8.7 Code to test SPI transmission and reception.

The main function initializes SPI1 and the GPIO ports for the LEDs, after which it calls the test code in Listing 8.7. This repeatedly sends out a character and lights the LED based on whether the received and transmitted values match.

Asynchronous Serial Communication

Protocol Concepts

Asynchronous serial communication works without a dedicated clock signal. Instead, both the transmitter and receiver have clock generators that must be configured to run at the same speed. The generic name for a peripheral that supports this is *universal asynchronous receiver/transmitter (UART)*.

> universal asynchronous receiver/transmitter (UART)
> *Peripheral for asynchronous serial communications*

Asynchronous communication typically allows transmission and reception to occur independently. This is different from SPI, where both the master and slave transmit and receive simultaneously. A UART contains separate hardware for the transmitter and receiver.

Start (0)	D0	DI	D2	D3	D4	D5	D6	D7	Parity	Stop (I)

Figure 8.14   Contents of asynchronous serial communication message.

A general UART message is shown in Figure 8.14 and contains these fields:

- Because there is no clock signal, the message includes a start bit (a logic zero) to synchronize the receiver's clock to the incoming message and start message reception.
- The data field of the message is typically 8 bits, but other sizes may also be supported. Data may be sent LSB first or MSB first.
- Parity helps detect errors in data transmission and can be enabled on UARTs. The parity of a message is determined by the total number N of one bits in the data character and the parity bit. If N is even, then the message has even parity. If N is odd, then the message has odd parity. The UARTs of the transmitter and receiver are configured to expect each received message to have the correct parity (e.g. odd). When parity is enabled, the transmitter computes the parity of the data and then adjusts the parity bit to one or zero to match the specified communication parity (e.g. odd). The receiver calculates the parity of the received data and parity bit, and verifies it matches the expected parity (e.g. odd). If it does not (e.g. there were an even number of ones received in the message), then the UART signals a parity error for the software to handle.
- One or more stop bits with a value of logic one are added to help the receiver detect timing errors. If a zero is received for any stop bit, then the receiver will indicate an error so the software reacts appropriately.

The UART hardware is more complex than the SPI hardware, with the addition of the hardware for the receiver clock generator, framing, and parity.

Figure 8.15 shows a sequence of three bytes ("1_2") transmitted by a UART.

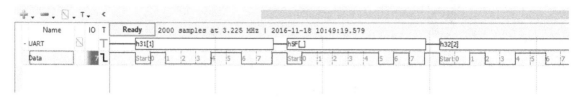

Figure 8.15 Example of serial data ("1_ 2") captured by logic analyzer.

KL25Z UART Peripherals

The KL25Z128 microcontroller has three UART peripherals. Here we cover UART0, which is similar to the other UART peripherals but has more features.

The UART contains a baud rate generator, a transmitter, and a receiver. The baud rate generator divides down an input clock signal to a lower frequency for UART communication. The transmitter uses a shift register to convert the input data (from UARTx_D), framing bits and optional parity information into a serial stream of bits. The receiver uses a similar shift register to convert the serial bit stream into a set of parallel bits. An edge detection circuit is used to identify the start bit and start shifting data in at the correct time. Error detection circuitry identifies framing, parity, and other errors.

The following fields in UART0_C1 (shown in Figure 8.16) are frequently used:

- The M field determines whether data is eight bits long (zero) or nine bits long (one).
- When one, PE field enables parity generation and checking.
- When parity is enabled (PE = 1), the PT field selects even parity (zero) or odd parity (one).

The following fields in UART0_C2 (Figure 8.17) are frequently used:

- TIE, TCIE, RIE, and ILIE control whether certain events trigger interrupts, and are discussed in subsequent pages.
- The transmitter and receiver can be enabled or disabled with TE and RE fields. They must be disabled to access some control registers.

The following fields in UART0_C3 (Figure 8.18) are frequently used:

7	6	5	4	3	2	1	0
LOOPS	DOZEEN	RSRC	M	WAKE	ILT	PE	PT

Figure 8.16 Contents of UART0_ C1 control register.

7	6	5	4	3	2	1	0
TIE	TCIE	RIE	ILIE	TE	RE	RWU	SBK

Figure 8.17 Contents of UART0_ C2 control register.

7	6	5	4	3	2	1	0
R8T9	R9T8	TXDIR	TXINV	ORIE	NEIE	FEIE	PEIE

Figure 8.18 Contents of UART0_C3 control register.

- ORIE, NEIE, FEIE, and PEIE control whether certain errors trigger interrupts, and are discussed in further pages.

The UARTx_D register is used to access both the transmit buffer and the receive buffer. A write-to UARTx_D writes to the transmit buffer whereas a read-from UARTx_D reads from the receive buffer.

Baud Rate Generator

Each UART has a clock that determines the baud rate for the transmitter and the receiver. The bus clock (e.g. 24 MHz) is divided by a 13-bit value from SBR to determine the oversampling clock frequency, which is then divided by the oversampling factor to set the actual baud rate for communication.

The SBR value is split across two registers: BDH holds the upper five bits of SBR and BDL holds the lower eight bits. The oversampling rate can be set to any value N between 4 and 32 by writing N-1 to the OSR field. A 16x oversampling rate is the default. The resulting baud rate is:

$$\text{Baud Rate} = \frac{f_{\text{BusClock}}}{\text{SBR} \times (\text{OSR} + 1)}$$

Status and Interrupts

The UART peripheral indicates when events have occurred using status flags and interrupts. The UART0_S1 (Figure 8.19) status register holds the following flags for transmission:

- The TDRE flag indicates when the transmit data buffer has room to accept another character (via UART_D).
- The TC flag indicates when transmission is complete.

UART0_S1 holds the following flags for reception:

- The RDRF flag indicates there is data to read from the receive buffer (via UART_D).
- The IDLE flag indicates the receive data line is idle.

7	6	5	4	3	2	1	0
TDRE	TC	RDRF	IDLE	OR	NF	FE	PE

Figure 8.19 Contents of UART0_ S1 status register.

UART0_S1 holds the following flags for errors:

- The PF flag indicates a parity error was detected during reception.
- The FE flag indicates a framing error was detected during reception.
- The OR flag indicates that the receive buffer's data was not read before new data was received.
- The NF flag indicates noise was detected by the receiver. This can occur when oversampling is enabled, in which the receiver samples each bit multiple times.

7	6	5	4	3	2	1	0
LBKDIF	RXEDGIF	MSBF	RXINV	RWUID	BRK13	LBDKDE	RAF

Figure 8.20 Contents of UART0_S2 status register.

The following fields in UART0_S2 (Figure 8.20) are frequently used:

- MSBF determines if data is transmitted MSB first (one) or LSB first (zero).
- When set to one, RXINV inverts received data.

A UART can generate an interrupt in response to these three types of events if the appropriate interrupt enable bits are set.

- Transmit events: Setting TIE to one enables interrupts when the transmit data register is empty (TDRE is one). TCIE enables interrupts when transmission is complete (TC is one).
- Receive events: Setting RIE to one enables interrupts when the receive data register is full (RDRF is one). Other receive events are possible as well, but are not discussed further here.
- Error events: Setting ORIE, NEIE, FEIE, PEIE to one enables interrupts when the corresponding error flag is set:

Other Features

There are many other features available that we do not cover here, such as single-wire mode, loop mode, transmit data inversion, communication protocol support, wake-up on idle line, address mark or match address. Further information is available in the reference manual [5].

Example: Communicating with a PC

Let's see how to use asynchronous serial communication between the KL25Z MCU and a terminal program on a PC. The FRDM-KL25Z development board connects the target MCU's UART0 with a UART in the OpenSDA debug MCU, as shown in Figure 8.21. The debug MCU provides a virtual serial port service over its USB connection with the PC. The OpenSDA MCU's UART is configured to run at 115,200 baud, with no parity and one stop bit.

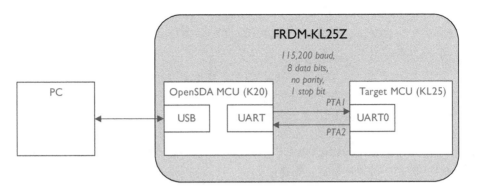

Figure 8.21   OpenSDA MCU provides a virtual serial port between PC and target MCU's UART0.

```
#define UART_OVERSAMPLE_RATE   (16)
#define SYS_CLOCK          (48e6)

void Init_UART0(uint32_t baud_rate) {
    uint16_t sbr;

    // Enable clock gating for UART0 and Port A
    SIM->SCGC4 |= SIM_SCGC4_UART0_MASK;
    SIM->SCGC5 |= SIM_SCGC5_PORTA_MASK;

    // Make sure transmitter and receiver are disabled before init
    UART0->C2 &= ~UART0_C2_TE_MASK & ~UART0_C2_RE_MASK;

    // Set UART clock to 48 MHz clock
    SIM->SOPT2 |= SIM_SOPT2_UART0SRC(1);
    SIM->SOPT2 |= SIM_SOPT2_PLLFLLSEL_MASK;

    // Set pins to UART0 Rx and Tx
    PORTA->PCR[1] = PORT_PCR_ISF_MASK | PORT_PCR_MUX(2); // Rx
    PORTA->PCR[2] = PORT_PCR_ISF_MASK | PORT_PCR_MUX(2); // Tx

    // Set baud rate and oversampling ratio
    sbr = (uint16_t)((SYS_CLOCK)/(baud_rate * UART_OVERSAMPLE_RATE));
    UART0->BDH &= ~UART0_BDH_SBR_MASK;
    UART0->BDH |= UART0_BDH_SBR(sbr>>8);
    UART0->BDL = UART0_BDL_SBR(sbr);
    UART0->C4 |= UART0_C4_OSR(UART_OVERSAMPLE_RATE-1);

    // Disable interrupts for RX active edge and LIN break detect, select one
    // stop bit
    UART0->BDH |= UART0_BDH_RXEDGIE(0) | UART0_BDH_SBNS(0) | UART0_BDH_LBKDIE(0);

    // Don't enable loopback mode, use 8 data bit mode, don't use parity
    UART0->C1 = UART0_C1_LOOPS(0) | UART0_C1_M(0) | UART0_C1_PE(0);
    // Don't invert transmit data, do enable interrupts for errors
    UART0->C3 = UART0_C3_TXINV(0) | UART0_C3_ORIE(1)| UART0_C3_NEIE(1)
            | UART0_C3_FEIE(1) | UART0_C3_PEIE(1);

    // Clear error flags
    UART0->S1 = UART0_S1_OR(1) | UART0_S1_NF(1) | UART0_S1_FE(1) | UART0_S1_PF(1);
```

```
    // Send LSB first, do not invert received data
    UART0->S2 = UART0_S2_MSBF(0) | UART0_S2_RXINV(0);

    // Enable UART transmitter and receiver
    UART0->C2 |= UART0_C2_TE(1) | UART0_C2_RE(1);
}
```

Listing 8.8 Code to initialize UART0.

The initialization code in Listing 8.8 will configure UART0 to communicate with the OpenSDA debug MCU. It does the following:

- Enables clock gating for UART0 and Port A.
- Disables UART receiver and transmitter to allow access to control registers.
- Selects oscillator clock source for baud rate generator.
- Connects PTA1 and PTA2 to U0Rx and U0Tx respectively.
- Sets the serial baud rate divider value to 48 MHz/(115,200 baud × 16), which rounds to 26.
- Sets the oversampling factor to 16.
- Configures for eight data bits, no parity and one stop bit.
- Enables the transmitter and receiver.

Program access to the UART can be based on polling or interrupts. Polled communication is simple but does not share the CPU's time as with interrupts.

Polled Communication

To demonstrate polled communication, we will use the program in Listing 8.9. The program first initializes the UART with the function from Listing 8.8 and then enters a loop. Within the loop, the program waits to receive a character. The function UART0_Receive_Poll will return the character after it has been received by the UART. The character is incremented by one and sent back with the function UART0_Transmit_Poll. We can try this program out on a PC with a terminal emulator program that communicates with the virtual serial port.

The function UART0_Transmit_Poll in Listing 8.9 needs to ensure the transmit buffer is empty before trying to write a character to that buffer. This is indicated by a TDRE flag value of one. At this point the code can write the data to transmit to UARTx_D (Figure 8.22). The code will not advance past the polling loop until the transmit buffer is empty.

The function UART0_Receive_Poll in Listing 8.9 needs to ensure there is data in the receive buffer before trying to read it out. This is indicated by an RDRF value of one. At this point the code can read the received data from UARTx_D. The code will not advance past the polling loop until the receive buffer is full (i.e. a character is received).

```
void UART0_Transmit_Poll(uint8_t data) {
    while (!(UART0->S1 & UART0_S1_TDRE_MASK))
        ;
    UART0->D = data;
}
```

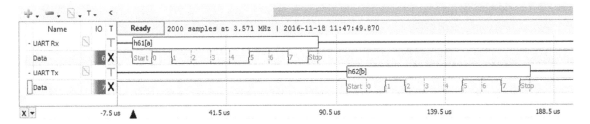

Figure 8.22   UART receives character "a," program adds one (changing character to "b") and transmits it out UART.

```
uint8_t UART0_Receive_Poll(void) {
        while (!(UART0->S1 & UART0_S1_RDRF_MASK))
          ;
        return UART0->D;
}

void main(void) {
    uint8_t c;

    Init_UART0(115200);

    while (1) {
        c = UART0_Receive_Poll();
        UART0_Transmit_Poll(c+1);
    }
}
```

Listing 8.9   Code for polled serial communication to echo back received character + 1.

Interrupt-Driven Communication

Now let us use interrupt-driven communication to create a program that will respond to each character received with a message "You pressed x." The program structure is shown in Figure 8.23. The TxQ queue will store outbound data from the main thread until the UART is ready to transmit it. The RxQ will store received data from the UART until the main thread is able to process it.

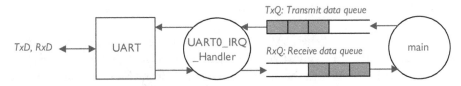

Figure 8.23   Overview of interrupt-driven UART communication.

```
uint8_t buffer[80], c, * bp;

while (1) {
    // blocking receive
    while (Q_Size(&RxQ) == 0)
            ; // wait for character to arrive
    c = Q_Dequeue(&RxQ);

    // blocking transmit
    sprintf((char *) buffer, "You pressed %c\n\r", c);
    // enqueue string
    bp = buffer;
    while (*bp != '\0') {
    // copy characters up to null terminator
            while (Q_Full(&TxQ))
                    ; // wait for space to open up
            Q_Enqueue(&TxQ, *bp);
            bp++;
    }
    // start transmitter if it isn't already running
    if (!(UART0->C2 & UART0_C2_TIE_MASK)) {
            UART0->C2 |= UART0_C2_TIE(1);
    }
}
```

Listing 8.10   Code in main thread for echoing serial input with interrupts; initialization code has been removed.

The main code is shown in Listing 8.10. An infinite loop waits until there is data in the receive queue. At that time a character is dequeued and a message to transmit is formed and loaded into the transmit queue. Note that this example code explicitly blocks on the receive queue until a character is received, or on the transmit queue until there is space available. A practical approach would use a state machine or scheduler to share the processor rather than block.

```
    Q_Init(&TxQ);
    Q_Init(&RxQ);

    NVIC_SetPriority(UART0_IRQn, 2); // 0, 1, 2, or 3
    NVIC_ClearPendingIRQ(UART0_IRQn);
    NVIC_EnableIRQ(UART0_IRQn);

    UART0->C2 |= UART_C2_RIE(1);
```

Listing 8.11   Additional code needed for Init_UART0() to use interrupts. This code is inserted immediately before enabling the UART transmitter and receiver.

We will configure the MCU so the UART generates an interrupt when ready to transmit a character, when a character has been received, or when there is an error. The initialization code of Listing 8.8 needs to be modified slightly, with the additions shown in Listing 8.11. To enable interrupt-driven reception, we set RIE to one in the configuration code so the UART generates an interrupt request when it has received new data. This occurs when the receive data register is full (RDRF is one).

For interrupt-driven transmission, we will set TIE to one so the UART generates an interrupt request when it is ready to accept new data to transmit. This occurs when the transmit data register is empty (TDRE is one). In fact, it will continue to generate interrupt requests until we write a new character to UARTx_D to transmit. If we do not have any data to transmit yet, then we should not enable transmit interrupts. Instead, we will enable transmit interrupts later, when there is data to send.

```
void UART0_IRQHandler(void) {
    uint8_t ch;

    if (UART0->S1 & (UART_S1_OR_MASK |UART_S1_NF_MASK |
    UART_S1_FE_MASK | UART_S1_PF_MASK)) {
        // clear the error flags
        UART0->S1 |= UART0_S1_OR_MASK | UART0_S1_NF_MASK |
            UART0_S1_FE_MASK | UART0_S1_PF_MASK;
        // read the data register to clear RDRF
        ch = UART0->D;
    }
    if (UART0->S1 & UART0_S1_RDRF_MASK) {
        // received a character
        ch = UART0->D;
    if (!Q_Full(&RxQ)) {
        Q_Enqueue(&RxQ, ch);
    } else {
        // error - queue full.
        // discard character
    }
    }
    if ( (UART0->C2 & UART0_C2_TIE_MASK) && // transmitter interrupt enabled
    (UART0->S1 & UART0_S1_TDRE_MASK) ) { // tx buffer empty
        // can send another character
        if (!Q_Empty(&TxQ)) {
            UART0->D = Q_Dequeue(&TxQ);
    } else {
            // queue is empty so disable transmitter interrupt
            UART0->C2 &= ~UART0_C2_TIE_MASK;
        }
    }
}
```

Listing 8.12 Interrupt handler for UART0 handles transmit, receive, and error.

Listing 8.12 shows the ISR for UART0. The handler could be triggered by several types of events, so the ISR needs to identify the cause (or causes) of the interrupt and service each.

The ISR can be triggered by multiple possible errors. The code checks to see if any of the error flags are set. If so, the code resets all the error flags by writing a one to each. It also reads the UART data register to reset the RDRF flag. The program might also handle the error, for example, by incrementing a counter of UART communication errors.

For reception, the ISR is triggered when the receive data register is full (RDRF is one). The ISR checks to see if RDRF is set, in which case it is time to read the received character from UARTx_D

Figure 8.24   Logic analyzer displays received character "a" and resulting transmitted message "You pressed a".

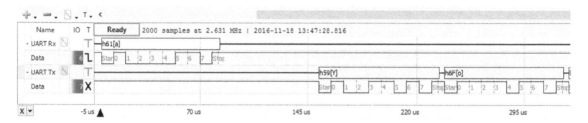

Figure 8.25   Logic analyzer shows delay between character reception, and the start of message transmission is about 60 μs.

and store it in the receive queue RxQ if there is space. If the queue is full, then the character is read from UARTx_D and discarded. Reading from UARTx_D resets RDRF.

For transmission, the ISR is triggered when the transmit data register is empty (TDRE is one). The ISR checks to see if TDRE is set, in which case it is time to load another character into the transmit data register. The ISR reads the new data from the transmit queue TxQ and writes it to UARTx_D. Writing to UARTx_D clears TDRE. If there is no new data to transmit, then the ISR needs to disable the transmitter interrupt so the UART ISR is not retriggered again until needed.

The communication activity of the completed system is shown in Figures 8.24 and 8.25. We see that there is a slight delay between the reception of the character and the transmission of the response.

Inter-Integrated Circuit Bus (I²C)

Protocol Concepts

I²C is a synchronous protocol that uses a serial data (SDA) signal and serial clock (SCL) signal. I²C is a master/slave protocol. The master initiates all communications, and slave devices transmit only when the master allows them to. A major feature of the protocol is device addressing: each message includes device addressing information, and each device on the bus has a unique address. Only the addressed device will respond to a message. This allows a system to be built that shares the SDA/SCL bus as shown in Figure 8.26 without using additional control signals (such as slave selects for SPI).

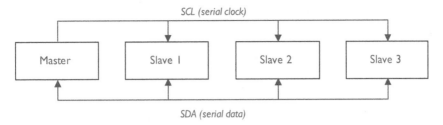

Figure 8.26 Overview of I²C system with master and three slave devices.

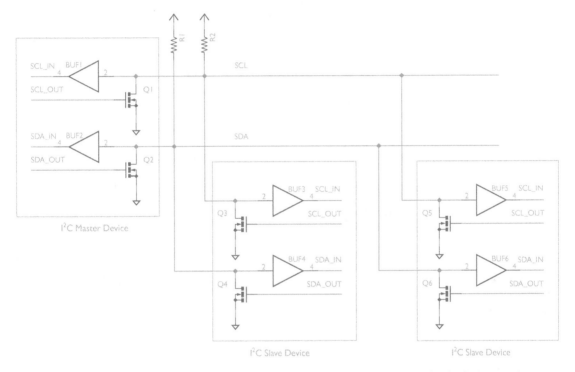

Figure 8.27 I²C signal drive circuits use "open drain" configuration to allow multiple devices to drive signals safely.

The circuits driving the SDA and SCL signals are shown in Figure 8.27 and are designed so that multiple devices can drive the signal simultaneously without damage. Each device's drive circuit consists of a transistor connected between the I²C bus signal (SDA or SCL) and ground. A separate pull-up resistor is connected between the signal and V_{DD}. For the master to send a 0 on SDA, the transistor Q2 is turned on, pulling SDA to ground. To send a one, the transistor Q2 is turned off, allowing the resistor R1 to pull SDA up to V_{DD}. If two devices attempt to transmit different data simultaneously, the SDA signal will be a zero.

I²C supports a range of communication speeds: 100 kbit/s (standard), 400 kbit/s (full speed), 1 Mbit/s (fast), 3.2 Mbit/s (high speed). The maximum communication speed for a given system implementation is limited by how quickly the pull-up resistor can pull SCL or SDA up to V_{CC}. This depends on the capacitance of the SCL or SDA signal, which is affected by the number of devices and the bus length. The maximum speed for a given device will be listed in its data sheet or reference manual.

Message Format

There are several types of I²C message, with the basic format shown in Figure 8.28. Each message contains several fields:

- The start condition indicates the start of a message.
- The slave device address identifies the target of the communication.
- The read/write bit indicates whether the following data is to be read from the slave or written to it.
- The acknowledgment bit has two uses: to indicate if the addressed slave is present, and whether more data will be read. These are explained later in this section.
- One or more data bytes. For some I²C slave devices, the first data byte will be interpreted as a register address.
- A stop condition indicates the end of a message.
- An optional repeated start condition is used in some types of messages.

Communication operations are structured as sequences of conditions (e.g. start, stop) and data transfers (one byte and one acknowledgment bit). We will see this in the code example mentioned.

		Slave Device Address								Data Byte									
Start	AD7	AD6	AD5	AD4	AD3	AD2	ADI	R/W	ACK	D7	D6	D5	D4	D3	D2	DI	D0	ACK	Stop

Figure 8.28   Basic fields of a simple I²C message with 7-bit addressing and one data byte.

Device Addressing

The master uses the device address to select a particular slave device on the bus. There are two addressing modes, one with 7-bit addresses and another with 10-bit addresses. For simplicity we will just discuss the 7-bit mode.

The first byte in the message has two parts, as shown in Figure 8.28. The device address is held in the upper seven bits, and the R/W bit is the LSB. This bit indicates whether the master will read from the slave (one) or write to it (zero). In practice, this byte is formed by shifting the slave address left by one bit and then adding the R/W bit.

Master	Start	Slave Dev. Add.	W(0)		Data		Data		Stop
Slave				ACK (0)		ACK(0)		ACK(0)	

Figure 8.29   Message format for master writing two bytes to slave device. Text indicates transmitting device. Blank indicates listening device.

Figure 8.29 shows the operations involved for a master to write two data bytes to a slave device.

- The master first sends the start condition, the slave device address, and a write command (zero). If the addressed slave is present, it will assert the ACK bit. If the ACK bit is not asserted, then the master will terminate the message with a stop condition.
- The master sends the first byte of data.
- The slave sends an ACK to indicate it has been received.
- The master sends the second byte of data.
- The slave sends an ACK to indicate it has been received.
- The master sends the stop condition, indicating to all slaves that the message has completed.

Master	Start	Slave Dev. Add.	R(1)			ACK(0)		NACK(1)	Stop
Slave				ACK(0)	Data		Data		

Figure 8.30   Message format for master reading two bytes from slave device.

Figure 8.30 shows how the master can read two bytes from the slave.

- The master first sends the start condition, the slave device address, and a read command (one). If the addressed slave is present, it will assert the ACK bit. If the ACK bit is not asserted, then the master will terminate the message with a stop condition.
- The master clocks the first byte of data out of the slave.
- The master sends an ACK to indicate it will read more data.
- The master clocks the second byte of data out of the slave.
- The master sends a NACK (one) to indicate that it does not want to read any more data in this message.
- The master sends the stop condition, indicating to all slaves that the message has completed.

Register Addressing

I^2C also supports register addressing, in which each device is structured as a series of addressable registers that can be read or written. This standardizes information organization and simplifies system development. The first data byte is interpreted by the slave device as a register address. Figures 8.31 and 8.32 show examples of writing and reading to a register in a device.

Master	Start	Slave Dev. Add.	W(0)		Slave Reg. Add.		Data		Stop
Slave				ACK(0)		ACK(0)		ACK(0)	

Figure 8.31   Message format for master writing one byte to a specific register in the slave device.

Master	Start	Slave Dev. Add.	W(0)		Slave Reg. Add.		Start	Slave Dev. Add.	R(0)			NACK(1)	Stop
Slave				ACK(0)		ACK(0)				ACK(0)	Data		

Figure 8.32   Message format for master reading one byte from a specific register in the slave device.

KL25Z I²C Peripherals

The KL25Z128 microcontroller has two I²C peripherals, called I2C0 and I2C1. Each I2Cx peripheral contains a baud rate generator, a shift-register-based transmitter/receiver, bus interface circuitry, and extensive control logic. The hardware handles each message as a sequence of bytes. The software must also be structured accordingly, as we will see shortly.

General Control

Clock gating must be enabled for the appropriate I2Cx peripheral using the SIM register SIM_SCGC4.

The I²C control register one (I2Cx_C1, shown in Figure 8.33) controls various aspects of the peripheral's operation. The relevant fields for master mode are these:

- IICEN enables the peripheral to operate.
- IICIE enables interrupts from the peripheral.
- MST sets master or slave mode and also generates start and stop conditions on the bus. Changing MST from zero to one generates a start and selects master mode. Changing MST from one to zero generates a stop and selects slave mode.
- TX selects if the peripheral will transmit (one) or receive (zero).
- TXAK controls whether to transmit an ACK (zero) or a NACK (one) after a byte is received.
- Writing a one to RSTA makes the peripheral generate a repeated start condition on the bus.
- DMAEN enables DMA transfers.

7	6	5	4	3	2	1	0
IICEN	IICIE	MST	TX	TXAK	RSTA	WUEN	DMAEN

Figure 8.33 Contents of I2Cx_C1 control register.

Status and Interrupts

The I²C status register (I2Cx_S, shown in Figure 8.34) indicates the status of the peripheral. The relevant fields for master mode are these:

- TCF indicates that a byte and acknowledgment bit transfer has completed.
- BUSY indicates the bus is busy.
- IICIF indicates that an interrupt is pending, for example, because a transfer has completed.
- RXAK indicates that an acknowledgment bit was received (one) after transmitting a byte. A zero indicates no acknowledgment was received.

7	6	5	4	3	2	1	0
TCF	IAAS	BUSY	ARBL	RAM	SRW	IICIF	RXAK

Figure 8.34 Contents of I2Cx_S status register.

The I²C data register (I2Cx_D) holds data to transmit or receive. When the master reads this register, the hardware starts to transmit or receive the next byte of data, depending on the value of the TX bit in I2Cx_C1.

Baud Rate Generator

The communication speed (I²C baud rate) is set by the bus clock frequency and factors determined by the I2Cx_F register, shown in Figure 8.35.

$$\text{I}^2\text{C baud rate} = \frac{\text{bus speed}}{\text{mul} \times \text{SCL divider}}$$

The MULT field defines the value of mul, which can be 1, 2, or 4. The SCL divider value is determined indirectly by the ICR field. The ICR value indicates which value of SCL divider to use from a table of 64 alternatives (see "I²C divider and hold values" in the documentation [5]). For example, an ICR value of 32 (0x20) will result in an SCL divider of 160. ICR also defines hold times for various signals.

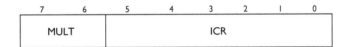

Figure 8.35 Contents of I2Cx_F control register.

Other Features

The I²C peripheral has many other features not covered here: the ability to operate as a slave (with an address match comparison), DMA, general call messages, and system management bus (SMB) support. There is a low-power mode that can operate while the rest of the MCU is in sleep mode.

Example: Communicating with the FRDM-KL25Z's Three-Axis Inertial Sensor

The FRDM-KL25Z board includes a three-axis inertial sensor (MMA8451Q) that detects acceleration and gravity. The sensor is connected to the MCU's I2C0 I²C bus, on pins PTE24 and PT25. The SCL and SDA signals are pulled up to 3.3 V with pull-up resistors. The sensor also has two outputs that can trigger MCU interrupt requests, indicating to the MCU that a certain condition has occurred.

PTE24 and PTE25 are not connected to any expansion headers, making it difficult to connect the signals to a logic analyzer. However, we can add a header that taps into SCL and SDA at the lower end of the pull-up resistors R16 and R18 (shown in Figure 8.36). We can now observe the bus activity on the logic analyzer.

Let's see how to access the accelerometer through I²C using NXP's polling-driven starter code for the board [6]. For interrupt-driven code, the MCU documentation provides an example flowchart for the ISR [5].

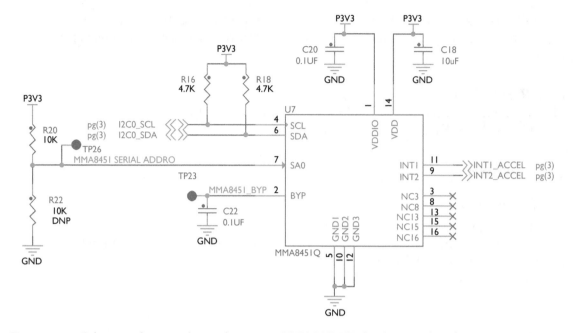

Figure 8.36   Schematic diagram of inertial sensor on FRDM-KL25Z development board. Image courtesy NXP Semiconductors.

```
void i2c_init(void)
{
    //clock i2c peripheral and port E
    SIM->SCGC4 |= SIM_SCGC4_I2C0_MASK;
    SIM->SCGC5 |= SIM_SCGC5_PORTE_MASK;

    //set pins to I2C function
    PORTE->PCR[24] |= PORT_PCR_MUX(5);
    PORTE->PCR[25] |= PORT_PCR_MUX(5);

    // set to 400k baud
    // baud = bus freq/(scl_div+mul)
    // 24MHz/400kHz = 60; icr=0x11 sets scl_div to 56
    I2C0->F = I2C_F_ICR(0x11) | I2C_F_MULT(0);

    //enable i2c and set to master mode
    I2C0->C1 |= (I2C_C1_IICEN_MASK);

    //select high drive mode
    I2C0->C2 |= (I2C_C2_HDRS_MASK);
}
```

Listing 8.13 Code to initialize I2C0 peripheral using pins PTE24 and PTE25.

The i2c_init function shown in Listing 8.13 initializes the I2C0 peripheral.

Building Blocks

Let's look at how the I²C operations are implemented. The code uses the pieces in Listing 8.14 as building blocks to simplify code development.

- The first three macros (I2C_M_START, I2C_M_STOP, and I2C_M_RSTART) instruct the I2C0 peripheral to send start, stop, or repeated start conditions.
- The I2C_TRAN and I2C_REC macros set the peripheral to transmit or receive mode.
- The I2C_WAIT macro contains a blocking loop that waits until the interrupt pending flag is set. This indicates that a byte and acknowledgment have transferred. The macro then clears the flag by writing a one to it.
- The NACK and ACK macros configure the peripheral to send either a NACK (no acknowledgment) or an ACK.

```
#define I2C_M_START     I2C0->C1 |= I2C_C1_MST_MASK
#define I2C_M_STOP      I2C0->C1 &= ~I2C_C1_MST_MASK
#define I2C_M_RSTART    I2C0->C1 |= I2C_C1_RSTA_MASK

#define I2C_TRAN        I2C0->C1 |= I2C_C1_TX_MASK
#define I2C_REC         I2C0->C1 &= ~I2C_C1_TX_MASK

#define I2C_WAIT        while((I2C0->S & I2C_S_IICIF_MASK)==0) {} \
                            I2C0->S |= I2C_S_IICIF_MASK;

#define NACK            I2C0->C1 |= I2C_C1_TXAK_MASK
#define ACK             I2C0->C1 &= ~I2C_C1_TXAK_MASK
```

Listing 8.14   Macros used as building blocks in sample code for I²C communication.

Write Byte

```
void i2c_write_byte(uint8_t dev, uint8_t reg, uint8_t data)
{
    I2C_TRAN;                   /*set to transmit mode */
    I2C_M_START;                /*send start */
    I2C0->D = dev;              /*send dev address (write)*/
    I2C_WAIT                    /*wait for ack */

    I2C0->D = reg;              /*send register address */
    I2C_WAIT

    I2C0->D = data;             /*send data */
    I2C_WAIT
    I2C_M_STOP;
}
```

Listing 8.15   Function to write a byte of data to I²C device register.

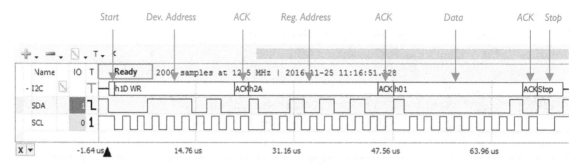

Figure 8.37 Signals and sequence of operations to write a single byte.

Listing 8.15 shows the code to writing a byte to a specific device register. The function arguments are device address (dev), the register address (reg), and the data. Figure 8.37 shows the corresponding bus activity.

The code switches the I2C0 peripheral to transmit mode and then sends a start symbol followed by the device address with the write flag set. I2C_WAIT causes the code to busy-wait until the byte transfer has completed. The code sends the register address and awaits its completion. It then sends the data and awaits completion. Finally the code sends the stop condition to end the transaction.

```
int init_mma()
{
    //check for device
    if(i2c_read_byte(MMA_ADDR, REG_WHOAMI) == WHOAMI) {
        Delay(40);
        //set active mode, 14 bit samples and 800 Hz ODR
        i2c_write_byte(MMA_ADDR, REG_CTRL1, 0x01);
        return 1;
    } else {
        //else error
        return 0;
    }
}
```

Listing 8.16 Code to initialize MMA8451Q inertial sensor.

The init_mma function in Listing 8.16 uses the i2c_write_byte function to configure the sensor to a sample rate of 800 Hz and a sample resolution of 14 bits. This is done by writing the appropriate byte to control register one (0x2a).

Read Byte
Reading is more complex; it consists of writing the device and register addresses and then reading the register value from the slave. Listing 8.17 shows the code to read one byte from a specific device register. The function arguments are the device address "dev" and the register address "reg". Figure 8.38 shows the corresponding bus activity from the logic analyzer.

```c
uint8_t i2c_read_byte(uint8_t dev, uint8_t reg)
{
    uint8_t data;

    I2C_TRAN;                   /*set to transmit mode */
    I2C_M_START;                /*send start */
    I2C0->D = dev;              /*send dev address (write)*/
    I2C_WAIT                    /*wait for completion */

    I2C0->D = reg;              /*send register address */
    I2C_WAIT                    /*wait for completion */

    I2C_M_RSTART;              /*repeated start */
    I2C0->D = (dev|0x1);        /*send dev address (read) */
    I2C_WAIT                    /*wait for completion */

    I2C_REC;                    /*set to receive mode */
    NACK;                       /*set NACK after read */

    data = I2C0->D;             /*dummy read */
    I2C_WAIT                    /*wait for completion */

    I2C_M_STOP;                 /*send stop */
    data = I2C0->D;             /*read data */

    return data;
}
```

Listing 8.17 Source code to read a single byte.

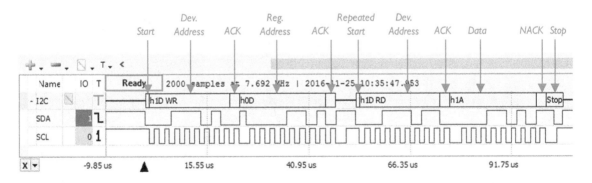

Figure 8.38 Signals and sequence of operations to read a single byte.

The code begins by switching the I2C0 peripheral to transmit mode and then sending a start symbol followed by the device address with the write command. Upon receiving the ACK, the code sends a repeated start condition followed by the device address with a read command. Upon receiving the ACK, the code switches the I²C peripheral to receive mode.

In order to indicate to the slave that only one byte of data will be read, the peripheral is configured to send a NACK after receiving the data. The code then performs a dummy read of the I²C data register to start the receive operation. I2C_WAIT makes the code wait for the operation to complete, and at this point the hardware also sends NACK. The STOP condition is sent and the received data is read out of the data register to be returned to the calling function.

The init_mma function in Listing 8.16 uses the i2c_read_byte function to verify that the sensor is present. The "Who am I" register (address 0x0d) will return a value of 0x1a when read.

Reading and Writing Multiple Bytes

Reading or writing multiple bytes is similar to reading a single byte. Listing 8.18 shows how the sample code reads the X, Y and Z accelerations from the sensor using the functions i2c_read_bytes (which is shown in Listing 8.19) and then formats the data bytes into the three acceleration vectors. Figure 8.39 shows the corresponding bus activity. Writing multiple bytes is similar, but is not covered here.

```
void read_full_xyz()
{
        int i;
        uint8_t data[6];
        int16_t accel[3];

        i2c_read_bytes(MMA_ADDR, REG_XHI, data, 6);

        for( i=0; i<3; i++) {
                accel[i] = (int16_t) ((data[2*i]<<8) | data[2*i+1]);
        }

}
```

Listing 8.18 Function read_full_xyz reads 6 bytes of data from sensor starting with register REG_XHI.

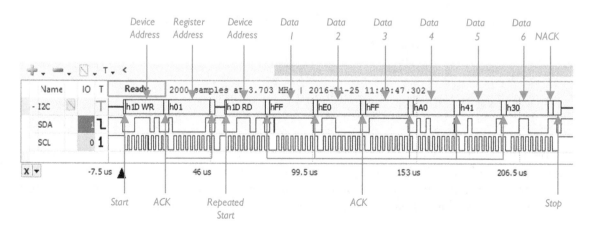

Figure 8.39 Signals and sequence of operations to read multiple bytes.

```
int i2c_read_bytes(uint8_t dev_adx, uint8_t reg_adx, uint8_t * data, int8_t
data_count) {
    uint8_t dummy;
    int8_t num_bytes_read=0;
    I2C_TRAN;                           /* set to transmit mode */
    I2C_M_START;                        /* send start */
    I2C0->D = dev_adx;                  /* send dev address (write) */
    I2C_WAIT                            /* wait for completion */
    I2C0->D = reg_adx;                  /* send register address */
    I2C_WAIT                            /* wait for completion */
    I2C_M_RSTART;                       /* repeated start */
    I2C0->D = dev_adx|0x01;             /* send dev address (read) */
    I2C_WAIT                            /* wait for completion */
    I2C_REC;                            /* set to receive mode */
    ACK;                                /* tell HW to send ACK after read */
    dummy = I2C0->D;                    /* dummy read to start I2C read */
    I2C_WAIT                            /* wait for completion */
    do {
        ACK;                            /* tell HW to send ACK after read */
        data[num_bytes_read++] = I2C0->D;/* read data */
        I2C_WAIT                        /* wait for completion */
    } while (num_bytes_read < data_count-2);

    NACK;                               /* tell HW to send NACK after read */
    data[num_bytes_read++] = I2C0->D;   /* read data */
    I2C_WAIT                            /* wait for completion */
    I2C_M_STOP;                         /* send stop */
    return 1;
}
```

Listing 8.19 Source code to read multiple bytes.

Listing 8.19 shows the i2c_read_bytes function. The code sends the device address and waits for the byte transfer completion. The code then sends the register address and waits until it is complete. The code then sends a repeated start condition followed by the device address (with the read command flag set). Upon completing the transmission, the code switches the I2C0 peripheral to receive mode. The code then performs a dummy read of the I²C data register to start the receive operation and waits until it completes. A loop reads each data byte except the last, using an ACK for each byte. The last data byte is read with a NACK to indicate no more data will be read. After the last read transfer operation completes the STOP condition is sent.

Summary

In this chapter, we have seen the motivation for communicating information serially and the core issues that must be tackled to do so. We examined helpful development tools and software structures. We have studied three different types of communication protocols (asynchronous serial, synchronous serial, and I²C) and how to implement them using the peripherals of the MCU.

Exercises

1. Examine Chapter 10 (Signal Multiplexing and Signal Descriptions) of the KL25 Sub-Family Reference Manual to determine the answers to the following questions. Assume that an MCU in an 80 QFP package is used.
   a. Which port bits can be used for SPI0?
   b. Which port bits can be used for SPI1?
2. Show the register settings needed to configure SPI0 to operate as a master at 12 MHz, 8 data bits (MSB first), SPI mode zero (Clock Phase CPHA = 0, Clock Polarity CPOL = 0). Assume the bus clock is 24 MHz. Enable interrupts for transmission, reception, and errors. Use the /SS pin as a slave select output.
3. Draw a timing diagram showing the bytes 0x31 0xF1 being transmitted by SPI at 1,000,000 baud, with SPI mode zero. Indicate the time of each signal transition.
4. Examine Chapter 10 (Signal Multiplexing and Signal Descriptions) of the KL25 Sub-Family Reference Manual to determine the answers to the following questions. Assume that an MCU in an 80 QFP package is used.
   a. Which port bits can be used for UART0?
   b. Which port bits can be used for UART1?
   c. Which port bits can be used for UART2?
5. Show the register settings needed to configure UART1 to transmit and receive at 71,433 baud, eight data bits (LSB first), one stop bit and odd parity. Assume the bus clock is 24 MHz. Enable interrupts to indicate that the transmit data register is empty, the receive data register is full, or any error has occurred. The UART should not trigger any DMA activity.
6. Assume a UART has both TIE and TCIE set to one and a program writes a byte to the UART D register for transmission. Which interrupts will occur, and when?
7. Draw a timing diagram showing the bytes 0x31 0xF1 being transmitted by a UART at 115,200 baud, with LSB first, odd parity, and one stop bit. Indicate the time of each signal transition.
8. Examine Chapter 10 (Signal Multiplexing and Signal Descriptions) of the KL25 Sub-Family Reference Manual to determine the answers to the following questions. Assume that an MCU in an 80 QFP package is used.
   a. Which port bits can be used for I2C0?
   b. Which port bits can be used for I2C1?
9. Show the register settings needed to configure I2C1 to communicate at approximately 800 kbaud. Assume the bus clock is 24 MHz. What is the actual communication frequency?
10. Draw a timing diagram of the following I²C message: a value of 0x31 being written to device 0x36 register 0x55. Assume 200 kbaud communications speed. Indicate the time of each signal transition.

References

[1] International Telecommunication Union, "Data networks and open system communications: open systems interconnection—model and notation," 1994.
[2] P. J. Koopman and T. C. Maxino, "The effectiveness of checksums for embedded control networks," *IEEE transactions on dependable and secure computing*, vol. 6, no. 1, pp. 59–72, 2009.

[3]   Digilent, Inc., "Analog Discovery 2 [Reference.DigilentInc]," [Online]. Available: https://reference.digilentinc. com/reference/instrumentation/analog-discovery-2/start?redirect=1. [Accessed November 25, 2016].

[4]   Dangerous Prototypes, "Bus Pirate—DP," Where Labs, LLC., [Online]. Available: http://dangerousprototypes. com/docs/Bus_Pirate. [Accessed November 25, 2016].

[5]   *KL25 Sub-Family Reference Manual*, KL25P80M48SF0RM, rev. 3 ed., NXP Semiconductor, B.V., 2016.

[6]   NXP, "FRDM-KL25Z and TWRKL25Z48M Sample Code Package," October 25, 2013. [Online]. Available: www. nxp.com/assets/downloads/data/en/lab-test-software/KL25_SC.exe. [Accessed November 25, 2016].

9

Direct Memory Access

Chapter Contents

Overview

This chapter presents the *direct memory access (DMA)* controller, a peripheral that is able to take control of the MCU's address and data bus in order to transfer data directly with read and write hardware operations, rather than relying on explicit load and store instructions in a program. Peripheral events (e.g. timer overflows) that can trigger interrupt requests can also be used to trigger DMA transfers. The DMA controller can eliminate simple ISRs, reducing the amount of software that the MCU must execute, which improves performance and responsiveness. In this chapter we see how to use DMA to copy memory data quickly, and also how to generate an analog waveform from data stored in memory using the DAC and a timer.

> direct memory access (DMA)
> *Type of memory access performed by peripheral hardware without using program instructions*

Concepts

A basic DMA transfer occurs as follows:

- A trigger event starts the transfer. This may be an explicit software write to a start field in a control register of the DMA controller, or an event such as a timer overflow or an ADC conversion completion.

- The DMA controller takes control of the MCU's address and data buses and control lines in order to read a data item from the source location (which is specified in the source address register). This source may be memory or a memory-mapped peripheral.
- The DMA controller then uses the address and data buses and control lines in order to write the data to the destination location (which is specified in the destination address register). The DMA controller releases the buses and control lines for the CPU to use.
- The DMA controller increments the source and destination address registers so the next items are addressed for the next transfer.
- The DMA controller updates a count register that tracks the number of items transferred. If there are more items to transfer, this process repeats.
- The DMA controller will indicate the final transfer has completed by setting a status flag and triggering an interrupt (if enabled).

There are two important variations of this basic transfer process:

- The source and destination address registers are usually incremented after each transfer to address the next locations. However, in some cases we wish to have the DMA controller to copy the same value into every destination, or read successive values from the same source. To enable this, each address register can be configured to advance or remain unchanged.
- DMA controllers typically offer two transfer modes. In the continuous (burst) mode, the DMA controller takes over the bus when it is triggered, transferring data nonstop until the transfer is complete. In the cycle-stealing (time-sharing) mode, the DMA controller shares the bus with the MCU, taking control once per trigger, transferring one item, and then yielding the bus. The system designer can select the appropriate mode for the application.

One obvious use for DMA is to transfer or fill a block of memory quickly. For example, this could be useful for erasing a buffer, initializing a data structure, or copying an image into a frame buffer. However, there are more sophisticated uses possible when combined with other peripherals. For example, DMA can be used to transfer a data value from a waveform buffer to the DAC in order to generate an analog waveform. Each transfer is controlled by a timer overflow, allowing precise timing with minimal CPU overhead. We will implement this example later in this chapter.

Using DMA transfers can also help reduce the energy or power used by the system. Because DMA transfers reduce the processing required of the CPU, it may be possible to place the CPU in a low-power sleep mode. Required peripherals will remain active, whereas the rest of the MCU will be disabled or powered down, reducing both the power and energy consumption of the system. Another option is to keep the CPU active but running at a lower clock frequency, which reduces power consumption.

KL25Z DMA Controller and Multiplexer Peripherals

As shown in Figure 9.1, the KL25Z MCU has a DMA controller peripheral that is connected to both the high-speed system bus and the low-speed peripheral bus.[1] The controller has four identical channels, numbered 0 through 3.

---

[1] The high-speed system bus uses a crossbar switch that allows simultaneous operation of multiple masters (Cortex-M0+ core, DMA controller, and USB peripheral) when accessing slaves (Flash memory controller, SRAM, and peripheral bridge).

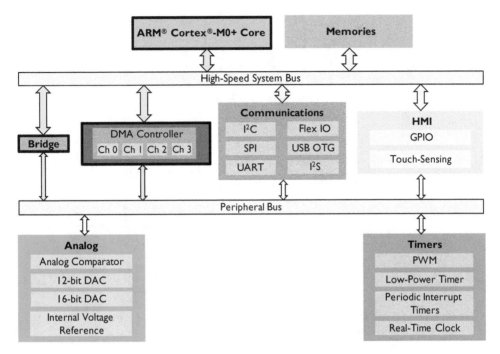

Figure 9.1 DMA controller can seize system or peripheral bus to transfer data between devices. Devices with **bold outlines** (core, DMA, bridge) can be bus masters. The high-speed system bus uses a crossbar switch to support simultaneous accesses.

Figure 9.2 shows the structure of a single DMA channel. DMA transfers can be started by a software write operation or a hardware trigger event. If the hardware trigger is used, the DMA_MUX multiplexer for that channel (on the left) selects one of many possible trigger event requests from the other peripherals and provides it to the DMA controller for that channel with the ERQ signal. The controller reads the data specified by the source address register (SAR). That data may need to be buffered and reformatted if source and destination are of different sizes, or if either is unaligned. The controller writes the data to the location indicated by the destination address register (DAR). DCR, BCR, and DSR are control or status registers that are discussed in further sections.

DMA Multiplexer and Trigger Sources

The DMA_MUX multiplexer specifies which hardware source will trigger the DMA channel. This subsystem is described in the direct memory access multiplexer chapter and chip configuration chapters of the MCU reference manual [1].

The DMAMUXx_CHCFGn control register (Figure 9.3) allows the selection of the hardware event that will trigger a DMA channel's transfer.

- The ENBL field enables the DMA channel when set to one.
- The TRIG field enables triggering of the DMA channel when set to one.
- The SOURCE field selects one of the trigger sources, as summarized in Table 9.1.

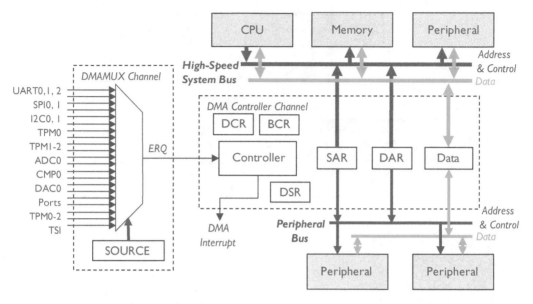

Figure 9.2   Events from other peripherals can trigger DMA controller channel to seize system or peripheral bus to transfer data.

7	6	5	4	3	2	1	0
ENBL	TRIG	SOURCE					

Figure 9.3   DMAMUXx_CHCFGn control register selects trigger source for DMA channel.

Table 9.1 Trigger Sources for DMA Transfers

Source #	Module	Description
0	–	Disabled
2–7	UART0,1,2	Receive, transmit
16–19	SPI0, 1	Receive, transmit
22–23	I2C0, 1	
24–29	TPM0	Channels 0–5
32–35	TPM1-2	Channels 0–1
40	ADC0	
42	CMP0	
45	DAC0	
49–53	Port control module	Port A-E
54–56	TPM0-2	Overflow
57	TSI	
60–63	DMAMUX	Always enabled

DMA Controller

The DMA controller is described in the DMA controller module of the MCU reference manual [1]. Each channel **n** has several control registers, as shown in Figure 9.2. The source address register DMA_SARn holds the first address to read from. The destination address register DMA_DARn holds the first address to write to.

The DMA_DCRn register, shown in Figure 9.4, configures the operation of the channel.

The DMA_DSR_BCRn register, shown in Figure 9.5, holds status flags and the byte count register.

31	30	29	28	27	26	25	24	23	22	21	20	19	18	17	16
EINT	ERQ	CS	AA		0		Res.	EADRQ	SINC	SSIZE		DINC	DSIZE	START	

15	14	13	12	11	10	9	8	7	6	5	4	3	2	1	0
SMOD				DMOD				D_REQ	0	LINKCC		LCH1		LCH2	

Figure 9.4 DMA_DCRn register defines DMA operation.

31	30	29	28	27	26	25	24	23	20	19	0
0	CE	BES	BED	0	REQ	BSY	DONE	0		BCR	

Figure 9.5 DMA_DSR_BCRn register holds status flags and the byte count register.

Let us examine the fields that define the basic aspects of the transfer.

- BCR defines the number of bytes to transfer (from 0 to 0x000f ffff). After each DMA transfer, the hardware decrements BCR by the number of bytes transferred.
- SSIZE and DSIZE specify the data sizes of the source and destination: 32 bits (00), 16 bits (10), or 8 bits (01). The source and destination sizes do not need to match, as the DMA controller will perform extra reads or writes as needed.
- SINC and DINC, when set to one, specify to increment the SAR or DAR by the data size after each transfer. A value of zero will result in no incrementing for that address register.
- SMOD and DMOD (when nonzero) define the address modulus in order to provide circular buffers. This feature modifies the address increment operation so that at the end of the buffer it automatically wraps back to the beginning. An SMOD or DMOD value of n specifies a buffer size of 2^{n+3} bytes, or 16 bytes to 64 kilobytes.
- CS controls whether the DMA controller performs cycle-stealing, in which it performs only one transfer per request, or if it makes continuous transfers until all bytes have been transferred.
- Setting AA causes the hardware to automatically align the addresses with the bus size, improving performance when transferring large amounts of data with continuous transfers.

Certain fields are related to how a transfer is started:

- Setting ERQ to one enables a peripheral request to start a transfer. This is used for a hardware-triggered transfer.
- Writing a one to START will start a transfer. This is used for a software-triggered transfer.

Certain fields indicate error conditions:

- CE indicates a configuration error has occurred.
- BES indicates a bus error when reading the source.
- BED indicates a bus error when writing the destination.

These fields indicate the progress of the transfer:

- The REQ status flag is one when a transfer has been requested but not started.
- The BSY status flag is one from the time the channel starts a transfer until the time when it completes.
- The DONE status flag is one when the channel has completed all of its transfers. If the DMA channel triggered an interrupt, this flag needs to be cleared in the ISR by writing a one to it, which will also clear all the status bits.

Completing a transfer can trigger an interrupt.

- EINT enables the DMA interrupt when the transfer has completed.

Channels can be linked to trigger each other. For example, channel 0 can trigger channel 1 after each cycle-stealing transfer. Channel 1 could trigger channel 2 after channel 1's byte count register reaches zero.

- LINKCC specifies how to link channels together.
- LCH1 and LCH2 specify the other channels for this channel to trigger.

Basic DMA Configuration and Use

The following steps are used to configure and use the DMA controller and multiplexer:

- Enable clock gating to the DMA module in SIM register SCGC7.
- If hardware triggering is used, enable clock gating to the DMAMUX modules in SIM register SCGC6.
- If hardware triggering is used, disable the DMA channel by clearing the channel's CHCFG field in DMAMUX0 to zero.
- Initialize the DMA control registers for channel n.
- Load SARn and DARn with the source and destination addresses.
- Load BCRn with the number of bytes to transfer.
- Clear the DONE flag in DSRn to clear the controller.

- If hardware triggering is used:
  - o Enable the DMA channel by writing the trigger source number to the channel's CHCFG field in DMAMUX0.
  - o Enable peripheral triggers by setting the ERQ flag to one.
- If interrupts are used, set the EINT flag to one.

Next, the transfer will be triggered. To trigger the transfer with software, set the START flag in DCRn.

Finally, await the end of the transfer. For polling, wait until the DONE flag in DSRn changes to one. For interrupts, the DMAn_IRQHandler will run after the transfer completes.

Examples

Let's examine two different ways to use the DMA controller: copying data and generating an analog waveform.

Bulk Data Transfer

How quickly can the processor copy a block of data in memory? Let us start with a simple software solution. Listing 9.1 shows the C source code to copy ARR_SIZE words from source array s to destination array d.

```c
#define ARR_SIZE (256)
uint32_t s[ARR_SIZE], d[ARR_SIZE];

void Test_SW_Copy(void) {
        uint32_t * ps, * pd;

        ps = s;
        pd = d;
        for (i=0; i<ARR_SIZE; i++) {
                *pd++ = *ps++;
        }
}
```

Listing 9.1 C code to copy data from source array s to destination array d.

```
000000 4a2a                    LDR         r2,|L1.172|
000002 482b                    LDR         r0,|L1.176|
;;;20        for (i=0; i<ARR_SIZE; i++) {
000004 2100                    MOVS        r1,#0
                |L1.6|
;;;21            *pd++ = *ps++;
000006 ca08                    LDM         r2!,{r3}
000008 1c49                    ADDS        r1,r1,#1
00000a c008                    STM         r0!,{r3}
00000c 29ff                    CMP         r1,#0xff
00000e d9fa                    BLS         |L1.6|
;;;22        }
```

Listing 9.2 Assembly code generated by compiler for code to copy data.

Compiling this code with optimization enabled generates the assembly code in Listing 9.2. The loop consists of five instructions (LDM at address 000006 through BLS at address 00000e). Let us assume each instruction will take one clock cycle to execute, so the loop should take five clock cycles per iteration. The time needed for 256 iterations of five clock cycles each at 48 MHz is 26.7 μs.

We run the code on the MCU and measure the timing, finding that it takes 44 μs to copy 256 words. This translates to a transfer rate of six million words/second, or eight clock cycles per loop iteration.

Why does the loop take eight cycles instead of five? The CPU's technical reference manual details the number of cycles needed to execute each type of instruction [2]. Most instructions take only one cycle, but some take more. LDM and STM each take two cycles (and would take more if they had more registers to load or store). BLS take two cycles each time the branch is taken back to |L1.6|, but only one cycle when it is not taken.

Let's use the DMA controller to get rid of this loop and its instruction overhead. We will use channel 0 of the DMA controller to perform bulk transfers of words using software triggering and polling for completion detection. The function Init_DMA_To_Copy in Listing 9.3 performs generic initialization for any copy. It first enables the clock for the DMA module, and then configures DCR0 to increment both the source and destination pointers and to transfer 32 bits at a time.

The function Copy_Longwords then configures the DMA controller for the specific transfer, based on the parameters (source pointer, destination pointer, and word transfer count). The code stores the source and destination pointers in the source and destination address registers. The code multiplies the word "transfer count" by four to indicate the number of bytes to transfer and stores it in the byte count register. Next the code clears the DONE flag and starts the transfer by setting the START flag. Finally the code sits in a polling loop to busy-wait until the DONE flag is set by the DMA controller, indicating the transfer has completed.

```c
#define ARR_SIZE (256)
uint32_t s[ARR_SIZE], d[ARR_SIZE];
void Init_DMA_To_Copy(void) {
    SIM->SCGC7 |= SIM_SCGC7_DMA_MASK;
    DMA0->DMA[0].DCR = DMA_DCR_SINC_MASK | DMA_DCR_SSIZE(0) | DMA_DCR_DINC_MASK |
    DMA_DCR_DSIZE(0);
}
void Copy_Longwords(uint32_t * source, uint32_t * dest, uint32_t count) {
    // initialize source and destination pointers
    DMA0->DMA[0].SAR = DMA_SAR_SAR((uint32_t) source);
    DMA0->DMA[0].DAR = DMA_DAR_DAR((uint32_t) dest);
    // byte count
    DMA0->DMA[0].DSR_BCR = DMA_DSR_BCR_BCR(count*4);
    // verify done flag is cleared
    DMA0->DMA[0].DSR_BCR &= ~DMA_DSR_BCR_DONE_MASK;
    // start transfer
    DMA0->DMA[0].DCR |= DMA_DCR_START_MASK;
    // wait until it is done
    while (!(DMA0->DMA[0].DSR_BCR & DMA_DSR_BCR_DONE_MASK))
        ;
}
void Test_DMA_Copy(void) {
    uint16_t i;
    Init_DMA_To_Copy();
```

```
    for (i=0; i<ARR_SIZE; i++) {
            s[i] = i;
            d[i] = 0;
    }
    Copy_Longwords(s, d, ARR_SIZE);
}
```

Listing 9.3 Code to use DMA controller to copy 32-bit words quickly.

The driver function is called Test_DMA_Copy. It initializes the DMA controller, the source data (with incrementing integers), and the destination data (with zeros). The function then calls Copy_Longwords. Running this code and measuring the timing in Copy_Longwords (using an oscilloscope and a debug twiddle bit) reveals that it takes about 10.8 μs for the DMA controller to transfer 256 words. This means the transfer rate is nearly 24 million words per second (96 megabytes/second), which is the full speed of the bus.

Compare this with the software solution, which manages only 6 million words per second due to the overhead of executing instructions (to load and store values, increment source and destination pointers, increment the counter, and conditionally branch to repeat the loop).

Analog Waveform Generation

The second example targets the running example of the analog waveform generator introduced in Chapter 6 that uses the digital-to-analog converter (DAC). In Chapter 7 we saw how to use the timer to generate a regular interrupt. The timer ISR updates the DAC in order to generate the waveform. Using an ISR provides precise timing while separating the waveform generator code from the rest of the program.

In this chapter we will remove the timer ISR and use channel 0 of the DMA controller to periodically transfer a data item from a memory buffer to the DAC. Note that the DMA controller can copy data but cannot generate it. We therefore will precompute the waveform samples and store them in an array from which the DMA controller will read.

Using DMA will reduce CPU loading by eliminating the timer ISR. Using the DMA to transfer data will also improve the timing stability even further, as the transfers will not be delayed by other ISRs (which might happen with the timer ISR approach).

Design
Figure 9.6 shows the sequence of events in waveform generation. The timer peripheral in the first column (TPM) generates a periodic event to trigger a DMA transfer, rather than an ISR as used in Chapter 7. The DMA controller is configured to transfer one sample (16 bits) per timer overflow event. The DMA controller will generate an interrupt after performing the last transfer to the DAC. The DMA ISR will update the DMA controller for the next set of transfers.

The top-level code (in Listing 9.4) initializes the LEDs, the DAC, the sample array (TriangleTable), the DMA system, and the timer TPM. It then starts the TPM and DMA system. At this point all waveform generation work is performed by the DMA system and its ISR, so the function can return, do other work, or even enter an infinite loop (as shown here).

Listing 9.5 shows the data sample array called TriangleTable, and its initialization function Init_TriangleTable. This function takes advantage of the symmetry of the triangle wave to load up the array from both the front and back in each loop iteration.

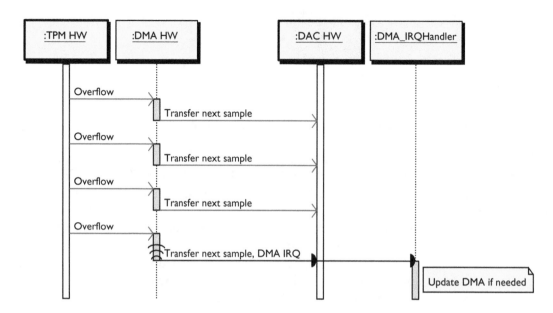

Figure 9.6 Sequence of events that generate analog waveform using timer, DMA, and DAC. Diagram shows DMA IRQ occurring after 4 transfers for readability, but in code IRQ occurs after 512 transfers.

```
void Play_Tone_with_DMA(void) {
    Init_RGB_LEDs();
    Control_RGB_LEDs(0,0,0);
    Init_DAC();
    Init_TriangleTable();
    Init_DMA_For_Playback(TriangleTable, NUM_STEPS);
    Init_TPM(10);
    Start_TPM();
    Start_DMA_Playback();
    while (1)
            ;
}
```

Listing 9.4 Top-level code for generating analog waveform.

```
#define MAX_DAC_CODE (4095)
#define NUM_STEPS (512)

uint16_t TriangleTable[NUM_STEPS];

void Init_TriangleTable(void) {
    unsigned n, sample;

    for (n=0; n<NUM_STEPS/2; n++) {
        sample = (n*(MAX_DAC_CODE+1)/(NUM_STEPS/2));
        TriangleTable[n] = sample; // Fill in from front
        TriangleTable[NUM_STEPS-1-n] = sample; // Fill in from back
    }
}
```

Listing 9.5 Code to initialize data buffer TriangleTable with waveform samples.

```
void Init_DMA_For_Playback(uint16_t * source, uint32_t count) {
    // Save reload information
    Reload_DMA_Source = source;
    Reload_DMA_Byte_Count = count*2;

    // Gate clocks to DMA and DMAMUX
    SIM->SCGC7 |= SIM_SCGC7_DMA_MASK;
    SIM->SCGC6 |= SIM_SCGC6_DMAMUX_MASK;

    // Disable DMA channel to allow configuration
    DMAMUX0->CHCFG[0] = 0;

    // Generate DMA interrupt when done
    // Increment source, transfer words (16 bits)
    // Enable peripheral request
    DMA0->DMA[0].DCR = DMA_DCR_EINT_MASK | DMA_DCR_SINC_MASK |
    DMA_DCR_SSIZE(2) | DMA_DCR_DSIZE(2) | DMA_DCR_ERQ_MASK | DMA_DCR_CS_MASK;

    // Configure NVIC for DMA ISR
    NVIC_SetPriority(DMA0_IRQn, 2);
    NVIC_ClearPendingIRQ(DMA0_IRQn);
    NVIC_EnableIRQ(DMA0_IRQn);

    // Set DMA MUX channel to use TPM0 overflow as trigger
    DMAMUX0->CHCFG[0] = DMAMUX_CHCFG_SOURCE(54);
}
```

Listing 9.6 Code to initialize DMA system for playing back waveform.

Listing 9.6 shows the code to initialize the DMA controller for waveform playback. The function is passed a pointer to the beginning of the source data (TriangleTable in this example) and the number of samples to transfer. These parameters will be needed each time DMA playback is started, so they are stored in variables Reload_DMA_Source and Reload_DMA_Byte_Count (after multiplication by two to reflect the two bytes per data sample).

The function next enables the clock gating for the DMA and DMAMUX modules, then disables the DMA channel (0) to allow configuration. The channel is configured to transfer 16-bit words, increment the source address but not the destination address, perform one transfer (cycle stealing mode) when a peripheral request is received, and generate a DMA interrupt when done with all transfers. The NVIC is configured to accept DMA interrupt requests, and finally the peripheral request trigger for DMA channel 0 is connected to the TPM0 overflow signal (specified by code 54).

```
void Start_DMA_Playback() {
    // initialize source and destination pointers
    DMA0->DMA[0].SAR = DMA_SAR_SAR((uint32_t) Reload_DMA_Source);
    DMA0->DMA[0].DAR = DMA_DAR_DAR((uint32_t) (&(DAC0->DAT[0])));
    // byte count
    DMA0->DMA[0].DSR_BCR = DMA_DSR_BCR_BCR(Reload_DMA_Byte_Count);
    // clear done flag
    DMA0->DMA[0].DSR_BCR &= ~DMA_DSR_BCR_DONE_MASK;
    // set enable flag
    DMAMUX0->CHCFG[0] |= DMAMUX_CHCFG_ENBL_MASK;
}
```

Listing 9.7 Code to start or restart DMA playback of specific data buffer to DAC.

Listing 9.7 shows the code to start the waveform playback using DMA. The source address register is loaded with the address of the data buffer, and the destination address is loaded with the address of the DAC0 data register. The byte count register is loaded with the number of bytes to transfer. The Done flag is cleared to clear flags, and then the channel is enabled by setting the enable flag.

```
void DMA0_IRQHandler(void) {
    // Turn off blue LED in DMA IRQ handler
    Control_RGB_LEDs(0,0,0);
    // Clear done flag
    DMA0->DMA[0].DSR_BCR |= DMA_DSR_BCR_DONE_MASK;
    // Start the next DMA playback cycle
    Start_DMA_Playback();
    // Turn on blue LED
    Control_RGB_LEDs(0,0,1);
}
```

Listing 9.8 Interrupt service routine for DMA0 sets up DMA system to play back buffer again.

Listing 9.8 shows the interrupt service routine that executes after the DMA controller completes its transfer of all data. The first step is optional—changing the blue LED so we can see when the ISR runs by using an oscilloscope or logic analyzer. Next, the code clears the DMA peripheral's done flag to tell the peripheral the interrupt is being serviced. Then the code calls Start_DMA_Playback to set up the DMA controller to transfer the contents of the data buffer again. The last step is optional, turning off the blue LED to indicate the ISR has completed.

Analysis

Let's verify the code and peripherals generate the waveform correctly. Figure 9.7 shows the analog waveform output (upper trace) and the DMA ISR activity (lower trace). The DMA ISR runs once every 512 samples (NUM_STEPS) to set up the DMA to play the buffer again, resulting in an ISR frequency of 194 Hz.

In Figure 9.8 we zoom in and see the ISR is active for about 2.8 μs. There is a minor overhead to enter and exit the ISR, adding roughly 20 cycles, or about 0.4 μs at 48 MHz. We can determine how much of the CPU's time is left for other processing. The total CPU load from the DMA ISR is (2.8 μs + 0.4 μs) × 194 Hz = 0.000621, or 0.00621%. In addition, the DMA controller takes over the bus to transfer each sample, preventing the CPU from using the bus. Each transfer takes two cycles every 10 μs, so the fraction of time that DMA uses the bus is 2/(48 MHz × 10 μs) = 0.004167, or 0.4167%. Adding these two values together shows that this waveform generator takes only 0.4787% of the CPU's time, leaving over 99.5% available for other processing.

Compare this with the approach from Chapter 7 based on the timer ISR. The timer ISR is active for about 1 μs and runs every 10 μs (100 kHz frequency). The total CPU load including interrupt overhead is (1 μs + 0.4 μs) × 100 kHz = 0.14 = 14%. Using the DMA system has reduced overhead by a factor of about 30.

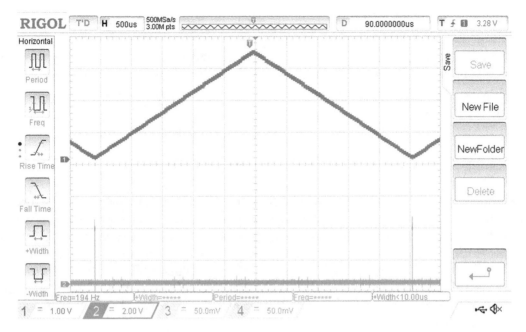

Figure 9.7 Analog output signal (above) and DMA ISR activity (below) show correct waveform generation.

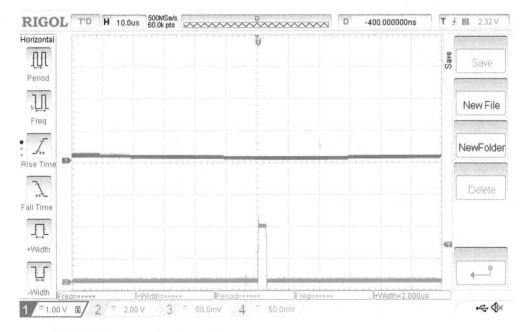

Figure 9.8 DMA ISR is active for about 2.8 μs.

Summary

The DMA system can transfer information among peripherals and memory quickly. In many cases this can eliminate the need to use software on the CPU, improving system responsiveness, predictability, and throughput while freeing up time for the CPU either to use on other activities or to save power by sleeping.

Exercises

1. Determine and present the register configuration needed so that the next 1024 bytes of data received on UART1 are saved by the DMA controller in memory starting at address DestAddress. When the transfer is complete, the DMA controller must generate an interrupt.
2. Consider the memory transfer example. Rewrite the code to copy the contents of array s–d without using pointers and measure its timing. How long does it take per array element, and how does this compare with the transfer using DMA? Enable maximum optimization for speed in the compiler, rebuild the code, and repeat the measurement. Are the results different, and if so, how do they compare with the transfer using DMA?
3. Determine and present the DMA and DMAMUX control register configuration needed so that the next 15000 ADC results are sent out through SPI channel 1 using DMA channel 3. Assume the ADC has been configured to perform 8-bit conversions and generate an interrupt upon completion.
4. We wish to increase the sampling rate for the analog waveform generator in this chapter. What is the maximum sampling rate possible that leaves 50% of the CPU's time for other processing?
5. How quickly can the DMA controller copy 8192 bytes of data from Port A (bits 0–7) to RAM? Explain the timing.

References

[1]   *KL25 Sub-Family Reference Manual*, KL25P80M48SF0RM, Rev. 3 ed., NXP Semiconductor, B.V., 2016.

[2]   *Cortex-M0+ Technical Reference Manual*, DDI 0484C, r0p1 ed., ARM Ltd., 2012.

[3]   J. Yiu, *The definitive guide to the ARM Cortex-M0 and Cortex-M0+ processors*, 2nd ed., Oxford: Newnes, 2015.

[4]   *Cortex-M0+ Devices Generic User Guide*, DUI 0662B, r0p1 ed., ARM Ltd., 2012.

[5]   *Kinetis KL25 Sub-Family Data Sheet*, KL25P80M48SF0, Rev. 5th ed., NXP Semiconductor, B.V., 2016.

Appendix

Measuring Current, Power, and Energy on the FRDM-KL25Z

Appendix Contents

Overview

This appendix describes how to measure and reduce power and energy consumption on the FRDM-KL25Z evaluation board.

FRDM-KL25Z Power System Architecture

The power system architecture for the FRDM-KL25Z development board is shown in Figure A.1. For full details, refer to the reference manual and schematic diagram [1] [2].

Most of the circuitry on the board runs at 3.3 V. There are four power inputs available, one linear 3.3 V voltage regulator, and three separate output power domains. Each output domain runs at the same nominal 3.3 V, and may be disconnected or measured separately. J3, J4, and J20 are headers for connecting jumpers to short out the parallel component(s).

Figure A.2 is an excerpt from the schematic diagram showing the circuit that implements the power system [2]. Note that the components marked DNP (do not populate) are optional and not present on the PCB. Also, certain resistors (R73, R74) are used as small, low-cost, removable jumpers. These resistors have a value of 0 Ω and simply short their two terminals together.

Power Inputs

There are four power inputs available:

- The two USB connectors (J5 and J7) can each supply 5V to power the board if connected to a USB port. J5 is connected to P5V_KL25Z and J7 is connected to P5V_SDA.
- The P5-9V_VIN input is located on the expansion header (J9, pin 16), allowing an expansion shield to supply power to the FRDM-KL25Z.
- The fourth power input is an optional coin cell BT1 that is connected to signal P3V3_BATT. To use a battery, first add the battery holder and diode D7 to the PCB and then insert the battery.

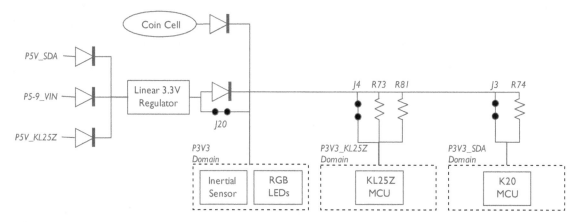

Figure A.1 FRDM-KL25Z power system architecture.

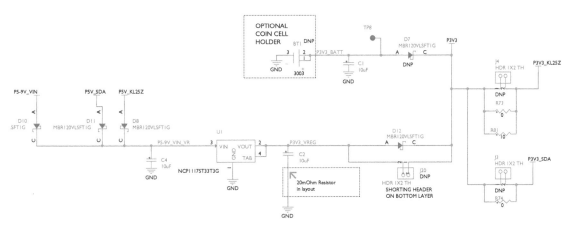

Figure A.2 Power supply portion of FRDM-KL25Z schematic [2].

Voltage Regulation

The first three power inputs are combined with diodes to create the signal P5-9V_VIN_VR. This then powers the linear voltage regulator U1 (NCP1117), which creates a stable 3.3V [3]. The P3V3_BATT input is not regulated.

There are two important power-related issues for the NCP1117 to consider. First, the NCP1117 has a dropout voltage of slightly under 1 V, so the input voltage must be at least 4.3 V. Second, the NCP1117 draws a large quiescent current (roughly 8 mA) in addition to any current drawn by from its output. For low-power applications this current may be many times larger than the average current drawn by the MCU and the rest of the circuit. Instructions on disconnecting the regulator are given later in this Appendix.

Power Domains

There are three output power domains:

- The P3V3_KL25Z domain powers the KL25Z MCU (U3).
- The P3V3_SDA domain powers the OpenSDA debug MCU (U6) and interface circuit (U4).
- The P3V3 domain powers the RGB LED (D3), the inertial sensor (U7), and the two domains above (P3V3_KL25Z and P3V3_SDA).

Current Measurement and Power Calculation

Measuring the entire board's current is a useful starting point. The entire FRDM-KL25Z board's current draw can be measured by powering it with a modified USB cable as shown in Figure A.3. Cut the red wire within the cable (the 5V supply line), strip the insulation off each end, and connect a *multimeter* in *ammeter* mode. The *power* consumed is the product of the current and the voltage. Be sure also to measure the USB supply voltage with a *voltmeter*, as it can vary between 4.8 and 5.1 V.

multimeter
Multi-function test equipment which can measure electrical values such as voltage, current, and resistance

ammeter
Test device which can measure current value through circuit. Multimeters typically have ammeter modes available.

power (P)
Rate at which a device uses energy. Measured in Watts (W). Symbol is P.

voltmeter
Test device which can measure voltage value across circuit. Multimeters typically have voltmeter modes available.

More precise current measurements require circuit modifications to isolate portions of the circuit; these are described in later sections. Please refer to the section titled "Circuit Modification Summary" for a summary of the modifications and the component locations on the PCB.

Finally, remember that when calculating power you must multiply the current by the circuit's operating voltage, which may be 5 V, 3.3 V, or something else. Measure when you are in doubt.

Figure A.3 Modified USB cable allows measurement of entire board's current draw.

Measuring Target MCU Current

To isolate the target MCU's current, remove resistor R73 (0 Ω). The MCU's current will flow through a 10 ohm resistor (R81), producing a voltage drop of 10 mV drop for every 1 mA of current. Populate J4 with a two-pin header.

To measure MCU current, connect a **voltmeter** across the two pins of J4. Divide the measured voltage drop by 10 to determine MCU current. Do not put an ammeter across J4, as that will give an inaccurate reading. The ammeter's internal shunt resistor will be in parallel with R81, reducing the effective resistance, voltage drop, and current reading.

Measuring OpenSDA Debug Circuit Current

To isolate the OpenSDA debug circuit's current, remove resistor R74 (0 Ω). Populate J3 with a two-pin header. Insert a shorting jumper on J3 in order to use the OpenSDA circuit (e.g. to program or debug the target MCU).

To measure the OpenSDA circuit's current consumption, remove the jumper and connect an **ammeter** across the two pins of J3.

Measuring Voltage Regulator Output Current

To isolate the voltage regulator output current, cut the trace on the back of J20. Populate J20 with a two-pin header. Insert a shorting jumper on J20 when you wish to short out the protection diode D12 and eliminate its voltage drop (roughly 300 mV depending on the current).

To measure the output current, remove the jumper and connect an **ammeter** across the two pins of J20.

Power Reduction

The following board modifications and procedures can be used to reduce power consumption.

Disconnecting OpenSDA Debug MCU Power and Reset Line

The OpenSDA debug MCU uses a significant amount of power. To disable it, you must disconnect its power and also disconnect it from the target MCU's reset line.

Disconnect the power to the debug circuit by removing resistor R74 (0 Ω). Populate J3 with a two-pin header.

- Insert a shorting jumper on J3 in order to use the OpenSDA circuit (e.g. to program or debug the target MCU).
- Remove the shorting jumper to disable the OpenSDA circuit.

The OpenSDA MCU controls the target MCU's reset line. If the OpenSDA MCU is not powered, then it will hold the target MCU's reset line low and prevent it from running.

Disconnect the target MCU's reset line from the debug MCU by cutting the trace shorting J14 on the back of the PCB. Populate J14 with a two-pin header.

- Insert a shorting jumper on J14 to use the debugger.
- Remove the jumper to allow the target MCU to run without the OpenSDA debug MCU being powered.

Disconnecting Voltage Regulator U1

The voltage regulator U1 draws about 8 mA of quiescent current. To avoid this current consumption, power the circuit through P3V3_BAT or P3V3 with a voltage that will not exceed the 3.6 V maximum supply voltage rating of the ICs. Exceeding this level will damage the hardware.

Be sure to cut the shorting trace across jumper J20 (on the bottom of the PCB) to allow diode D7 to prevent the P3V3 rail from powering U1 (as described in the section "Disconnecting Voltage Regulator U1").

If applying power through P3V3_BAT, add diode D7 to the PCB. D7 is not populated, as indicated with DNP (do not populate) on the schematic diagram.

Energy Measurement

Measuring *energy* consumption involves integrating the instantaneous power consumption over the time period of interest. This can be challenging for digital circuits because switching activity makes the power consumption vary with a high frequency.

> energy (W)
> *Capability of a system to do work on another system. Measured in Joules (J). Symbol is W (work).*

Capacitor-Based Measurement

A simple way determine the energy use is to power the circuit with a capacitator for a certain amount of time. The total energy used during that time (W, measured in Joules) is proportional to the capacitance and the difference between the squares of the capacitor's starting and ending voltages.

$$W = C\frac{V_1^2 - V_2^2}{2}$$

Dividing this energy by the time over which it is used gives the **average rate of power consumption** (P, measured in Watts).

$$P = C\frac{V_1^2 - V_2^2}{2t}$$

A small ultracapacitor (e.g. 0.1 or 0.33 F, rated for at least 5 V) will provide an adequate amount of energy for many low-power applications based on the FRDM-KL25Z. Assuming a starting voltage of 3.3 V and an ending voltage of 2.0 V, a 0.47 F capacitor will provide 1619 mJ of energy. This is enough to supply 161.9 mW for 10 seconds. Note that the larger the voltage difference is, the more energy is available.

The following bounds are useful when estimating the time to discharge a capacitor. A constant current load I will take t seconds to discharge the capacitor from V_1 to V_2:

$$t = \frac{C}{I}(V_1 - V_2)$$

A constant resistance load R will take t seconds to discharge the capacitor from V_1 to V_2, where ln is the natural logarithm

$$t = -CR\ln\frac{V_2}{V_1}$$

Implementation

Connect the capacitor to the P3V3 rail and ground, both of which are available on connector J9. Be sure to cut the shorting trace across J20 to allow diode D7 to prevent the P3V3 rail from powering U1, as described in "Disconnecting Voltage Regulator U1." If desired, disconnect the OpenSDA MCU power and reset line as well.

The capacitor will take some time to charge up to the P3V3 rail voltage. The capacitor's voltage will drop slightly after it is disconnected from the rail as charge is redistributed within the capacitor. These times and levels should be investigated because they depend on the capacitor's equivalent series resistance, previous level of charge, and capacitance tolerance.

It is important to measure the initial and final voltages of the capacitor accurately in order to calculate energy correctly. The initial voltage (P3V3 rail) will be approximately 3.3 V if J20 is shorted (bypassing D7), or significantly less (e.g. 3.1 V) if J20 is not shorted. The final voltage is determined by the highest of the minimum operating voltages for the devices of interest. For example, the MCU requires 1.71 V to operate, the inertial sensor needs 1.95 V, while the blue LED needs over 2.5 V [4]–[6]. For some applications it will be practical to measure this voltage directly using a multimeter, while other applications will require other methods.

Circuit Modification Summary

Table A.1 shows which modifications are needed to perform different measurement operations. Table A.2 shows how to use the jumpers and headers for different operations.

Figures A.4 and A.5 show the locations of components used in the modifications and measurements.

Table A.1 Summary of Circuit Modifications for Different Operations

		Run target MCU, disconnect debugger	Measure target MCU current	Measure debugger current	Measure regulator output current	Disconnect regulator output	Power board with coin cell
Target MCU power	Remove R73, add J4		Yes				
Debug MCU power	Remove R74, add J3	Yes		Yes			
Target MCU reset line	Cut J14 shorting trace, add J14	Yes					
Regulator output diode bypass	Cut J20 shorting trace, add J20				Yes	Yes	Yes
Coin cell components	Add D7, BT1						Yes

Table A.2 Summary of Jumper Settings for Different Operations

	Run, debug, or program target MCU	Run, target MCU, disconnect debugger	Measure target MCU current	Measure debugger current	Measure regulator output current	Disconnect regulator output	Power board with coin cell
J4: Target MCU power			Open. Measure voltage across J4, divide by 10				
J3: Debug MCU power	Short	Open		Open. Measure current through J3			
J14: Target MCU reset	Short	Open					
J20: Regulator output diode bypass					Open. Measure current through J20	Open	Open

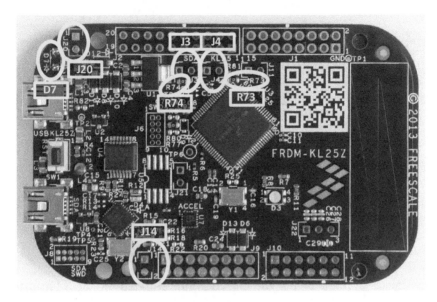

Figure A.4 Locations of jumpers, resistors, and diode on the front of PCB for circuit modifications.

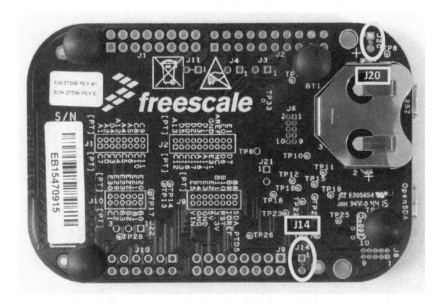

Figure A.5 Locations of jumpers, resistors, and diode on the back of PCB for circuit modifications.

References

[1] *FRDM-KL25Z User's Manual*, rev. 2.0, NXP Semiconductor, B.V., 2016.
[2] *FRDM-KL25Z Schematic SPF-27556*, TX, NXP Semiconductor, B.V., 2013.
[3] *NCP1117, NCV1117 Voltage Regulators Datasheet*, On Semiconductor, 2013.
[4] *Kinetis KL25 Sub-Family Data Sheet*, KL25P80M48SF0, rev. 5th ed., NXP Semiconductor, B.V., 2016.
[5] *MMA8451Q 3-Axis, 14-Bit/8-Bit Digital Accelerometer Data Sheet*, NXP Semiconductors, B.V., 2016.
[6] *Cree PLCC4 3-in-1 SMD LED CLV1A-FKB Product Family Data Sheet*, Cree, Inc., 2015.

Glossary

Acknowledgment Device response indicating successful reception of message

Activation record Temporary storage in memory for function's preserved registers, arguments, local variables, return address, etc. Exists only from function's start to end.

Aliasing Distortion of signal resulting from sampling at too low of a frequency

Ammeter Test device which can measure current value through circuit. Multimeters typically have ammeter modes available.

Analog Able to represent an infinite number of possible values

Analog-to-digital converter (ADC) Circuit which converts an analog value (e.g. voltage) to its corresponding digital value

And Multi-input binary logic operation with output of one only if all inputs are one, else output is zero

Anode Positive terminal of a polarized component (LED, battery, etc.)

Arithmetic/logic unit (ALU) Hardware circuit in CPU which performs a machine instruction's arithmetic and logic operations

Assembler Software tool which translates assembly language code into machine code

Assembly language Human-readable representation of machine code

Asynchronous Activities which are not synchronized with each other, or a protocol that does not send clocking information

Atomic Indivisible, cannot be interrupted or preempted

Baud rate Rate at which communication symbols are transmitted. Also called symbol rate.

Big-endian Describes byte ordering convention in which the most significant byte is stored first in memory

Binary Base-two numbering system. Each digit can have one of two values (zero and one).

Bitwise and Operation in which output bit is logic and of corresponding input bits. C operators are & and &=.

Bitwise one's complement Operation in which output bit is inverse (one's complement) of corresponding input bit. C operators are ~ and ~=.

Bitwise or Operation in which output bit is logic or of corresponding input bits. C operators are | and |=.

Blocking State in which a task is waiting for an event to occur. Also called waiting.

Burst-mode Mode in which DMA controller performs all transfers in a burst without sharing bus with CPU

Busy-waiting Wasteful method of making a program wait for an event or delay. Program executes test code repeatedly in a tight loop, not sharing time with other parts of program.

Byte Value which is eight bits long

Byte-addressable Memory in which each address identifies a single byte

Call graph Diagram showing subroutine calling relationships between functions in a program

Call stack Stack of activation records/stack frames of functions which have started executing but have not yet completed

Cathode Negative terminal of a polarized component (LED, battery, etc.)

Central processing unit (CPU) Hardware circuit that executes a program's instructions

Clear To change a bit to zero

Clock gating Method to disable circuit by blocking clock signal, reducing power consumption

CMSIS-CORE Portion of CMSIS that provides C-language interface to processor core and peripherals

Comparator Circuit that compares two values to determine equality or identify larger value

Compiler Software tool that translates high-level source code to assembly language code

Condition code flag Indicates whether result of instruction is negative (N) or zero (Z), or whether instruction resulted in carry (C) or overflow (V)

Control register Register used to configure operation of hardware in CPU or peripheral

Cooperative multitasking Scheduling approach where tasks share CPU by voluntarily yielding it to other tasks

Cortex Microcontroller Software Interface Standard (CMSIS) Definition of hardware/software interfaces and debugging interfaces that simplify the development of systems with Cortex-M processors

Counter Digital circuit which counts number of input pulses

CPU overhead Portion of time CPU spends executing code that does not perform useful work for the application

Critical section Section of code that may execute incorrectly if not executed atomically

Cycle-stealing Mode in which DMA controller shares bus with CPU, taking turns to transfer data

Data race Situation where ill-timed preemption of a code critical section can result in incorrect program result

Decimal Base-ten numbering system. Each digit can have one of ten values (0 through 9).

Demultiplexer Electronic selector switch that routes input signal to one of N outputs

Deserialization Conversion of information from serial to parallel form

Digital Capable of taking on a limited number of values

Digital-to-analog converter (DAC) Circuit that converts a digital value to its corresponding analog value (e.g. voltage)

Direct memory access (DMA) Type of memory access performed by peripheral hardware without program instructions

Directive In assembly language, an order to control how assembler operates. Does not represent an instruction.

DMA controller Peripheral that performs DMA

DMAMUX Multiplexer that selects DMA event source

Do not populate (DNP) Indicates that a PCB component is optional and is not installed

Duty cycle Fraction of time that a PWM signal is asserted

Endianness Property that describes the order of bytes in multi-byte structures stored in memory

Energy (W) Capability of a system to do work on another system. Measured in Joules (J). Symbol is W (work).

Epilog Final code in function which restores preserved registers, prepares return values, frees activation record and returns control to caller function

Event-triggering Approach in which software runs when an event occurs

Exception Event that causes a program to deviate from normal flow of control. Examples include illegal instruction, illegal memory access, and interrupt.

Field A group of one or more bits defining a data item. A register may hold multiple fields.

Finite state machine (FSM) A type of state machine with all states and transitions defined

Framing symbol Symbol used to indicate start or end of message

General-purpose input/output port (GPIO port) Peripheral with digital input and output bits

General-purpose register Register located in CPU used for data processing by instructions in program

Halfword Value that is 16 bits (two bytes) long

Handler Software routine that runs in response to interrupt or exception request

Hexadecimal Base-sixteen numbering system. Each digit can have one of sixteen values (0 through 9, A, B, C, D, E and F). Symbols A through F represent values of ten through fifteen.

Immediate value Data value that is stored as part of a machine instruction

Infrared (IR) Electromagnetic energy immediately past the visible portion of the spectrum; also called invisible light

Input GPIO port bit Portion of GPIO port that enables program to read a single-bit input signal

Instruction Command for processor to execute. Consists of an operation and zero or more operands.

Instruction set architecture (ISA) Description of instructions, registers, and memory accessing modes that a CPU supports

Integrated circuit (IC) Electronic circuit with components built into a single piece of silicon, enabling extreme miniaturization, mass production, and cost reduction

Integrated development environment (IDE) PC-based program supporting development activities such as code editing, building, downloading, debugging

Inter-Integrated circuit bus (I^2C) A type of synchronous serial communication bus with addressing and acknowledgments

Interrupt Event used to trigger specific program activity

Interrupt request (IRQ) Hardware signal indicating that an interrupt is requested

Interrupt service routine (ISR) Software routine that runs in response to interrupt request. Also called a handler.

Invert To change a bit to the opposite value. Also called toggle.

Kernel Scheduler with support for task features such as communication, delays, and synchronization

Label Symbol in assembly language which represents an address

Least-significant Having the smallest place value. The least-significant byte of a two-byte value represents values of 0–255.

Light-emitting diode (LED) Electronic component which emits light. Used for indicators, back-lighting, and general illumination.

Link register (LR) ARM CPU register that holds return address for subroutine calls or return code for exception handlers

Linker/Loader Software tool that combines separate object code modules and links cross-references to create single executable program file

Little-endian Describes byte ordering convention in which least-significant byte is stored first in memory

Local variable Variable that is visible and accessible only within its declaring function

Machine language Code in which each instruction is represented as a numerical value. Processed directly by CPU.

Media access control (MAC) Rules controlling when a node can transmit a message on shared media

Microcontroller unit (MCU) Integrated circuit containing CPU, peripherals, support circuits, and often memory

Mnemonic In assembly language, text abbreviation used to describe operation performed by instruction

Modularity Measure of how program is structured to group related portions and separate independent portions

Most-significant Having the greatest place value. The most-significant byte of a two-byte value represents values of 0 to 65,280 which are multiples of 256.

Multimeter Multi-function test equipment which can measure electrical values such as voltage, current, and resistance

Multiplexer Electronic selector switch that routes one of N inputs signals to the output. MCU pin multiplexer is bidirectional (includes demultiplexer).

Multitasking Approach in which program consists of multiple tasks with independent control flow interleaved over time

Native data type Primary data type used by ALU and registers; 32-bit integer for ARM Cortex-M CPUs

Non-preemptive scheduler Scheduler that does not allow tasks to preempt each other

Operand Part of an instruction: parameter used by operation

Operating system Kernel with support for application-oriented features such as file systems, networking support, etc.

Operation Part of an instruction: specifies what work to do

Or Multi-input binary operation with output of one if any inputs are one, otherwise output is zero

Output GPIO port bit Portion of GPIO port that enables program to write a single-bit output signal

Parallel Organization in which multiple items are simultaneously available or active

Pending Requested but not yet serviced (e.g. interrupt)

Peripheral Hardware that helps CPU by interfacing or providing special functionality

Polling Software approach in which program explicitly checks a condition

Pop Instruction which reads a data item from the top of the stack (last used location) in memory and updates the stack pointer

Power (P) Rate at which a device uses energy. Measured in Watts (W). Symbol is P.

Preemption Pausing the execution of a task to allow another task to run

Preemptive scheduler Scheduler which supports task preemption

Printed circuit board (PCB) Board which holds electronic components and conductive traces for interconnection

Prioritization Favoring one item over another. For example, running task A before B to reduce A's latency at the expense of B.

Program counter (PC) CPU register used to specify address of instruction to execute next

Program status register (PSR) Register holding condition code flags

Programmer's model Specifies a CPU's characteristics, including instructions, data types, registers, addressing modes, and operating modes

Prolog Initial code in function which preserves registers and prepares activation record

Pulse-width modulation (PWM) Method for encoding information onto a single digital signal based on duty cycle

Push Instruction that writes a data item to the next free stack location in memory and updates the stack pointer

Quantization Process of selecting a discrete digital value to represent an analog value

Real-time kernel Kernel designed for real-time systems

Real-time operating system (RTOS) Operating system designed for real-time systems

Real-time system System that must respond to events before specified deadlines

Register Hardware circuit which can store a data value

Register file Holds CPU's general purpose registers

Responsiveness Measure of how quickly a system responds to an input event

Return address Address of next instruction to execute after completing a subroutine

Root function A task's main software function, which may call other functions as subroutines.

Sampling Process of converting a continuous-time signal to a series of discrete-time samples

Scheduler Mechanism to control which task runs on a processor at a given time

Sequence diagram Diagram showing sequence of operations and communications between two or more actors (e.g. threads, peripherals)

Serial Organization in which items are available or active sequentially, not simultaneously

Serial peripheral interconnect (SPI) A type of synchronous serial communication bus

Serialization Conversion of information from parallel to serial form

Set To change a bit to one

Signed Numbering system that is able to represent positive and negative values and zero

Spaghetti code Code which is poorly structured because it entangles unrelated features, complicating development and maintenance.

Stack Last-in, first-out data structure. Data items are removed (popped) in the opposite order they were inserted (pushed).

Stack pointer (SP) Pointer to data item on top of stack (last in, first out)

State machine State-based model of system with rules for transitions between states

Status register Register that indicates the status of hardware in CPU or peripheral

Subroutine Program function that can be called by another function

Supply voltage Level of voltage applied to electronic circuit to enable operation. Also called VDD or VCC.

Symbol (communication) A waveform or state transmitted on a communication channel to represent one or more bits of information.

Symbol (program) Text name representing a value (e.g. address, data value) in a program

Synchronous Activities which are synchronized with each other, or a protocol which sends clocking information

SysTick timer Timer peripheral available in Cortex-M CPU cores, typically used to generate periodic time tick

Task Function and its subroutines that perform an activity. Each task has its own flow of control.

Task preemption Scheduling approach where a task is paused to allow a different task to run. Eventually the first task resumes execution where it was paused.

Timer/counter Peripheral that measures time or counts events

Timer/PWM module (TPM) Timer peripheral in Kinetis KL25Z MCU which can also generate PWM signals

Top-of-stack Next item that can be popped from stack

Transfer function Mathematical equation describing relationship between input and output values

Transistor Basic electronic component which operates as switch or amplifier

Universal asynchronous receiver/transmitter (UART) Peripheral for asynchronous communications

Unsigned Numbering system that is able to represent positive values and zero

Vector Address of an exception handler

Vector table Table of vectors used to process different exceptions

Volatile data Data that can change outside of program's normal flow of control

Volatile memory Memory that loses its contents if power is lost

Voltmeter Test device which can measure voltage value across circuit. Multimeters typically have voltmeter modes available.

Waiting A state in which a task is waiting for an event to occur. Also called blocking.

Watchdog timer (WDT) Hardware peripheral used to reset out-of-control program

Word Value that is 32 bits (four bytes) long

Index

CPSIA information can be obtained
at www.ICGtesting.com
Printed in the USA
BVHW062352120619
550817BV00003B/20/P